Eastern Practices
and Individuation
Essays by Jungian Analysts

Edited by Leslie Stein

CHIRON PUBLICATIONS • ASHEVILLE, NORTH CAROLINA

www.ChironPublications.com

Interior design by Danijela Mijailovic
Cover design by Celeste Stein
Printed primarily in the United States of America

ISBN 978-1-68503-056-8 paperback
ISBN 978-1-68503-057-5 hardcover
ISBN 978-1-68503-058-2 electronic
ISBN 978-1-68503-059-9 limited edition paperback

Library of Congress Cataloging-in-Publication Data

Names: Stein, Leslie A., editor.
Title: Eastern practices and individuation : essays by Jungian analysts / edited by Leslie Stein.
Description: Asheville, North Carolina : Chiron Publications, [2022] | Includes bibliographical references. | Summary: "Are Eastern practices useful for psychological growth? Is psychoanalysis an aid on an Eastern path? Carl Gustav Jung had the realization of the existence of a center deep within our being, the Self, the discovery of which is the goal of individuation: the process of psychological development. Unable to find analogies to the Self in Christianity, he turned to Eastern religions, uncovering and finding a reflection of this miracle in Daoism and Hinduism, while also examining Buddhism and Sufism. Eastern paths and their practices, such as meditation, mindfulness, and yoga, have been absorbed into Western culture. It is thus timely to approach the contemporary relevance of Eastern religions and practices to the Jungian path of individuation. These essays are personal, engaging, and contain a refined analysis of whether these two paths may work together or are pointing to different end points. Contributors: Ashok Bedi, Lionel Corbett, Royce Froehlich, Karin Jironet, Patricia Katsky, Ann Chia-Yi Li, Jim Manganiello, Judith Pickering, Leslie Stein, Murray Stein, Polly Young-Eisendrath"-- Provided by publisher.
Identifiers: LCCN 2022041524 (print) | LCCN 2022041525 (ebook) | ISBN 9781685030568 (paperback) | ISBN 9781685030575 (hardcover) | ISBN 9781685030582 (ebook)
Subjects: LCSH: Individuation (Psychology)--Religious aspects. | Self--Religious aspects. | Jungian psychology. | Psychology and religion. | Asia--Religion--Influence.
Classification: LCC BL65.S38 E27 2022 (print) | LCC BL65.S38 (ebook) | DDC 204/.4--dc23/eng20221121
LC record available at https://lccn.loc.gov/2022041524
LC ebook record available at https://lccn.loc.gov/2022041525

Table of Contents

The Buddhist no-self

Eastern Practices and the Matrix

....

List of Contributors

Ashok Bedi, M.D., is a Jungian psychoanalyst and a board-certified psychiatrist. He is a member of the Royal College of psychiatrists of Great Britain, a diplomate in Psychological Medicine at the Royal College of Physicians and Surgeons of England, a Distinguished Life Fellow of the American Psychiatric Association. He is a Clinical Professor in Psychiatry at the Medical College of Wisconsin in Milwaukee and a training analyst at the Carl G. Jung Institute of Chicago. His books include *In the Eye of the Storm — Staying Centered in Personal and Collective Crisis; The Spiritual Paradox of Addiction; Crossing the Healing Zone; Awaken the Slumbering God*dess: *The Latent Code of the Hindu Goddess Archetypes*; *Retire Your Family Karma: Decode Your Family Pattern*; and *Find Your Soul Path and Path to the Soul.* He is the liaison for the International Association of Analytical Psychologists (IAAP)for developing Jungian training programs in India and travels annually to India to teach, train the consult with the Jungian Developing groups at several centers in India, including Ahmedabad and Mumbai. He leads the annual "A Jungian Encounter with the Soul of India" study group to several centers in India under the auspices of the New York Jung Foundation and the Carl Jung Institute of Chicago. His publications and upcoming programs may be previewed at www. pathtothesoul.com

Dr. Lionel Corbett trained in medicine and psychiatry in England and as a Jungian Analyst at the C.G. Jung Institute of Chicago. He is a professor of depth psychology at Pacifica Graduate Institute, in Santa Barbara, California. He is the author of six books including: *Psyche and the Sacred: The Religious Function of the Psyche*; *The Sacred Cauldron: Psychotherapy as a Spiritual Practice*; *The Soul in Anguish: Psychotherapeutic Approaches to Suffering*; *Understanding Evil: A Guide for Psychotherapists*, and *The God-image:*

From Antiquity to Jung. He is the coeditor of four volumes of collected papers: *Psyche's Stories*; *Depth Psychology, Meditations in the Field*; *Psychology at the Threshold*; and *Jung and Aging.*

Royce Froehlich is a Jungian analyst in private practice in New York City, an instructor, supervisor, and training analyst at the C.G. Jung Institute of New York, and a member of the faculty at the Jung Foundation for Analytical Psychology. He holds graduate degrees from the European Graduate School (Ph.D.), Union Theological Seminary (M.Div.), Columbia University (M.S.S.W.), and The New School for Social Research (M.A.). A former audio engineer at ABC Radio Networks, he holds an interest in the philosophy of media and the questions it generates concerning its effects on the human psyche.

Karin Jironet, Ph.D., studied linguistics and ethnology (M.A.) as well as speech pathology (B.M.Sc.) at Lund University, Sweden. She earned her Ph.D. in Theology, Psychology of Religion at the University of Amsterdam, the Netherlands, in 1998. As a postdoctoral researcher, she published on Sufi mysticism (Leiden University, the Netherlands). Jironet who was trained as a Jungian psychoanalyst in Zurich (ISAP), is a member of IAAP and AGAP and served at the board of NAAP, the Dutch Association for Analytical Psychology. She is an internationally published author of several peer-reviewed articles and of nine books, of which one, *Female Leadership,* was nominated for the Gradiva Award in 2011, New York. Her orientation is toward spirituality in leadership, corporate as well as personal. She serves on Ph.D. committees internationally, travels and works with groups and individuals globally and in her private practices in the Netherlands and in Italy.

Dr. Patricia Katsky received her Ph.D. from UCLA. She trained as a Jungian Analyst at the C. G. Jung Institute of Los Angeles and is now a member of the C. G. Jung Institute of San Francisco. She is a professor of depth psychology and former provost at Pacifica Graduate Institute in Santa Barbara, California. She has had a lifelong interest in Eastern spiritual practices, focusing on yoga, Tibetan Buddhism, and Chan Buddhism. She co-founded a not-for-profit counseling center in Los Angeles in 1976 and continues to serve on the board. She lectures nationally and internationally on the intersection of Jungian and post-Jungian thought and Eastern spiritual traditions. She published an article titled "Enlightenment, Individuation, and Nonduality: Reflections on a Dream," in the *Jung Journal*, Winter 2021.

Jim Manganiello, Ed.D., is a licensed clinical depth psychologist and therapist. He has an academic rank of associate professor. He has been the Director of the New England Mindbody Institute and the Director of the Center for East-West Psychology and Contemplative Healing, (a Dzogchen psychology organization). He has lectured internationally on the sacred dimensions of depth psychotherapy. He is the author of articles and books in this area, including *Unshakable Certainty* and *Your Creative Imagination Unlocked, Become Who You Truly Are*, (with abstract painter and sculptor Frank Arnold). Jim lives in Massachusetts' rural North Shore, with his wife, Wanda Stevens, and their animal family: Nicholas, the cat pack leader, and two dogs, Bella and Maxie.

Dr. Judith Pickering is a Jungian Training Analyst, Psychoanalytic Couple and Family Therapist, and Psychoanalytic Psychotherapist working in private practice in Sydney, Australia. She is the author of *Being in Love: Therapeutic Pathways Through Psychological Obstacles to Love* (Routledge, 2008) and *The Search for Meaning in Psychotherapy: Spiritual Practice, the Apophatic Way and Bion* (Routledge, 2019), a 2020 American Board & Academy of Psychoanalysis (ABAPsa) book award winner, as well as numerous articles on analytical psychology, psychoanalytic psychotherapy, and couples therapy. She holds tertiary degrees in Religious Studies, Asian Studies, Music Education, Musicology, Psychotherapy, and Analytical Psychology and has a doctorate in Psychology. She has been a practitioner of Buddhist meditation for over 40 years and holds a deep interest in interreligious dialogue and contemplative and apophatic mysticism.

Leslie Stein is a Jungian Analyst in private practice in Sydney, Australia. Professor Stein is a native New Yorker and a graduate of the C. G. Jung Institute of New York. His works that relate to the topic of this book of essays are: *Becoming Whole: Jung's Equation for Realizing God* (Helios Press); *Working with Mystical Experiences in Psychoanalysis: Opening to the Numinous* (Routledge); *The Self in Jungian Psychology: Theory and Clinical Practice* (Chiron); and the novel, *The Journey of Adam Kadmon: A Novel* (Arcade).

Dr. Murray Stein is a Training and Supervising Analyst at the International School of Analytical Psychology Zurich (ISAP-ZURICH). He has been President of the International Association for Analytical Psychology (IAAP) and President of ISAP-ZURICH and lectures internationally. He is the author of *Jung's Map of the Soul; Minding the Self; Outside Inside and All Around,* and many other books and articles. Four volumes of his Collected Writings have been published to date. He lives in Switzerland and has a private practice in Zurich and from his home in Goldiwil.

Ann Chia-Yi Li, M.A., is from Taiwan where she studied Chinese Literature and English Literature. She is a training analyst of ISAP ZURICH and maintains a private practice in Zurich. Ann has served on the ISAP Program Committee since 2013. Her interest lies in the relationship between Daoist practice, Alchemy, and Analytical Psychology. She has an article published in 2018, "The Receptive and the Creative: Jung's Red Book for Our Time in the Light of Daoist Alchemy," in *Jung's Red Book for Our Time: Searching for Soul under Postmodern Conditions, Vol. II,* edited by Murray Stein and Thomas Arzt.

Polly Young-Eisendrath, Ph.D., is a psychologist, writer, speaker, and Jungian analyst who has published 19 books, including, *The Self-Esteem Trap: Raising Confident and Compassionate Kids in an Age of Self-Importance,* and *Love Between Equals: Relationship as a Spiritual Path.* She is the co-author, with Jean Pieniadz, Ph.D., of *Dialogue Therapy for Couples and Real Dialogue for Opposing Sides: Methods Based on Psychoanalysis and Mindfulness.* She hosts the popular podcast *ENEMIES: From War to Wisdom,* which provides a fresh look at human hostilities and what to do about them. She is a lifelong Buddhist practitioner and a Mindfulness teacher.

....

Note on the Collected Works

As the Collected Works of C. G. Jung are cited extensively and repeatedly in this work, for the purpose of convenience, all references are of the Volume and Paragraph number: e.g., CW 7, § 388. The citation of the Collected Works is:

Jung, C. G. *Collected Works of C.G. Jung.*
R.F.C. Hull, Trans. Bollingen Series XX.
Princeton: Princeton University Press.
19 Volumes + Index + Vol. A. and B.

Introduction

Leslie Stein

It is accurate to say that it is inconceivable to profess a real interest in the works of C.G. Jung without having or developing a powerful curiosity about the numinous, the religious or spiritual dimension that exists beyond logic. Psychological growth in the vast corpus of Jungian psychology is indeed described and grounded in the promise of the healing power of this numinous dimension, so much so that Jung ascribed the therapeutic approach to the numinous as the "real therapy."[1]

Many hesitate at the gate of this mystical, unknowable dimension of our existence. The urge may be there, even prompted by a deep longing, but it may not be pursued because that mystery is ultimately irrational, indescribable, heretical for some religions, unscientific, and at most appears only as a philosophical or psychological idea. This hesitancy, even for those few who even contemplate the possibility that there is more to existence than just pursuing ego satisfaction, can also be because the inquiry appears hopeless, engendered by a feeling that it will be in vain, beyond our capabilities, as made obvious in a poem by the German philosopher Hans-Georg Gadamer:

> Man runs; and before him flees
> The ever-receding goal.
> In vain does he pull and tug
> At the curtains that drapes heavily

---

[1] Jung, 1973, Vol 1, p. 377

Over the mystery of life, over days and
nights.[2]

Yet, there are also those who are not content to remain at the
gate, who instead believe or intuit that there must exist some means to
approach the numinous, and therefore they begin to give some level
of priority to opening to that mystery. The reasons for the differences
between the hesitant and the emerging mystic are speculative. It could
be that those who give attention to that dimension do so because of
developmental issues and resultant complexes, perhaps as a reaction
to overwhelming trauma, or even arising from a deep pathology. It
also could be, more benevolently (and, in my view, more accurately),
an inexplicable higher-order calling, an innate aesthetic subtlety, and
a consequent desire for the refinement of consciousness. This may be
brought on spontaneously or even by a momentary glimpse of that
which touches the spirit, a vague hint that there may be that exciting,
yet remote possibility of a more expansive reception to that mystery.

The numinous dimension of psyche came forcefully, patently,
and indelibly to Jung in a dream wherein he encountered the Self
as a center and a centering process in our being that is constantly
nudging us toward order and homeostasis. When that miracle is
realized to any extent as an ancient, preexisting force deep within
us, which it is, it will not appear to come from our mind or body, but
rather is alien to our logical mind that therefore suggests a powerful,
spiritual possibility. Jung was so moved by his discovery of the Self,
he sought constantly to understand its numinous power through
his profound scholarship, searching for analogs far and wide: in
Hinduism, Daoism, Alchemy, Gnosticism, Christian mysticism,
Sufism, and Kabbalah. By discovering parallels to the Self in these
Eastern analogies, then having them multiplied and reexplained by
his continued insights, he makes the numinous nature of the Self the
ultimate centerpiece of psychological growth, the process he calls
individuation.

It is to Eastern practices that he turns to ground the Self in
human history as he could not find that support or recognition in
Christian doctrine. The religions of the East, defined for this work
as the practices of Hinduism, Buddhism, Daoism, and Sufism, the

[2] Gadamer, 1994, p. 62

non-Western traditions he examines, align with the Self as they all direct our basic religious instincts inward in order to reveal our true being. The Self and these Eastern traditions propose a numinous goal for our longing and the trail that is followed in that direction is the apex of human development. The promise of these Eastern practices for a Westerner, for those who pass that gate of hesitancy and attend to the numinous, is compelling by offering what appears as a logical means to turn inward, and a defined, well-laid-out discipline for the fulfillment of that longing, not found in Western religion.

Numinosity, spirituality, mystical experience, a deep moment of peace, a glimpse of wholeness, even when presented as a vague feeling, orients one away from the constant vicissitudes of the conscious mind. The numinous is therefore not just a nice idea or an interesting metaphysical concept to serve as a possible basis for psychological growth, but rather it is the critical fulcrum to modulate psychological opposites. It serves this function by fostering awareness of the wider interconnectedness of things, the possibility of a unity, thus raising the possibility of healing ourselves, our community, and our planet. Numinosity is the pivot point of civilization, wherever it can be found and in whatever form it arrives and is understood.

There is, therefore, no logical inconsistency between seeking the numinous through psychological individuation or by immersion in any Eastern practice; that greater dimension of human potential lies in both. It explains so clearly why Jung turned to the East for analogies to explain the Self. Eastern practices and Jungian psychoanalysis can then be said to naturally augment each other, as they turn the mind toward an exploration of inner truths, the only possibility for balance in an often dark and confused world.

This is not, however, so easily answered, as they exist on different metaphysical platforms and levels of sophistication. The teachings of the East are ancient, exquisitely detailed, a complex diamond, each facet polished and repolished, reflecting centuries of wisdom and refinement, while the Western description of the process of psychological change, individuation, is relatively new and very scarce in comparison.

In addition, Jung's writings are often vague as to what he intends to be the relationship between Eastern practices and individuation, causing many authors to struggle with the appropriate weight Jung intends to give to these practices, considering his continuous reference to their importance as analogies, yet his clear reluctance to integrate them too deeply into his psychology. A hesitancy can be detected in his writings, even when he relies on Eastern practices to explain the Self, because it may cause some possible dilution of the psychological process of individuation, overwhelming the ego, essential to realizing the Self.

There may, in fact, be more contrasts than similarities, as these essays suggest, and therefore specific questions arise, such as: Is being deeply engaged in an Eastern practice helpful to the process of individuation? Conversely, will psychoanalysis be useful on the path of an Eastern practice? Does Jung's admonition that individuation, rather than Eastern practices, is the path for a Westerner still have relevance?

An effective way to address these and other questions that flow from the comparison is to obtain a deeper understanding of Eastern practices as a prelude to answering how they relate to psychological growth. If the ideas and goals of an Eastern practice are made clear, then its interaction with the numinosity of the Self will be better understood.

These are, in this time when Eastern technologies of meditation, mindfulness, yoga, and Eastern inspirational books and videos are fully part of mental health, perhaps academic questions. Many analysands and analysts are in fact fully engaged in Eastern practices. And this is natural and how it should be because in this very troubled and complex world, the numinous represents a pressing hope that we can reach a higher level of awareness and greater consciousness. Western society will continue to seek out the techniques of Eastern practices as well as Western psychotherapy, to instinctively bring us back to a center point, where the noise of the world and our own mind can be stilled.

It is clear, therefore, that there can be no easy or conclusive enunciation of the exact means by which Eastern practices and the Jungian process of individuation can be joined, overlap, or be of mutual benefit. All we really know is that they easily appear to be aligned as responding to the psychological need for looking inward for meaning, partaking of the numinous, and containing the promise of achieving a unity, however described. To go further in that analysis, to understand how Eastern practices can absorb or are consistent with psychoanalysis, to bring the two closer together, requires, at least, four approaches.

The first approach is to find out how those who are engaged with an Eastern practice have used Jungian analysis to their benefit. This is approached by way of personal accounts of the way an Eastern practice has fit into and altered the life of a Jungian Analyst or the effect on those who come to psychoanalysis.

The second approach is to examine in more detail than previously available, how the complex paths of Hinduism, Daoism, and Sufism have relevance to psychoanalysis. This requires going deeper into the detail and true nature of those practices to determine what elements will be aligned with Jungian analysis.

The third approach is to address the specific problem of the Buddhist practice of no-self, a practice of over half a billion people, to determine if it has any room for the Jungian concept of the Self. It is fair to say that this is an issue that has not yet been resolved and requires reexamination.

The fourth approach is to bring the idea of Eastern practices into focus in the modern Western life, where chaos appears to be dominant. Is it possible for a Westerner to really partake of an Eastern practice, or is it better to heed Jung's warning to stay within the Western version of psychological growth?

For this difficult task, I approached each Jungian Analyst deliberately and carefully to answer these issues for reasons that may be helpful to explain. The copious writings of Polly Young-Eisendrath clearly have proclaimed her deep involvement with Eastern practices, and she generously opens her mind and heart to reveal the effect of those practices on her path of individuation, through a career as a Jungian Analyst, a scholar, and a force of never-ending inquiry. I also took upon myself to write the second essay to approach my 50-year practice within a Tantric path, not only to provide a narrative of the confusion it brought, but also to trace why indeed I and others chose an Eastern path, and to raise the eternal question of what stands in the way of its completion. The Analyst, Pat Katsky, broadened our subjective, personal experiences by performing a study of patients with Eastern practices to indicate how that weaved into their analysis and thus to point to the role of those practices in psychoanalysis.

In order to examine individuation through the prism of Eastern practices, I approached those who could penetrate into those practices to give the most comprehensive, accurate picture of what they really provide and how that relates to Jung's ideas. Starting with the Atman of Hinduism that Jung chose as the primary analogy of the Self, Ashok Bedi, a Jungian Analyst steeped from birth in the structure and substance of Hinduism, provides a detailed background that must be understood before that issue can be brought into focus. Lionel Corbett, known for his own profound writings on the sacred and the numinous, undertakes the most thorough analysis of the Atman and nonduality, as well as the efficacy of how they were used by Jung. He leaves no doubt of how that connection should be understood.

The same thoroughness and conclusive analyses are provided by the Jungian Analyst Karin Jironet as to Sufism, which Jung treated as in the same category of other Eastern religions, as one of the "exotic religious systems."[3] She is a lifelong practitioner of Sufism and indicates the structure and nature of that system to allow the comparison with individuation to be made.

Jung was influenced by the Daoism expressed in *The Secret of the Golden Flower* at the time that he first realized the Self, the central archetype of our psyche. Ann Chia-Yi Li, a Jungian Analyst and an expert in the tradition of Daoism, in exquisite detail, provides a discourse that makes that connection with individuation understood and beyond doubt.

The yet unanswered, frustrating question as to how the Buddhist doctrine of emptiness and no-self can accommodate the idea of the Jungian Self remains. Jung wrote the Foreword to D.T. Suzuki's *Introduction to Zen Buddhism* and draws upon Buddhist ideas over a hundred times in his writings. Yet, how to square the idea of a nonconceptual, ego-absent, no-self with Jung's Self that only has importance to the extent that is realized by the ego, remains uncertain. Does this Eastern religion align with the concepts of individuation?

To put this complexity to rest, Judith Pickering, who has written extensively on Buddhist spiritual practice and the apophatic way (spiritual knowledge through negating concepts of God), unravels the issue. Murray Stein, the foremost Jungian Analyst who has concentrated on explaining Jung's process of individuation, takes this further by probing questions to and dialogue with a Western Tibetan Dzogchen practitioner, Jim Manganiello, that indicates the uncertain relationship of no-self to the doctrines of individuation.

---

[3] Jung, CW 11, § 861

The last approach, the outstanding question of whether it is possible for a Westerner to advance to the end goal of an Eastern practice, may not be answered by proclamations by some of enlightenment. Royce Froelich, a Jungian Analyst who focuses on the effect of technology on psychoanalysis, provides the perfect ending to whether, in our noisy, technological world, the practice of Eastern religion and spirituality may be too difficult for Westerners, as Jung suggests.

It appeared to be the right time to provide this work, other than just in aid of an intellectual desire to draw a more precise connection between Eastern practices and individuation. Not only is this a particularly intimidating time in history when we all are seeking some solace and peace and need to know where to turn, but it is also a period when spirituality is becoming scientifically relevant. I do not wish to make this proposition work too hard, but research in spirituality and altered states as an adjunct to psychoanalysis is burgeoning with the emphasis on mindfulness, as well as the concept of "psychospiritual" integration, the blending of spirituality and psychology. In recent years, what was an important but peripheral attention to the numinous has become a focal point for research into quality-of-life issues, pastoral care, and models for dealing with trauma. Here, the numinous is finding a contemporary place in what appears to be an increasing pattern of absorbing and legitimizing Eastern practices into mental health theory and clinical work. This makes Jung's comments on the importance of the numinous and the relationship of psychology to Eastern spiritual practice more urgent and necessary.

The true spirit of Jung, that which places his form of psychoanalysis as a critical component of mental health, lies primarily in the numinous dimension. It is a dimension where the conflicting opposites, the tragedies of modern living, can find a resting place. To understand Jung's analogs in Hinduism, Daoism, Sufism, and his engagement with Buddhism, amplifies the nature of the numinous and brings us closer to the goal of our work as Analysts and explains the longing we see in every analysand and ourselves.

References

Gadamer, H-G. (1994). *Literature and Philosophy in Dialogue: Essays in German Literary Theory.* R. H. Paslick, Trans. Albany: SUNY Press

Jung, C.G. (1973). *C.G. Jung Letters.* Vol 2. G. Adler & J. Jaffe, Eds. Princeton: Princeton University Press

PERSONAL
ENCOUNTERS

1

From Akron to Bodhgaya:
Suffering and Individuation

Polly Young-Eisendrath

In this brief essay, I explore the range of my spiritual discoveries over a lifetime of individuation from the perspectives of theories of the unconscious mind in Buddhism and psychoanalysis. My main discovery is that I have never been especially interested in my own identity or inner conflicts but instead have been motivated first by the suffering I witnessed around me in my childhood and then by the conditions of my physical and social contexts in adult life. While I am profoundly introverted, my "discoveries" of Self have come through my inquiries into the intersubjective world in which I have found myself and not especially into my own individual identity. Only in the "backward look" over my own development have I been able to perceive the patterns of the archetypal Self as it emerged through my spiritual and psychological engagements with human consciousness in relationship.

As a Jungian analyst since 1986 and a practicing Buddhist since 1971, I have had many different views of and particular answers to the question "Will somebody *please tell me what's going on here*, anyway?!" as I have formulated the overarching question about human existence on my path of individuation. It's a phrasing

3

I embraced early on in adulthood based on a similar statement expressed by the American writer Annie Dillard.[1] In this chapter, I examine retrospectively some early stirrings of this fundamental inquiry, as well as my attempts to respond to it over the decades.

These cogitations take me from my working-class childhood in Akron, Ohio, to a Buddhist retreat on Phowa (conscious dying) in Bodhgaya, India, and through many decades of training and practice as a Jungian psychoanalyst and clinical psychologist, and more decades of training and practice in Zen and Vipassana meditation forms. I am telling my story here to those I imagine to be my professional peers who are psychotherapists, Jungians, psychologists, and perhaps also serious spiritual seekers. If I were addressing a different audience, I would shape it differently.

Here, my orientation is largely personal, although I try to define specialized terms in a manner I believe is consistent with their formal or proper meaning in their field — specifically, Buddhism or analytical psychology. My aim is to expose the personal dilemmas and vulnerabilities that led to my spiritual and psychological searches and to attempt to discover where I have ended up in this search at the present time as a psychoanalyst, Buddhist, feminist, psychologist, author, and podcaster, as well as a mother, grandmother, and life partner!

Accepting Jung's definition of *individuation* in adulthood to mean the embracing of one's "psychic totality" or "becoming a psychological individual," I emphasize, as Jung did, my "collective considerations and obligations" as well as my own unique "combination or gradual differentiation, of functions and faculties which in themselves are universal."[2] As a young child, with a father who suffered from borderline personality disorder with transient states of psychosis, I found myself steeped in situations that provoked painful observations and questions. Even in childhood, I began to investigate my experience and look for answers, as I illustrate below.

---

[1] Dillard, 2015, p. 139
[2] Jung, CW 7, § 267

The Archetype of Self: Context and Constraints

From a Buddhist perspective, we are born into certain "causes and conditions" (karma and *sankaras*) that connect with the "mind stream" or "storehouse/home consciousness" that travels with us from incarnation to incarnation through diverse lifetimes. Or, to be more precise, we travel through space-time within these unknown circumstances that potentiate and constrain our possibilities in meaningful ways (as in, "This life was designed *just for you!*") that may perplex and perturb us throughout our years ("Why me? Why this?") but are not entirely or perhaps at all under our control or the control of others. While we are responsible for our own intentional actions and speech, we may mistakenly take credit for our mental formations or even traits ("*my* creativity") or disavow our actions ("my temper is *not my* fault"). Using a Jungian term here, these causes and conditions comprise the "archetype of Self" for one's particular incarnation: the bedrock constraint of our individual subjectivity, shaping the potentials for being a particular embodied Self. I define this archetype as the fundamental imprint of our individual humanity/subjectivity that drives or compels the formation of a particular ego complex (including a body) within the relationships of family of origin and other significant situations of early development (birth through seven years, or so).

The flag I now fly under (psychoanalyst, Buddhist, feminist) may sound very complicated because it has a host of identifiers, but it boils down to one observation that I came upon around seven years old: "People (around me) seem intent on destroying themselves and their relationships" and an accompanying question, "Is it possible for people to know/respect/love each other?" Although these things were not formed in such precise terms when I was seven years old, growing up in a working-class family in Akron, Ohio, they were already discernible to me and carried some compelling emotional effects. These perceptions and questions were (as I look back at all this now) the reason that I stopped speaking and became an "elective mute" (now called "selective mute") on my second day of the second grade

5

in elementary school. Diving into my subjectivity, and inhabiting my own fantasies and stories, I thereafter spent each school day with my head tucked deeply into my desk (hidden under its flip top) and my afternoons and evenings at home alone in my bedroom, lying still and quiet with my eyes closed, as much as possible. I ate little and needed less. This was possibly my first "spiritual retreat." It was also the first time I felt truly powerful. No grown-up, no teacher or parent, could *make me say* anything. I felt a freedom to be myself in silence, a freedom I had not previously felt.

The age of seven is significant for consciousness: it's the first time we become wholly conscious or aware of our individual identity: "Oh, I am *me!*" This *me* becomes something we can reflect on. It seems somehow apart from the "I" observing it. The developmental researcher Jean Piaget says the period of six to seven years old is the beginning of "concrete operational thought," meaning that we can "operate" on our own thoughts and feelings, using them instrumentally and comparing them in a rudimentary way to others' thoughts and feelings. At seven, I began to get the hang of not speaking while reviewing the images and words in my mind for myself, trying to answer the question of what was going on in the situation I found myself in. Was I a budding Zen Buddhist or a budding psychoanalyst or a budding schizoid personality? Whatever the answer, I felt the power of "thought review" and removed myself from ordinary social environments.

My parents, who themselves had had only eighth-grade educations and were in their early 40s at the time, were driven completely mad by my behaviors. Although I had had a very secure and emotionally close relationship with my mother in my early years, I was an odd child (socially awkward and quiet) and was known to the school principal, as my mother later told me when I was 50 years old, as "highly gifted" (assessed from standardized tests). This information apparently created worry for teachers and the principal as I seemed not to respond enthusiastically to most school environments. Were they failing me? Was I failing them? Everything became more and more dramatic for me (and the adults around me) in the second grade. For example, some months into my silence, my father stayed home from his factory job for an entire week so that he could "spank Polly every day." His spankings were not painful or vindictive, and I could tell that he was embarrassed to be taking these actions against me. He was frustrated because he could not *make me do what he wanted*. I could also tell that I had more power than he did because I was *withholding* something. The spankings led to nothing. Then my mother took to the couch in the living room where she seemed to be at all times when she was not in the kitchen. I could feel her despair. I felt sorry for her but couldn't do anything (because I wasn't speaking), so I just headed for my bedroom.

Eventually, near the end of second grade, I overheard my parents talking about how they'd been in meetings with some authorities at my school and that I would be sent to a "psychiatrist" at Akron University (seems to me I heard the word at that time and knew its meaning). I then began to consider the broader implications of my behavior: Although I was discovering many things in my private inquiry, I was apparently going to be in a lot more trouble if I continued the silence.

My internal stories and fantasies were about bringing an end to human hostilities, to war. The silence began when I had come to understand "war" from my father's stories of being in World War II. I understood that in war, humans *willingly killed each other*. Many times, I had overheard people in my family say something like "*I'll kill you* if you do that again!" but I had not seen anyone act on that threat. I had seen my aunt beaten up, even perhaps "beaten to a pulp." But my aunt would talk about what had happened in a kind of carefree jokey manner, telling her story dramatically, with a cigarette in hand, sipping a "good cup of coffee" at my mother's kitchen table.

I worried early on about the overtones of violence around me. I thought the threats were serious, but not terrifying, until I heard about people killing each other willingly in war. I felt terrified of war. This "war" and the killings seemed to me to be a Big Problem that no one talked about, certainly not the adults around me who threatened each other often. I would have to solve this problem myself, I thought.

I dove into silence with the belief that saints (I was Catholic) often sacrifice their lives and I could perhaps sacrifice my childish life, imitate a saint, and persuade adults to end war. In my silence, I was imagining a way to express my sincere insights about the mistake humans were making in their willingness to use aggression, hostility, and violence to try to get their way with each other.

As the summer after second grade wore on, I began to see that my plan was not working well. I began to resign myself to living an ordinary life, not a saintly one. It was hard to shake myself out of the silence because it felt so right and powerful. But then I also began to see that I needed to express myself in order to develop any plan to end violence. Entering hesitantly back into speech, I discovered that my words — both written and spoken — often came to me automatically, almost fully formed, especially when I was passionate and principled. I could always count on having something to say because I did not have to "think it up." I had apparently discovered some secret source of guidance: an articulate and informed voice speaking into my inner ear.

I came quickly to see myself as someone who could stand up and say certain things (not personal, but principled) without hesitation, in front of others, even while I was often very shy within my personal self. There was a lot about my young mind — its schizoid style and fantasies, for example — that I would now say could be categorized as somewhat psychotic although it seemed to me to be spiritual at the time. Mine was not a conventional mind. I did not experience childhood or my family life as safe, predictable, cozy, or "ordinary." Instead, I felt my identity and surroundings to be precarious, confusing, and unpredictable. My mother's warmth and attention were a stable, steady force, but they were surrounded by a sea of chaos and mystery. From my earliest memories, I felt ill-suited for "life on Earth" or whatever it was that I had landed in, and yet, when I spoke and wrote my thoughts and insights, I was warmly praised and welcomed by teachers and mentors. Events entirely unknown to me had in many ways shaped my childhood mind.

Experience of the Archetype of Self

My father, who had fought in World War II, had a dark and hidden past in the sense that his story was left out of all family narratives and suppressed by him under all circumstances. I never saw his parents or heard about them or saw pictures of them. Although we lived next door to his brother, my uncle, and his wife and their five children, I knew next to nothing about my father's family of origin. I knew they were from West Virginia. I knew his parents were dead. When I asked about them, my father would say, "They died before you were born" without details, and sometimes he would add, "You remind me of my mother." My next-door cousins were a rowdy crew who seemed full of life and energy — fighting, running in the woods, playing rough games, starting fires, getting into trouble with authorities. They expressed the opposite of my own schizoid approach to life, and I was fascinated by their style.

They were also a contrast to my mother's well-organized, tidy Slovenian Catholic family of 10 siblings and two parents. My mother, who met my father when they were both working in the same tire factory in Akron, regularly boasted about and extolled the virtues of her clan. She clearly felt "above" my father's nasty crew. My mother's seven sisters and two brothers were what I knew as "our family." Holidays, celebrations, and other family occasions were with her family. There were lots of grandchildren at these events and lots of chores and tasks that girls like me were meant to carry out while the boys got to do other things (hang out at the Slovenian club, for instance, or drink homemade wine in the garage with the men).

My grandparents did not speak English, and my grandmother often called me "Barbara" because I had a cousin named Barbara who also lived in Akron. My grandparents lived in Verona, Pennsylvania, close to the steel mill where my grandfather had worked after he left the coal mines of West Virginia. This Slovenian family felt impersonal to me, as though they could not know me as an individual, especially because my grandmother rarely knew my name. No one, not my parents or my cousins, seemed to care that my grandmother got my name wrong, and I eventually learned to respond to "Barbara." No one in that family ever asked me a personal question — not even "How are *you*?" — although a few of my aunts hugged me and bought presents for me on outings. I was grateful for their food, stability, and stories "of the old country." But I did not identify with the clan.

I identified with the other side: my father's ragtag crew. While my mother was a good caregiver and a well-organized homemaker (she stopped working after I was born), my father was weird, disturbed, and yet compelling in many ways. He left for his factory job at 4:30 a.m. on weekdays, and returned home at 5 p.m. when dinner was already on the table. Erratic and ornery, he was also a "good wage earner," by my mother's report. He also was extremely intelligent (had a very high score on the Army Alpha IQ test), wrote poems, and spent hours looking out into the fields in our backyard, silent. At night, he was gripped by anxieties and sometimes delusions. Often he raged at night, accusing my mother and me of doing things to him, of being disloyal or against him.

On our small "farm," he was kind and attentive to the domestic animals (dogs, cats, chicken, ducks, sometimes goats), tended our vegetable gardens, built sheds, and loved to join in with the children (my cousins and neighbors) in our pretend games and stories. He played like a child (a large man at 6 feet 2 inches tall and 220 pounds) and helped us create shows and carnivals. He was a leader of our gang and a petulant and competitive member; there were no other adults playing with us like my dad. I was proud of him even though his involvement could seem embarrassing if he was childish.

The significant events of my father's hidden past were revealed to me only in adulthood and only now, in my 70s, do I know the details. My father, as his brother told me in my 30s, was born into a West Virginia mining family to a father who was a "member" of the erstwhile "Jesse James Gang." My grandfather, Cecil Young, was found floating in a river with a bullet in his back when my father was six years old. Recently, a cousin of mine, from Ohio, researched this death and unearthed some poignant newspaper accounts. On September 7,

1917, *The Chillicothe Gazette* reported, "Floater is Identified as Akron Man; Leaves Wife and Four Children." The article reports that a body was exhumed, one that had been unable to be identified because it was so badly decayed after floating in the river for almost a week. But, on "Friday morning two brothers and the father identified the floater found in Paint Creek as Cecil E. Young ... they said he was married and left a wife and four children. That he was a carpenter at Camp Sherman and was survived by his mother and three sisters." The narrative continues, "Young, it will be remembered, was the man for whom his wife and children were searching, five or six weeks ago, when work at the camp opened. They claimed at the time that they were starving and were searching for the husband. ... Whether he met death by suicide, accident or foul play, is not known." According to my uncle, my father's older brother, Cecil Young was found "with a bullet in his back for cheatin' at gambling."

And the story continues in the news. Four years later, on October 29, 1921, another newspaper, *The Akron Beacon Journal,* tells what happened to the four children and the mother, my grandmother (whom I reminded my father of):

> The body of Mrs. Louise Young ... who died Friday at the Peoples Hospital from the effects of poison, self-administered Tuesday evening in a fit of despondency, will be taken to her old home in Gassaway, West Virginia. ... Mrs. Young was 35 years old, and the widowed mother of four children, two living with her, one with relatives, and one an inmate of the Boys Industrial School. She had been receiving a pension from the county for the care of the two children living with her, but because she had been giving the authorities considerable trouble, and had been neglecting her children, Judge H. C. Spicer, in juvenile court Tuesday morning, committed her two children to the county home for children and revoked her pension.

Later that day, my grandmother poisoned herself with arsenic. My father, 10 years old, was living with his aunt at the time while his 12-year-old brother was in the Boys Industrial School. My father *never spoke* of any of this and said only that his parents had died before I was born.

These unknown conditions shaped much of the emotional and unconscious meaning of my childhood and of my father's madness — creating a calling in me both to speak and not to speak: to become a psychoanalyst, as well as a Buddhist. The torture of my father's mind, as well as the intelligence and vulnerability of his spirit, opened questions in me instead of closing off my perceptions. My trauma was largely observed trauma and not directly experienced. The violence and beatings I witnessed (but never endured myself), taught me about the destructive hostilities in families. Intuitively, I knew the adults around me meant well. I knew they were held captive to some forces they could not resist and did not understand. That's why I wanted to contemplate, in my own mind, the problem of "war" when I was seven years old.

Of course, it might have gone differently if I not been a serious, introverted child who was wholly dedicated to questions about human suffering. It would certainly have gone differently if I had not had access to one solid and engaged caregiver: my mother. The elective mutism provided my first retreat and gave me the incentive to work within my mind to find a pathway to discernments, and then to hear my inner voices and their wisdom, as distinct from their anxieties. From my earliest childhood, I have memories of many spiritual experiences, including levitation. Without a doubt, I was born into the archetype of the Wounded Healer and I embraced it with all my heart as a spiritual path.

The Wounded Healer, Catholicism, and Buddhism

My mother's Slovenian family was deeply, rabidly, and devotedly Catholic. My mother was my own personal god until I was about 12 years old. I asked her about everything, reported everything to her, and generally felt grounded by her instructions and ideas. Catholicism worked well for me as a structure holding both the interpersonal chaos and my inquiring mind, giving me a way to understand and digest my spiritual experiences without becoming too otherworldly, as well as a way to access art (stained glass windows and sculptures) that was otherwise absent, as well as music and crowds of grown-ups acting kindly and being quiet. Reading about the lives of the saints and contemplating my own dedication to Big Questions, I felt that perhaps I "had a vocation" as a nun. I spoke about this idea only to my mother, who steadfastly discouraged it (I was her only child, and she wanted grandchildren). I held the notion in my heart as I felt I had some special role in bringing peace to humans through God's insights.

When I was around 12 to 13 years old, I surpassed my mother's education and I began to develop my own friends and move away from my mother as my best friend and my father as a playmate. My mother took this badly. As I look back, I realize she was envious of what was developing for me. At the time, it seemed that she was irritated and unhappy with my achievements and ideas. "Don't let yourself get a big head!" and "You don't need all those BOYS around all the time!" were the kinds of feedback she began giving me. Nonetheless, I moved on and out into the world because my many (truly) fine and inspiring teachers and mentors in the public schools in East Akron were aware of my gifts and leaned into me to develop them. I was a star student and even — shockingly, given my oddities — a student leader.

My mother and father were not happy about my popularity when it took me away from them, even though they were proud to boast about it occasionally. By my junior year in high school, I was at the top of my class of 401 and had also been sought out by Akron Bell Telephone to become a telephone operator. Twenty hours a week, in addition to classes and leadership, I worked as a telephone operator and made substantial earnings that I brought home to my parents to help with the household. I got some spending money from my employment, but more importantly, I felt independent. I knew

I could make my own living long before I graduated high school. Nearing graduation, I applied to some colleges, got scholarships everywhere but also reserved the possibility of life in a convent instead of the world.

The week after I graduated, I entered a convent for one week and considered the possibility of initiation into a vocation. It was a convent of Dominican (the "Gray Nuns") Sisters, who were largely educators and social workers. After one week, I knew that life in the convent was not for me. Spiritual questions and conversations were discouraged, and many of the novices were depressed and withdrawn. I wanted an adventure, not a lockdown in the spiritual world.

In the fall of 1965, I entered the freshman class (of around 4,000 students) at Ohio University in Athens, Ohio. I thought that I wanted to become a psychologist so that I could help people with mental illness. I wanted to get to bottom of what I had witnessed as hidden motivations and longings in the adults around me. I was wholly sincere without an ounce of irony. I wanted to end war and stop the relentless destruction among humans in their relationships with each other. Taking undergraduate courses in psychology and sociology quickly informed me that these subjects carried neither knowledge nor wisdom of the sort I was seeking. In my honors sophomore seminar in psychology, we were "running" rats and nonsense syllables, not speaking with people. Even though I could easily join in the discussion of behaviorism in the research labs, I was not interested. I fled briefly to studio art (as a painter) and then into French literature (spent a year abroad in France), and finally finished with a degree in English literature with a specialty in medieval studies, writing my honors thesis on the image of the Virgin in the European Middle Ages — taking my cues especially from a theorist I stumbled onto: Erich Neumann, a Jungian analyst. Through him, I discovered the archetype of the Great Mother, allowing me to unpack some of my projections into my own mother and to embrace firmly the natural force carried by female humans. In my senior year, my roommate said, "If you really want to find out about Carl Jung, read *Memories, Dreams, Reflections.*" I did and I fell in love with Jung. He quickly stepped into my father's shoes and fulfilled my fantasies of an Oedipal love affair.

But just when it seemed as though I would dive fully into the world of Jungian psychology, I was waylaid by a spiritual breakdown. Reading *In Search of the Miraculous* by Petr Ouspensky,[3] in the summer of 1970, I once again took to silence and to my bed. I felt overwhelmed by the challenge of self-awareness (self-responsibility and agency) posed by Ouspensky and his teacher, G. I. Gurdjieff, as a means of developing the consciousness needed to reincarnate in a human life, especially for poor working-class people like my relatives who would surely slide into some terrible wormhole in the cosmos because they lacked even a modicum of self-awareness. I could feel the heavy burden of karma: the darkness of habitual thoughts and actions as they carried humans into deeper and deeper miseries. I wanted to help. I felt compassion for my family. I could find nothing in the Jungian or medieval works I had been studying that could be applied to the suffering of the members of my family.

My (first) husband, who was a philosopher, a depressive, and a Zen practitioner, took one look at my predicament and said, "Stop mucking around in your thoughts. If you really want to help with the suffering of the world, you will need to learn some Zen!" And so, in the late fall of 1970, I went up to the Rochester Zen Center in Rochester, New York, from Greensboro, North Carolina (where I lived), for my first introductory workshop. I was 23 years old. There, I met Roshi Philip Kapleau, the head teacher, who was recently back from 14 years of training in Japan. In his brief talk, Kapleau said some profoundly wise things with the utmost simplicity and practicality: For instance, "Make your bed when you get out of it in the morning. That is when it is most relevant to you. And then, when you return to your bed at night, you will be surprised that someone has made it for you." And, "Listen to the bell without thinking where can I buy one like it?" Useful and immediate spiritual insights about arising of

---

[3] Ouspensky, 2001

15

daily life had been sorely lacking for me; they reverberated through ripples of meaning, out beyond my complex scholarly studies of the medieval cosmos and Jung's psychology.

With zero knowledge of Buddhism, I dove into the world of Zen the same way I had dove into my wooden desk in the second grade of elementary school. I was all in. Sitting meditation in Zen practice is very demanding and physically exhausting. I had encountered nothing like it in any spiritual practice or religion I had explored. After fleeing the convent, I began exploring the world's religions by practicing them, imitating the religious scholar Huston Smith. Only in Zen did I find the combination of embodied engagement and mental challenge that has kept me occupied for these 50 years. In my early practice days and months, I was confronted by massive psychological distress, as well as wrenching physical pain. Sometimes my experiences were connected to observing my fellow practitioners in the Zendo. Their apparent pain and suffering would leave me distressed about the missing kindness and compassion in the practice. Was Zen practice traumatizing people in their attempts to find truth through experience? Roshi Kapleau was a firm and kind teacher who guided me well through these inquiries and reassured me about the necessity of awakening for true compassion.

After about four years of practicing at the Rochester Zen Center, I decided to take a break from formal Zen practice because I wanted to go to personal psychotherapy, and Kapleau would not permit his students to go to psychotherapy while they were in training with him ("follow only one master" was the dictum). In my conversations and relationships with fellow Zen practitioners, I gradually discovered that most of us suffered difficult psychological wounds in our childhoods and had strong "father hunger," by which I mean we did not feel fathered well by our own fathers. Kapleau's sweet, avuncular style was a welcome antidote for our hunger. And yet, there was not any personal psychological help available to us. Instead, we were thrown back to practicing on our meditation cushions when we raised questions about the psychological side of human suffering.

Also, I noticed that certain kinds of idealization were popular among Zen students, and they had to do primarily with the value of fierce sitting practice. I never heard about the value of fierce compassion or loving kindness. In the spirit of wanting to fulfill my Bodhisattva vows, many times I fainted or otherwise collapsed in the Zendo, and as soon as I could, I would calmly return to my cushion and my practice with zero curiosity about the reason for my collapse. I felt no mercy for my weaknesses. I began to wonder about this kind of compulsion in myself and others. I also witnessed a certain kind of brutal fierceness in the Zendo managers who wielded the "stick" at retreats with regular whacks to keep us awake.

And so, it began to seem that my natural therapeutic strivings that began with my childhood observations of my father's mental illness and my own longing to alleviate it had a valid place in my spiritual adventures. While therapeutic insight was no substitute for awakening, I saw that it played a role in compassion, allowing suffering individuals to commiserate with and embrace each other. I could also see that I personally needed to go to psychotherapy in order to discern what might be useful in helping myself and others with emotional and mental suffering. I spoke to my teacher to say that I would need to leave formal practice in order to find my own way. He generously said, "Sometimes, individuals need to go their own way, and I hope you can find your way on the path." A decade or so later, I was reunited with Roshi Kapleau and practiced with him until the end of his life. I grew close to him and was privileged to help him publish some of his unpublished talks. When we were serendipitously reunited after our decade apart, Kapleau commented sagaciously: "When you are walking through a field of high grasses, it looks as though there is no path. But when you look back over your shoulder, it's a different story. You were following a path all along." It seems to me now that this wise comment is a summary of my spiritual development throughout my entire lifetime. I have been following a path that I have not known or seen.

Birth and Death: The World and the Self

Two other aspects of my life in the first part of the 1970s are worth mentioning on the path of spiritual development through individuation. In 1971, the year I first took my formal Zen vows, I also had an ectopic pregnancy, and my life was suddenly and acutely at risk. In the experience of being saved through emergency surgery, and then later giving birth to my first child in 1972, I faced my first serious encounters with death in these occasions of birth. During the diagnosis of my ectopic pregnancy, I saw immediately how birth and death are different sides of the same coin. I was pregnant, but if I carried the pregnancy even a few days longer, I would very likely die from hemorrhage, as a result of the exploding of my fallopian tube; the fetus was already dead, drowned in the blood in the fallopian tube. In my first live birth, I gave birth to a 10-pound baby who was one month overdue. This is my daughter, now in her late 40s. In the 14th hour of childbirth, I saw a bright light at the end of a dark tunnel. I became confused as to whether I was the baby being born or the mother dying. I could feel into both of them. The absolute interface of birth and death is a central teaching of Buddhism: What is born will die, and what dies will be reborn within the cycles of samsara.

In my outer life in Greensboro, I was actively involved in antiracism as a part of the Black Power movement, and I lived and worked in the Black community. My husband was a professor of philosophy at Bennett College, a black women's college. I considered myself to be a political radical; I wanted my life to be integrated with the lives of people of diverse skin colors and backgrounds, having grown up in an integrated school and neighborhood in Akron. I knew from my experience (as I had known from the beginning) that I needed to discover how humans could learn to live together peacefully with their differences. I also knew from becoming a mother that I needed to find out why women were robbed of their inherent power and heroism. Women risk their lives to give birth to all of us; there are no exceptions. Facing into birth/death in having children is heroism, plain and simple. At the age of 25, I became a first-time mother and a feminist simultaneously, as I dove into the writings of Adrienne Rich, especially her powerful, moving memoir *Of Woman Born*.[4] I was also deeply influenced by her iconic poem about psychoanalysis, "Diving Into the Wreck."

Looking back now, it seems to me that I began to study the Self through experiences of the outer world, instead of any particular interest in my subjectivity. My interest in feminism and psychoanalysis came to me by way of childbirth, not by way of my concern about being a woman or having a female identity. Instead, I had an experience of childbirth that brought the female hero to my door, and I was interested in the ways that she inhabited the space between life and death. My interest in world peace and the creative use of conflict came to me both through my time as a political activist and in my early life as an observer of domestic violence.

Exploring my own psyche was the last thing on my list but, in my analysis (with June Singer), I began to understand and appreciate that my "self" was more or less the product of experiences and processes that were unconscious. While I was led to psychoanalysis and to feminism by experiences in life rather than an interest in my identity or my inner conflicts, in the end, I discovered that I knew very little about myself from my conscious perceptions and preoccupations and that I could not learn much about myself simply through meditation and contemplation.

Psychoanalysis and Buddhism

In the many years, I have followed the unseen path of my life through the wild, high grass of my experiences. I have come to feel that engagement with others, especially through significant close relationships (including psychotherapy and love relationships) is the *via regia* to self-understanding. The challenge and particularity of our closest others, as we travel the human path of impermanence and imperfection with them, permit us to know ourselves through the

---

[4] Rich, 1996

questions asked and the observations offered in dialogue together. The reflections we see of ourselves in others' eyes stand next to the thoughts and feelings we have about ourselves. We need to hold our self-narratives lightly and make room for how we are reflected.

Human life is a social engagement (I say this as a lifelong introvert who lives on a Vermont mountain) because we come into it as a pair, a dyad, and we depend on another from the beginning in order to know ourselves, to see ourselves, and to hear ourselves. Meditation and contemplation give us insights into the universal conditions of our existence, but they cannot tell us much about the particularity of our own subjectivity — the archetype of the Self. We cannot see ourselves easily, no matter how long we stare at those tangled grassy fields in front of us.

And so, I have engaged fully in love, both romantic and parental. I was lucky to have had at least one true love in my partnership and marriage to Ed Epstein. Together, Ed and I had many spiritual and life adventures, and many opportunities to explore our reflections in each other's eyes. Ed was a psychotherapist and a practitioner of psychodrama. Over the years, I learned a lot from Ed, about myself, and about couple relationships. Throughout our time together, I became the more formal practitioner of psychology, psychoanalysis, and Buddhism, but Ed was there by my side, with all of his questions about the reality of the principles and practices I embraced. Whatever I came to in my studies and meditations, Ed would always come back to the practical. How was I applying what I knew to my everyday life?

When Ed was 59 years old, he was diagnosed with advanced Alzheimer's. He had begun developing early onset Alzheimer's at the age of 54. He died at the age of 66. During the decade of his slow erasure and decline, I learned how to love Ed in a different way. I learned to love him on a one-way street, without the reciprocation of his interest and witnessing of me. I have written extensively about this part of my life with Ed in my book *The Present Heart: A Memoir of Love, Loss, and Discovery.*[5] That book came out the day after Ed died in 2014. His transition into death was his greatest teaching to me. Ed stayed in conscious, eye-to-eye contact with me through his transition, although he had no cortex by the time that he died. He was conscious and responsive without a cortex.

It was, in fact, Ed's Alzheimer's and his dying process that brought me to the study and practice of Phowa, the Tibetan Buddhist method for the transfer of consciousness at the time of death. Because Zen and Vipassana did not teach much about the process of conscious dying, I turned to Tibetan Buddhism to find out. In the year 2007, I attended my first Phowa retreat in Garrison, N.Y., at the Garrison Institute, with the eminent master Ayang Rinpoche. By this time, I had studied a lot about early Indian Buddhism, as well as practiced extensively through retreats and close relationships with my teachers. Ayang Rinpoche teaches through both lectures and mind-to-mind transmission. I was very sensitive to such transmission, which had a powerful effect on my meditation. As a result, I had a personal meeting with Rinpoche, who insisted I should attend a Phowa retreat with him in Bodhgaya, India. He asked for my commitment to this meeting in India.

At this time in December 2007, Ed was quite ill with dementia although he was still living at home. He had retired from his psychotherapy practice. Friends of mine were rotating at my house through 10 days of Ed's care, so that I could attend this retreat at the Garrison Institute. I wanted to decline Rinpoche's invitation, but I found myself conceding and promising to come to India sometime in the near future to attend the retreat there. I was not deeply optimistic that I would be able to follow through. Not only was Ed at home ill, but he and I had encountered a financial disaster: Ed had thoroughly mismanaged our finances during the early years of his disease. I had no money. I had no freedom to travel. But some things changed in my personal life after Ed went into residential care in 2009, and through a variety of circumstances that I could not have anticipated,

---

[5] Young-Eisendrath, 2018

I went to Bodhgaya in 2012 and attended the retreat there with Ayang Rinpoche.

By the time of Ed's death in 2014, I had practiced Phowa with communities in India and Denver, Colorado. Consequently, I was informed and able to make arrangements for formal practice of Phowa during Ed's transition. Practices were done by masters in India and the U.S., and I am sure they contributed to Ed's capacity to remain conscious during the dying process. In my dreams following his death, I encountered Tibetan monks who informed me about what they were doing for Ed.

Without Ed's illness and death, I doubt that I would have looked deeply into these esoteric Tibetan practices and learned about the transition of consciousness at the time of death. As a consequence of all this, I was able to learn also from my direct experience of Ed while he was dying that consciousness does not depend on the cortex or on any brain function. I have recently discovered that the acute awareness at the time of death is called "terminal clarity" by those scientists who study Near-Death Experience.

In this last chapter of my individuation story, I embrace the validity of the two approaches to subjective experience that my life has emphasized, Buddhism and psychoanalysis. Buddhism has been the primary foundation for my spiritual development and life. My dedication undoubtedly has roots in the deaths of my grandparents, lost in the wild grasses of my childhood, as they affected my father. I have extended my interest in Buddhism now to my engagement with a community of scientists who are studying the "new science of consciousness," which hypothesizes that the brain is a filter, not a generator, of consciousness. They range from the researchers on reincarnation and parapsychology at the Division of Perceptual Studies at the University of Virginia at Charlottesville, to the scientists who study controlled psychedelic experiences at Johns Hopkins University, to the researchers who are studying Near-Death Experience throughout the world.[6] Some of these researchers are influenced by

---

[6] Greyson, 2021

the work of the cognitive scientist Donald Hoffman[7], who states that consciousness is generated not by anything material, but through an interactive conscious network that exists outside of space-time.

While I am thoroughly engaged in this new study, I have also been reinventing Dialogue Therapy, the couples therapy I began with Ed. Writing and teaching about couples developing skills to transform difficult conversations and polarizations is my current antiwar work. Psychoanalysis contributes importantly to this work because of the concept of "projective identification," a term that originates with Melanie Klein and refers to unconscious communication but also may be seen to include Jung's ideas about how we infect each other's unconscious dynamics. Projective identification begins in our earliest relational dyad in which the infant communicates its life/death needs without language or culture. Working with couples locked into complexes and with other polarizing conversations, I feel that I am finally completing the silent retreat I began in the second grade.

I have had an extraordinarily unconventional life that, in many ways, seemed to rise up around me. On the surface, no one could argue that my childhood as a working-class girl growing up in Akron, Ohio, in the 1950s, with parents who had not completed even a high school education, would predict a career in psychology, psychoanalysis, and couples therapy in which I have published 19 books that have been translated into more than 20 languages. No one would have predicted that I would be a 50-year practitioner of Buddhism, including esoteric Buddhism. No one could have imagined that I would be living on the side of a mountain in Vermont where I am able to interview some of the most extraordinary scientists and sages in the field of consciousness. The only thing that could have signaled my unfolding through this process is the unseen design of karma (the archetype of the Self) that puts together our subjectivity in a particular and individual way, moment by moment. This is the path that is hidden from us when we look at the wild grass ahead but is revealed when we look back over our shoulders.

---

[7] Hoffman, 2008

References

Dillard, A. (2015). *Pilgrim at Tinker Creek*. New York: Harper Collins

Hoffman, D.D. (2008). Conscious realism and the mind-body problem. *Mind & Matter, 6*(1), pp. 87-121

Greyson, B. (2021). *After: A Doctor Explore what Near-Death Experiences Reveal about Life and Beyond*. New York: St. Martin's Essentials

Ouspensky, P.D. (2001). *In Search of the Miraculous*. San Diego: Harvest Books

Rich, A. (1996). *Of Women Born: Motherhood as Experience and Institution*. New York: W.W. Norton

Young-Eisendrath, P. (2018). *The Present Heart: A Memoir of Love, Loss, and Discovery*. Emmaus, Pa.: Harmony/Rodale

2

Archetypal Forces and the Ego Structure for Eastern Practices

Leslie Stein

The lure of Eastern practices is the hope of attaining to another dimension beyond and above the struggles and vicissitudes of the conscious mind. This chapter explores the forces that take one away from a Western religion to find the answer in a new paradigm of an Eastern practice, with all its esoteric and impossible promises. It also explores, through a personal account, the struggles and questions that take place because of a strong Western ego and what then is necessary for the goal of an Eastern practice to be reached.

I slowly made my way out of the water after completely immersing myself for the Holy Dip at 10 p.m. on January 24, 2001, the auspicious bathing time and day: *Mauni Amavasya*, at the meeting of the Ganges and Yamuna Rivers, one dirty, one clean, that form a visible line of confluence that is said to be the mystical, virtual Saraswathi River. It is at this time, 10 p.m. until midnight that it is believed the water turns into divine nectar. I was standing dripping wet from that nectar in a loincloth in the midst of the *Maha Kumbha Mela* in Allahabad in north-central India, among 30 million Indian bathers gathered for the Dip at this one spot at that time of day. Great multitudes of worshippers who had been let into the water for the

Dip also gradually inched out onto the banks, the *Sangam*, already filled with countless lingering pilgrims, all silent as required. By this Holy Dip, we had all escaped the endless cycle of death and rebirth, and there was thus an air of jubilation. The compacted, shoulder-to-shoulder multitudes suddenly parted, and a naked monk, a *naga sadhu*, covered only in white funeral pyre ash, was let through, which was extremely unusual as there was no room to maneuver, and I watched as he made his way and then stopped in front of me. He grabbed both my shoulders and said in perfect English, ignoring the penetrating silence, "Time to call off the search," then walked away.

What indeed was I there for? What could I have been searching for? Why were hundreds upon hundreds of hours of psychoanalysis not enough? What was I lacking? What are any of us looking for in the mysterious East? Am I merely seeking an improved version of my ego, or is it to find a higher realm, a release, to transcend the confusion and conflicts of the burden of the "I"? How indeed could it be anything loftier if my limited, confused sense of myself, the *Nur-Ich-Sein*, cannot possibly know what it is looking for? In exploring this duality of the limited conscious mind searching for the complete unknowable, a commentator expresses the dilemma well:

> When we want something, normally we know
> well enough what needs to be done to get it.
> But what if the object I desire is something
> that can never become an object, because it is
> prior to the subject- object dichotomy? What if
> it can never be an effect, because it is always
> unconditioned? What means will enable me to
> attain an end that is impossible to grasp? I find
> myself in a dilemma. If I make no effort to do
> anything, it seems that the result will always be
> nothing, and there will be no progress towards
> the desired goal. But to the extent that I exert

myself to attain, I do not, for in this case all
effort is self-defeating.[1]

The ego is searching for the unknowable because the
conscious mind has failed to provide satisfaction. We seek then to
shed the solipsistic, solid-seeming ego that stands in the way to reveal
that which is beyond it through the agency of that ego, somehow
wrest itself from itself, go beyond itself, so we will always be caught
in this ultimate conundrum, as Satprem, the Frenchman who made
his life in India, explains: "*without* the 'I' one cannot live …; *with*
the 'I' one suffocates."[2]

But the "not-I," the mystery we try to envisage that lies
outside the conceptual mind, has no apparent shape, no nature, so if
we participate in an Eastern practice, we are conducting a search for
something unimaginable by following a well-laid, specific Eastern
path to this putative promised land. We then must cleave to that path,
to a program to be followed, to a teacher who proclaims to know,
irrespective of their conception or characterization of the endpoint:
nirvana, enlightenment, mystical union, individuation. We expect a
journey to someplace around a corner that we cannot yet see and,
most critically, cannot begin to comprehend. Sri Aurobindo explains:
"When we seek to envisage it by the mind we are compelled to
proceed through an infinite series of conceptions and experiences.
… yet there is no experience by which we can limit It, there is no
conception by which It can be defined."[3]

There are at least two approaches found in established Eastern
practices that are directed to resolving the paradox of engaging the
limited ego to serve as the bridge to approach the incomprehensible
dimension. The first form relies on the principle that within each of
us there is already limitless consciousness that stands behind the ego,
and therefore, there is nothing to be attained, only that reality to be

---

[1] Loy, 1988, p. 137
[2] Satprem, 1978, p. 52, emphasis supplied.
[3] Aurobindo, 2005, Vol 21, p. 38

realized, remembered, made clear; no need to search as we already have and are what we seek. The doctrines of *Advaita Vedanta* and Zen Buddhism, finely wrought over centuries, exemplify this first principle, although with different emphases. For *Advaita Vedanta*, the divine *Brahman* is involuted in all things and thus is in our hearts (as the *Atman*), so we can one day ultimately exclaim, "Tat Twam Asi," *That* thou art, in recognition of its eternal presence within us and its ultimate role as the catalyst for all our actions. This approach, therefore, discounts any need for the limited ego to struggle to climb higher and instead orients it to an acceptance of the incarnated truth by an intuitive, refined awareness that *Brahman* is found in all things and that it alone is behind all reality. Ramesh Balsakar, a proponent of *Advaita*, explains the reward of that realization that resolves all conflicts: "… whatever happens in that manifestation, in the functioning of that manifestation, can only happen because that is what the Source intends. The manifestation cannot exist without the Source, because the manifestation has come from the Source."[4] In Mahayana Buddhism, the "Buddha nature" is the phrase given to the internal seed or embryo that lies within us that seeks to be realized. In Zen Buddhism, as set out in the doctrines of the 13th century Dōgen, Buddha nature is in the form of the emptiness of an independent self as the true nature of mind. This is the pivot realization for practice that can be made apparent by dissolving the ego's delusions to reveal this essential nature of all things.

The second form of Eastern practice that reconciles the limited ego with a divine source maintains that duality until higher consciousness is found. It therefore offers a path of gradually developing the ego into the purified instrument of realization of a transcendent unity, as a continuous, mystical higher consciousness bringing bliss and liberation from suffering. This form requires a search, a long journey, a lifetime process through stages on a path, as we are ignorant of that unity and need to attain to it and condition

---

[4] Balsekar, 1998, p. 18

the ego by various, arduous practices. The length of that process, to have any cogency, is offered to be within this lifetime, even though it may never be achieved. Mirra Alfassa, who was called The Mother, a spiritual companion to Sri Aurobindo, explains:

> In almost, almost all cases, a very very sustained effort is needed to become aware of one's psychic being. Usually it is considered that if one can do it in thirty years one is very lucky—thirty years of sustained effort, I say. It may happen that it's quicker. But this is so rare....[5]

What is promoted in this second form is the need for a subtle identity shift from a limited, ego-based, rational view of existence to that offered by the slow drip of higher consciousness. This alteration of consciousness is also very much the position of the process of individuation in Jungian psychoanalysis, although framed differently as moving from unconsciousness to realization of the Self, the central, unifying core of our psyche, through self-examination. In Eastern practices, this form is predicated on the possibility that there exists the means to subjugate the power of the first-person point of view by creating another orientation through such practices as meditation, chanting, and austerities, to name a few, whereby the insights of a unifying dimension will arise and be realized.

Both forms may overlap to some degree conceptually and in practices but are always and inevitably phrased, explained, or symbolized to our ego in words or expressions that are, at their core, amorphous, because "enlightenment is intellectually incomprehensible; it cannot be understood or attained through conceptual knowledge, because it escapes all categories of thought."[6] Each Eastern practice, centuries old, has therefore developed its own

---

[5] Dalal, 1999, p. 104
[6] Loy, 1982, p. 65

explainable, linear version of a path for realizing the ultimate mystery and the shape and texture of the goal. All contradictions and doubts have been internally and logically reconciled, and the doctrines of each are able to be completely explicated. They all manage to provide perfect, self-referential solutions to the dimension beyond the ego, thus making them within the grasp of the conscious mind. The variations in path and goal are understandable in this regard, with each doctrine shaped by the different insights of its founder, because, as Sri Aurobindo explains, "It is so that he conceives his god; it is so that he constructs his heavens."[7]

The Urge to Search

The starting point of all searching, by an explanation that is beyond doubt, is that we all have, as Jung puts it, that "irresistible compulsion and urge to become what one is, just as every organism is driven to assume the form that is characteristic of its nature, no matter what the circumstances."[8] He does not refine that urge in us more specifically, and it appears in his writings as an evolutionary force akin to an instinct, a religious instinct. It is, as he expresses it, "an incorruptible essence potentially present in every human being, the divine pneuma."[9] Expressed at its highest by him: "It is the very ground of existence, the procreative urge …"[10] That urge, the divine spirit, can be suppressed but never lost, as Satprem reveals: "there is but one question in a man, a little interior cry which asks a perpetual 'what' — simply 'what'… One can remove anything yet this endures."[11]

Thus enters the shining lure for me and others, drawing us into Eastern practices that offer a form and shape to the "what," however expressed or conceptualized. It is a form that we can read

---

[7] Aurobindo, 2005, Vol. 21, p. 61
[8] Jung, CW 9i, § 634
[9] Jung, CW 11, § 359
[10] Jung, CW 11, § 258
[11] Satprem, 1978, p. 56

about, understand logically, observe the fervor of its followers, hear about the success of its practitioners, be awestruck by stories of those who have seized its goal, and even have immediate experiences that go beyond thought. Each form in turn explicitly promises to meet our deepest longing, our religious instinct, and the ache in our being for delivery from the oppression of the "I." How could one ever call off that search? We always will seek a means to bring our chaotic lives to a higher state of unity and oneness and thus seek the unknown, however described: enlightenment, bliss, peace, nirvana, the Self. That search, from a psychological viewpoint, becomes noble, as Jung suggests: "the urge to individuation gathers together what is scattered and multifarious, and exalts it to the original form of the One ..."[12]

The paradox that remains, however, that is lost in our enthusiasm for possible realization, is that we cannot conduct a search to become an enlightened or an individuated being, as we have no idea what that is, even if some claim it, we read and understand how it is described, or we are instructed how to attain it by a practice. How can we as Westerners evaluate the realizations of beings from an Eastern lineage as holding the answer we seek, except by how others situate them in the context of a highly defined practice? In the *Dhammadasa Sutta*, Buddha lists the characteristics of a "stream-winner" as one who possesses "unshakable" faith in the Buddha, Dhamma, the Sangha, and observes the Five Precepts. How can that be measured? In the *Path of Purification* of the *Theravada Abidhamma*, interpreted by the Burmese monk Mahasi Sayadaw,[13] the measurement is according to the completion of the seven progressive stages set out in the *Vissuddhi-Magga* and, as well, the 17 stages of the *Vippassana-Nana* that lead to Sainthood. Another example, if one is necessary, is the exquisitely detailed three-volume work, the Tibetan Buddhist *Steps on the Path to Enlightenment,* which refers

---

[12] Jung, CW 11, § 401
[13] Sayadaw, 1950/1965

to a precondition of an enlightened being as having completed the necessary starting point of "Be Patient, search for learning. Then stay in a forest, and Persevere in meditative equipoise."[14] Until enlightenment is reached, "there is no end to what you must study."[15]

The urge, however, fully matches the vague promise that we can win the spiritual lottery by climbing a path up an imagined mountain, somehow reorienting the ego structure toward what appears as a foggy ray of light. It is, no matter how the mind approaches it or how many insights or experiences we have, a hope of finding something beyond where and how we are: an idea or state that we possibly can glimpse that will guarantee that we no longer have discomfort and confusion. The urge requires us to seek a way to reach this state and to engage our life energy in that pursuit. We cannot call off the search once it is ignited. We also sense and experience glimpses in moments of stillness, so we get that drop of honey on our tongues. That is not what the sadhu could have meant. If I have breath, I will search. I am searching, even if I *try* to stop.

Psychological Consequences

There are specific attributes that are clinically observable in those who undertake Eastern practices that may offer some insight into their psychological effect. In these terms, it can be recognized that such individuals are manifesting the religious instinct, thus suggesting that they will possess a proclivity to orient to a wholeness or unity in psyche, however described by a practice. The idea of continued subjective states oriented to a synthesis is inherent in all practices so they are indeed drawing on what Jung calls, "the most important of the fundamental instincts, the religious instinct for wholeness."[16] The practices therefore fulfil the "authentic religious

---

[14] Sopa, 2004, Vol. 3, p. 510
[15] Ibid., p. 512
[16] Jung, CW 10, § 653

function" that is inherent in psyche,[17] and suggest that individuals engaged in such practices can align readily with the individuation process.

For all of those who are adherents of Eastern practices, the possibility of partaking in a transcendent dimension, the critical healing dimension in psychoanalysis, however expressed by a tradition, is patent. Each tradition offers up a chance for realization of the evolutionary force within each of us to become what one can be, creating a story or idea that is congruent with the Jungian Self or a unity that reflects a psychological purpose.

For experienced practitioners, as the ego is altered by a practice to embrace a wider dimension, a sense of wholeness will have moved somewhat to the foreground, so that the conflicts inherent in psychological opposites may retreat to the background to an extent. Eastern practices are therefore always a useful, skilful, focused approximation to wholeness, and the presence of such an experienced practitioner in the consulting room will suggest an openness to a similar refinement of the ego in the psychological process.

On the other hand, engagement in an Eastern practice may conflict with the form and function of psychological growth. This is because the nature of the religious instinct is to strongly cleave to a particular, exclusive form that explains that which is beyond the dimension of the conscious mind, possibly negating psychological constructs. In all Eastern practices, we are directed to an object or a concrete, bounded explanation to attach to that undefined goal. It is the case that from the strong impetus of the religious instinct and the need for a cognitive frame, we psychologically seek a definable object, as Jung puts it, in the form of "analogies" of that instinct derived from the interplay of feeling-tone complexes. The effect of directing the instinct to a specific analogy or form is that this canalizes the libido into a narrow pathway. The libido, the energy

---

[17] Jung, CW 11, § 3

of the complexes, is thus channeled away from itself, fully or in part, to be converted into or carried by the analogy.[18] Jung describes it as "a transfer of psychic intensities or values from one content to another, a process corresponding to the physical transformation of energy ...."[19] Thus, he adds: "The transformation of instinctual energy is achieved by its canalization into an *analogue of the object of instinct.*"[20] A specific Eastern practice, accordingly, inevitably creates a canalization of the religious instinct and, as a result, a "conviction becomes blind auto-suggestion, and the psychic field of vision is narrowed to one fixed point on which the whole weight of the unconscious forces is concentrated."[21] This may suggest a barrier to therapeutic characterizations through a defensiveness against re-framing the concepts of a tradition into a psychological narrative. Such a narrative may be seen as insulting the precepts of the practice or not in line with the words of the teacher or guru.

This depth of the conviction towards a particular, overriding Eastern form, rather than a psychological form, is most evident where the canalization of the religious instinct is occurring outside a native culture. This arises because choosing a specific Eastern practice stands in opposition to the constructs of the prevalent conventional religions. The movement to that one-sided direction is therefore more forceful and deliberate as the channeling, the canalization of the libido, creates a deep emotional commitment toward the new object.

This canalization, however, is a necessary phenomenon as the possibility of eschewing any object that serves the religious instinct is, especially for those where that instinct strongly breaks through, contrary to the workings of the unconscious. The canalization of the religious instinct is necessary and therefore provides the powerful, intense, energic urge, the search, because it is a fundamental

---

[18] Jung, CW 5, § 203
[19] Jung, CW 8, § 80
[20] Ibid., § 83, emphasis supplied.
[21] Ibid., § 87

unconscious process. If this was not the case, the archetypal religious instinct may flood psyche, leading to some other form of manifestation that may be destructive, such as drug addiction. In this context of canalization as a necessary process, psychotherapeutic encounters can be useful for an Eastern practice as the movement of the religious instinct towards the object, a movement in the unconscious, needs symbols, community, a path, and a goal, in order to be contained. The process of psychoanalysis therefore requires the ego to come to its aid by making a deliberate choice for its manifestation, establish a direction, offer some apparent certainty to that which is unknown and not yet crystalized. What remains is the question of why will a manifestation of the religious instinct be directed to an Eastern practice rather than it stay entirely within the succor of a Western religion?

According to the discipline of the psychology of religion, theories of choice of a religious practice include such factors as the extent to which a religion is perceived as able to reduce uncertainty,[22] the degree of consistency with an individual's world view determined empirically by challenges to meaning,[23] and other ideas arising from the passage through developmental stages of the ego structure. From a Jungian perspective and the Self, there is a different explanation.

The Characteristics of Choice

Many decades before I went to the *Kumbha Mela*, as a professor at the University of Toronto specializing in the capacity of urban planning to provide for improved psychological health and overall community well-being, I was in Varanasi, the holy city in northwest India, on a project for the United Nations. In 110-degree heat, I walked through ancient laneways down to the Ghats, the steps leading to the Ganges, and saw sadhus sitting in meditation in the midst of waves of heat, clouds of dust, and utter chaos. I observed in them a crystalline stillness that somehow appeared to be woven

---

[22] Hogg, et al., 2009
[23] Spilka, et al., 1985

into the fabric of this ancient city as if that could only exist in that madness. I felt it; I experienced it as within me as well. I initially considered it only as a curiosity, but as I left to walk back, I observed the passage of an older Western man sitting in exquisite ease on the back of a bicycle rickshaw who appeared integrated into the rhythm of the city and had a presence, a refined, almost beautiful equanimity. These sadhus and the Westerner carried a sacredness I had never experienced in a church or synagogue. It was in them, in fact in every gesture of every inhabitant.

The next day, I was walking again on the Ghats, seeking to repeat those feelings, and a sadhu dressed in ochre robes turned to me and said, "Ah, you've returned." He walked on, but I was dumbfounded, frozen in place. Why would that happen? What did he mean? I was then overwhelmed by the conscious thought that the sacredness I saw around me had always been within me, but I had forgotten it was there, suppressed by my neuroses, and so blinded to any other dimension.

Days later, I was in Patna in the northerly state of Bihar, a more commercial city, where I went to carry out research at the University of Patna, and, in passing, I spoke briefly to three German academics who had traveled widely in India. That night, as we had agreed, I took a rickshaw to meet them at their hotel for dinner. The journey dragged on for more than an hour as we meandered through alleyways in the dark night; it was almost pitch black aside from a few cooking fires. Finally, the driver came to a stop, left the rickshaw, and went into a small hut. I had no idea what to do, so I went to the hut after 10 minutes, and there he was having food with a family that I assumed was his. I stood there with a feeling of panic. After only a few minutes, a man approached me and said in English, "No need to be concerned. I know why you're here. Follow me." He took me on a 20-minute walk, which I assumed would lead to the Germans' hotel, until we came to a small gathering of sadhus, lounging against a wall of a temple. Their ochre robes were tattered, and they had matted hair and beards. I tried to explain in English to my guide and to them that I was looking for my German acquaintances at the Hotel

New Urvashi. One sadhu nodded his head in understanding and took me gently, almost affectionately, by the arm and led me toward the middle of what appeared to be a large open field. No one else was there that I could sense, even though in India every inch of ground is covered with humanity. His eyes were so wide and embracing that I felt that he was honest and I could trust him. I had no real fear and, instead, it seemed that I was in the right place. I could not tell where I was going, and he suddenly stopped and said, "Sit here — it's time — this is what you are looking for," and then he initiated me into a form of Tantric practice. In the darkness, I could only make out his wide, clear eyes, and, for a moment, I was overwhelmed, tearful, touched by knowing that this was what I have longed for always.

What I then started searching for was called, in his words, *Parama Purusha*, the ultimate all-embracing divine, as alien to my Bronx, New York upbringing as could be imagined. The way it came to me, as a mystery in the dark night, appeared to match my own unformed, inner direction toward a mystery. The numinous, the miraculous, the spiritual longing was at last met. Was this Indian culture the right place to look? As I was flying home a few days later, trying to meditate in business class, a joke I had heard some time before came to me about a man on his knees under a streetlight when a second man comes up to him and asks what he is looking for. The man on his knees looks up and explains, "I'm looking for my keys," and the second man, interested in helping, asks "Where did you lose them?" The man on his knees points down the street and answers: "I lost them way over there, but there is light over here."

The sweep of this experience, so long ago, contained several factors that propel one, propelled me, to Eastern practices. India, the setting, allowed my participation as part of pulsing humanity in the exotic madness where the unknown was in every particle of matter. The divine, the mystery of existence, was not a possibility far away on an altar or explained in a book or a prayer but was inside each person and the air, nothing like Western life. This was inherent in the society, the smell, the cacophony, in temples, in idols, in greetings, and in the gaze of others. It brought me into a sense of being part, a participant in, the drama of higher consciousness.

A second factor that settled on me was the hint that this was available to me, not just some robed monk: It sparked my imagination that I would obtain revelations, perhaps be able to share my internal, subjective experiences in a community, thus accepting other spiritual aspirants as compatriots. Here, before me, was also the proof of the journey: the sadhus sitting completely still in the chaos, another sadhu recognizing my return to myself, a distinguished Western man living that process, that striking, otherworldly monk who brought me into communion with the unknown in the middle of nowhere. The Westerner in the rickshaw became my symbol of a journey that I was about to take, one that overrode other religious training and interest, never to return to the religion of my birth.

There was perhaps a third factor, now reflecting on that time, that allowed me to move forward from that experience into establishing a daily practice. There was a sense that here was a well-worn path going back many centuries that I could traverse, ever closer to that higher consciousness, where each level and step was laid out for me and that could engage the ego in discipline. Discipline I already had, the benefit of being an intellectual Westerner, so an ego-directed goal was consistent with my thinking function with the promise that I would get more instruction as I progressed.

Archetypal Foundations

The choice of a religious practice is primarily and inevitably determined by a cultural complex. For most of the world's population, it is embedded in a closed, all-encompassing cultural system shaped by the historical, myriad interactions between education, politics, and other influences that result in a particular orientation, so as to become a "primary, non-reducible phenomenon."[24] Being brought up in the Islamic tradition in the Islamic Republic of Pakistan, as an example,

---

[24] Murken & Namini, 2006, p. 291

will lead to a singular choice of a cultural religious identity. In Western countries, however, an Eastern religion is but one subsystem within the vast array of choices available in a pluralist society.

A Westerner choosing to follow an established Eastern religion must, as I had to, turn away from the cultural religious dominant. This is not to deny the impact of Eastern technologies incorporated into Western daily life, such as meditation, mindfulness, and yoga employed as either secular or spiritual adjuncts. The blending of Eastern concepts in Western spirituality and psychology is now undeniably part of the global circulation of ideas, often modifying the Eastern practices presented to the West.[25] The significant difference between using these Eastern technologies, within the dominant, and pursuing Eastern spiritual lineages lies in the breakthrough of an archetype into consciousness that seizes an individual and redirects the instinctual energy into a particular practice.

A fateful turning toward Eastern religion arises from the breaking through of an ancient archetype that Jung describes as the "concept of the soul-force or soul-stuff, awakened out of the unconscious by a reactivation of archaic forms of thought."[26] These archaic forms, in ancient manifestations, are illustrated in shamanism, understood by Jung "as an archaic archetype important in earlier human prehistory which has emerged in recent times to compensate for the West's over development of rationalistic consciousness."[27] Shamanism is proposed by John Merchant as exemplifying primordial religious fervor[28] and is associated with the breakthrough into consciousness of mystical and religious experiences. It is asserted by another commentator that Jung's encounter with Mircea Eliade, who wrote extensively on shamanism, oriented Jung to find the emergence of the power of that ancient stream

---

[25] Borup, et al., 2017
[26] Jung, CW 10, § 21
[27] Merchant, 2012, p. 2
[28] Ibid., p. 29

of the mystical, shamanistic, dimension in Daoism, Tibetan Buddhism, Kabbalah, and the Book of Enoch.[29]

The scope and operation on consciousness of the primordial archetypal forces that specifically draw us deeply into the realm of Eastern practices are in fact elaborated upon and explained most clearly and usefully in the Book of Enoch. This may appear an obscure reference, but Jung made over a hundred mentions of the Book of Enoch, a work of several disparate parts presumed to have been written between 300 and100 B.C.[30] Recent commentary has enhanced its contemporary relevance since discovery of Aramaic fragments of the text in 1976.[31]

Jung engages with the figure of Enoch to distinguish him from Christ, as Enoch was just an ordinary man, the "Son of Man," not like Jesus, the Son of God, who Jung at one point even suggests adopted this concept of Enoch to advance his position.[32] The substantial references by Jung to Enoch are also, more relevantly, employed to explain the archetypal possibility of an ordinary person participating in the divine drama, opening his or her imagination through revelations, orienting to an inner voice, seeking desperately for psychic order, coming into the actual presence of God, experiencing the bliss of heaven, and being the harbinger of a continued transmission of wisdom through generations. It is indeed these ideas that suggest the power of the archetypal bases for committing to an Eastern religion.

The narrative of the book is a description of Enoch's visions, "which the angels showed me, and from them I heard everything,"[33] that begins with the chaos caused by the destruction of human order by the "Watchers." They are archangels who descend to the earth and

---

[29] Hunt, 2020, p. 3
[30] Knibb, 2008, Chap. Four
[31] Nickelsburg & VanderKam, 2004
[32] Jung, 1973, Vol. 2, p. 205
[33] 1 Enoch 1:2

"defiled themselves with women,"[34] who then gave birth to giants "who consumed them and devoured mankind."[35] This apocalyptic revelation derives particular significance for Jung because the news of this catastrophe was explicitly brought to the attention of Yahweh, but he was unaware of these events. Yahweh, Jung explains, "for some incomprehensible reason, has drawn no conclusions from his omniscience,"[36] a theme Jung also elaborates on in his essay, *Answer to Job*. Yahweh, upon hearing this catastrophe, decides to bring on the deluge of the flood and calls on Enoch to reprimand the Watchers. Jung's conclusion from this part of the narrative is that this led to a partnership between man and the divine caused by Yahweh's lack of awareness of the disaster and, thus, the need for man to be self-reliant. In this, Enoch,

> is not only the recipient of divine revelation but is at the same time a participant in the divine drama, as though he was at least one of the sons of God himself. This can only be taken as meaning that in the same measure as God sets out to become man, man is immersed in the pleromatic process.[37]

Enoch is rewarded by being brought into God's throne room and shown the divine tablets. This symbolically reflects that a representative of humanity must be intertwined with God to maintain the macrocosmic order. As Jung explains, he "must get into immediate proximity to God, and as the pre-existing Son of Man he is no longer subject to death."[38] This means for us, most importantly, "But in so far as he was an ordinary human being and therefore mortal, other mortals as well as he can attain to the

---

[34] 1 Enoch 12:4
[35] 1 Enoch 7
[36] Jung, CW 11, § 671
[37] Ibid., § 677
[38] Ibid., § 686

vision of God; they too can become conscious of their saviour, and consequently immortal."[39] His reason for explaining this view of Enoch is specifically, as mentioned, to contrast the relationship of humanity with Christ: "Christ by his descent, conception, and birth is a hero and half-god in the classical sense."[40] The connection of humanity with Christ is, therefore, more distant, in fact remote, and does not suggest the possibility of a direct merging with God, so there is no participation in the larger unfolding of the divine drama or the revelation of the macrocosm.

The visions of Enoch are revelations that are more graphic and extravagant than even those of the mystics, raising the distinct promise that an ordinary person can reach the divine through imagination and numinous experiences. Enoch's visions, most interestingly, at one point include a journey to the Far East wherein lies the Garden of Righteousness as well as the Tree of Knowledge.[41] Righteousness, as adopted in this context by Jung, is the appropriate term for the characteristic of one who is turned inward.[42] This inward turning to higher consciousness is presented by Jung as our duty in order for us to become self-reliant and fully conscious: "It is no accident that so much stress is laid on righteousness, for it is a quality that Yahweh lacks ..."[43] The problem is that this lack may cause God to "forget his justice," and "In this case his righteous son would intercede with him on man's behalf."[44] Becoming conscious for each individual, in the unfolding of this narrative is, therefore, necessary in order to repair that aspect of the divine drama that arises from unconsciousness. Jung also makes the point that Enoch is "a staff to the righteous,"[45] which indicates the possibility of such a person who has met God then can

---

[39] Ibid.
[40] Ibid., § 690
[41] 1 Enoch 32
[42] Jung, CW 14, § 20n136
[43] Jung, CW 11, § 678
[44] Ibid., § 682
[45] 1 Enoch 49:1-3

offer spiritual guidance so that each of us can reach that state, as it is described in Genesis of Enoch "walking with God."[46]

The possibility of that active relationship where each of us is a critical participant in the divine drama, that requires acts of turning inward to achieve righteousness, and to also bring order to chaos as we obtain strength from revelatory insights, is a result of and congruent with the indwelling Self as an active agent. The Book of Enoch employs these factors to create for us that possibility of a participatory role in a shared experience of transforming chaos to order that is just what is presented by Eastern practices as a series of progressive steps, a movement and a practice toward higher wisdom. As a commentator notes: "The plot also produces a sensation of causality, movement and progress. At several turns in the story, ritual performance becomes the trigger that causes the next sequence of events."[47] It thus offers an endpoint by a sequential path to finally participate fully in the mystery of the macrocosm and to achieve the absolute goal of walking with God in this lifetime.

The Book of Enoch also establishes the basis of being able to mediate the conflict of opposites, which is the goal of all esoteric and mystical traditions. The Watchers altered the divine order, the macrocosm, by interfering with the potential of humanity. This created a schism between evil and good, the essential set of opposites, that is solved when God instructs the Archangel Michael to bind *Shemihazah*, one of the leaders of the transgression. The Watchers then ask Enoch to intercede on their behalf with God. In this way, Enoch becomes the midpoint, the virtual center, that which mediates the opposites of good and evil in the vast Pleroma. Enoch is, incidentally, said to have lived 365 years, which is reminiscent of the essence of *Abraxas*, whom Jung uses as that midpoint in *Septum Sermones ad Mortuous*,[48] who is given the number 365, signifying that it contains all the opposites at the midpoint.

---

[46] Gen 5:23-24
[47] Werline, 2015, p. 327
[48] Jung, 1989, Appendix V

Enoch is killed by the Antichrist but then rises to heaven. The Book offers this final reward because of the participation of an ordinary man who has become a unity, the mediator of opposites, to counteract the underlying forces of disorder. It is suggested accordingly by a commentator, "These parables contain imagery and motifs common to those found in Near Eastern religions."[49] This is a sound observation as the story is of a higher spiritual dimension breaking through into the consciousness of an ordinary person by revelations who is thus able to participate in the activity of the divine by entering the highest truth, creating spiritual immortality by inward and right thinking, and turning chaos into order. The Son of Man is the potential in all of us to enter a dimension beyond the conscious mind. This is not offered in Western religion but is the basis for an immersion into Eastern practices.

The Book of Enoch illuminates the primal archetypal force that sustains a commitment to an Eastern practice: Seeking to be intertwined with the divine drama, however it may be conceived. Such a practice offers the possibility of reaching that higher dimension to be lived on a human scale in which each person has a part and an active role in obtaining wisdom. Such a practice also allows a reparation of the opposites of good and evil through realization of that dimension within each person's heart and mind. To become enlightened, however expressed, involves revelation, imagination, a substantive connection with the absolute, to be part of a community that is engaged in this process, and to have the insight into the interconnectedness of all things: macrocosm and microcosm. This holds the clear and welcome promise of a resting place for the enormous force of libido created by the religious instinct.

Purifying the Ego

The Jungian Self is the highest-order construct, the central archetype, as Jung calls it,[50] that provides the psychic function of

---

49 Latteri, 2015. p.68
50 Jung, CW 10, § 771

orientation and thus order in the chaos of opposites that are our lives. Its realization is the endpoint of psychological growth, and it also guides the process toward its own discovery. In guiding the process, it can be equated, without any precision, to a soul-force, God's will, an evolutionary instinct, a religious instinct, and the deep urge to become what can be, all of which seek wholeness and the peace that this can bring. In this form, it operates as the prime mover that compels the effort and longing for its discovery and is responsible for drawing us to individuation and the creation of a commitment to Eastern practices.

The appearance of the Self is in glimpses of unity and interconnectedness, a feeling of closeness to the divine, a sense of participation in the mystery of the macrocosm. These are the archetypal forces revealed in the Book of Enoch that are all aspects of the archetype of the Self. The forces and the archetypes are the same for Eastern practices and individuation.

The substantive difference relates to the process of the purification of the ego, the vessel for the reception of the Self and higher consciousness. The purification of the ego in order to discover the Self begins with the engagement of the conscious mind with the shadow, what Jung refers to as the process of the transformation of the Lower Adam.[51] Progress occurs at this stage by discrimination of the shadow elements in psyche through the analytic process of dissolution followed by synthesis.[52] This is the initial means for the induction of ego consciousness to the intimation of the unconscious and a centralizing or mediating force in psyche that is integrating the shadow elements. This always hints at that which is preexistent, universal, and impersonal.

The psychic purification of the ego as the starting point of individuation is also the initial stage for all Eastern and esoteric practices, such as Buddhism, Hinduism, Sufism, and Kabbalah.[53]

---

[51] Jung, CW 9ii, § 385
[52] Ibid., § 410
[53] Wilber, et al., 1986, Chap. 3

"Purification" is a universal term used in both *Theravada* and *Mahayana* Buddhism, as well as being the essential foundation of classical yoga.[54] Without that stage of the process, without wrestling with the defilements inherent in the development of ego consciousness, there can be no further spiritual transformation. However, this process alone, the mainstay of analytical practice, does not advance to the same level as that found in Eastern practices.

This distinction is well explained in the works of Sri Aurobindo that highlight a difference between this psychological process of purification and the greater aspirations of Eastern practices. Aurobindo writes about the need for a "triple transformation," specifically addressed in his form of yoga. The first transformation is of the defilements and egoism of the mind, which he calls the "psychic transformation." It is suggested by a commentator, in a psychological analysis of this stage, that this embraces the essential elements of a Jungian analysis: "In Jungian language this means becoming more conscious of the shadow, the anima/animus and one's relationship with the archetypal psyche, as well as the coalescing and directing quality of the heart-Self."[55] This is essential but limited, as Aurobindo explains, as the psychic being "is one's individual soul-being. It is not the Divine, though it has, of course, come from the Divine and develops towards the Divine."[56]

This psychic purification stage for Aurobindo is only a prelude to a higher dimension, the second transformation, that requires the power of the soul-being to occupy the foreground of the conscious ego and thus permeate consciousness:

> One may practise yoga and get illumination
> in the mind and the reason; one may conquer
> power and luxuriate in all kinds of experiences
> ...; but if the true soul-power behind does not

---

[54] Whicher, 1998
[55] Johnston, 2016, p. 98
[56] Aurobindo, 2012, Vol 28, p. 102

manifest, if the psychic nature does not come
into the front, nothing genuine has been done.[57]

This second step in his triple transformation, once that soul-power manifests, occurs by a spiritual transformation by advancing through various planes of consciousness that require the established platform of an already purified ego to orient the soul-being to the involution and grace of Divine Reality. It includes full realization beyond the Self by continued absorption in that Reality of "the world as one, a vast free consciousness, full of freedom, peace and light — it is that we speak of as the higher or divine consciousness."[58]

This second stage may appear that it will be psychologically a consequence of the gradual shift of the ego toward the primacy of Self, but it is much different. It is realization of and absorption into a truth that arises from seeing, without doubt or slippage, through the delusions of the conscious mind. This is evidenced by the cessation of an ego-based search, forsaking thinking and the reasoning that still evaluates the process, and therefore changing the ego's very structure. In an early journal entry of his own journey, Aurobindo explains what it means to move to the second stage:

> August, 1912, will complete the seventh year
> of my practice of Yoga. It has taken so long...
> for Nature beginning in the dark to grope her
> way to the light – now an assured, but not yet
> a full lustre, for the Master of Yoga to quiet the
> restless individual will and the presumptuous
> individual intelligence so that the Truth might
> liberate itself from human possibilities &
> searchings and the Power emerge out of human
> weaknesses and limitations.[59]

---

[57] Aurobindo 1958, p.199
[58] Aurobindo 2014, Vol. 30, p. 381
[59] Aurobindo, 2010 Vol. 10, p. 74

The power of divine intervention, the soul-power, which he refers to as the Master of Yoga, will humble the ego, cleanse it from delusion, call off the search, and accept fully one's human weakness and limitations. This is what the second stage requires. It is a stage for the ego going beyond what Jung suggests when he steps back from this aspect of the process:

> The human mind cannot step beyond itself, although divine grace may and probably does allow at least glimpses into the transcendental order of things. But I am neither able to give a rational accounts of such divine interventions nor can I prove them.[60]

The extent and nature of the purification of the ego that is required for Aurobindo's second state is not explained by Jung, although it lurks as an idea. Esther Harding offers a similar expression of the necessity of this degree of ego refinement:

> In order to find the Self ... one must be freed from ego desirousness and from the conflict of opposites. (First), the possibilities of ego consciousness must be fully explored, then it will be possible to perhaps to go a step beyond the accepted cultural level of the day and bring up from the depths of the unconscious a value that will produce an enlargement and transformation of consciousness itself.[61]

Being freed from ego desirousness is a high bar for the West and is not suggested by Jung. The closest he perhaps comes is drawing on the alchemical process of purification to add:

---

[60] Jung, CW 18, § 1591
[61] Harding, 1973, p. 235

> No longer the earlier ego with its make-
> believes and artificial contrivances, but
> another, 'objective' ego, which for the reason
> is better called the 'self.' No longer a mere
> selection of suitable fictions, but a string of
> hard facts, which together make up the cross
> we all have to carry or the fate of ourselves
> are.[62]

Artificial contrivances and fictions are the nature of the Western mind, so the standard he suggests for purification is the complete substitution of the ego with the unifying aspect of the Self where the mind rests in wholeness without variance. This makes the transformation of the psyche a necessary, preliminary step in both individuation and Eastern practices but does not provide how that can occur at the level of psychic transformation. Both psychological and Eastern processes strengthen the Jungian Self and the possibility of the creation of an aware or realized psyche in which the reality of union is constantly in the foreground. There is, however, a lacuna in not explaining the full extent of purification of the ego for the psychological process of realizing the Self. It prevents individuation from being the same as Eastern practices, as the latter seek to define the operation of the divine transformation or the realization of emptiness by detailing the precise form and content of the ego that is needed to obtain the higher realizations.

Form of the Ego

Eastern practices in every form offer attainment to a higher state as an ideal and a possibility through direct effort, as in forms of yoga, in Buddhism, or by removal of ignorance, as in *Advaita*. They thus are explicit about the specific practices and ideations that must be undertaken along the path at different levels of development. Even where there is nonduality, as in *Advaita*, the conscious mind needs to

---

[62] Jung, CW 16, § 400

be reconditioned through remembering. Altering the ego structure by specific injunctions is the ancient foundation of all Eastern practices, such as, to take a basic idea, the Five Precepts of Buddhism.

No Eastern practice requires a complete loss of the self-reflecting conscious mind but instead seeks a reorientation of the cooperating instrument of the ego away from a mundane, defiled state to an open, receptive clarity that accords with the nature of a higher dimension. Jung's admonition that complete absorption in oneness, samadhi, is a loss of ego antithetical to psychological growth as merely a dream state[63] would be correct if one remains in a constant state of samadhi. This is not the practical case, as that event provides the higher knowledge that becomes the sustained insight that is absorbed by a purified ego and initiates the process of moving it to the foreground of the mind. As explained in the writings of Mahasi Sayadaw, the culmination of the practice, that highest state, is "very short, and lasts for just an instant, like the duration of a single thought of noticing."[64] Thereafter, the ego reviews "the Deathless Nibbana"[65] that has been realized. It is, in reality, the descent from the samadhi experience and its contemplation that fosters a new subjective state that settles onto the waiting and prepared ego.

It is difficult for an ego in the abstract and in Jungian theory to understand how it should be purified. Humility, giving up contrivances, or loss of egoism remain only as vague ideas without specific guidelines and instruction. The need for purification that is the preparation of the ego to receive higher states, the descent of wisdom, is only implied by Jung through his use of the language of the alchemical text, *Aurora Consergens*, where it is expressed that wisdom is to be found on the "firm foundation of fourteen principal virtues."[66] These include, inter alia, humility, holiness, virtue, goodness, patience, temperance, and obedience. The form and shape

---

[63] Jung, CW 11, § 785
[64] Sayadaw, 1950/1965, p. 22
[65] Ibid., p. 23
[66] Jung, CW 12, § 382

of such an ego, how it is to be altered, how it operates, the position it takes in relation to these virtues are not explicated by him.

Transformation of the psyche, purification of the ego, in all Eastern practices is explicit with specific, subtle requirements to be followed so that the ego can make room and then step aside for the involution of the divine or insight into our true nature. In Sri Aurobindo's terms, psychic transformation includes distinct purification practices to "Eliminate egoism in all its forms; eliminate it from every movement of your consciousness."[67] What stands in the way is not the ego but rather *egoism* manifested through impulses for attention to all material and internal states as well as the entirety of our processes. The starting points, touching only gently again on the path of Mahasi Sayadaw, are therefore purification of conduct through contemplating the "five Groups of Grasping," then the contemplation of the processes of mind and body through the six sense-doors, the purification of all aspects of mind: one's view, one's doubts, and distinguishing what is for the path and what is not-path.

There is a need for this specificity in the process of the purification of the ego for it to be able to grasp the import of revelations, expressed well by the Kabbalist scholar Moshe Idel: "The introduction of the inner faculties in order to describe the psychological mechanism of revelation is important as it internalizes the revelatory event... ."[68] Eastern practices, all of which rely on revelation, therefore have particular practices to match purification to levels of spiritual development along a well-laid-out path in preparation for the ego to absorb this knowledge. In these practices, the process is phrased as to what is needed in freeing oneself from the progressive subjective states that arise in ever-refined insights. In the ninth century Tantric text, the *Spandakarika*, the ultimate goal of this process is: "Liberated in this way from the impulses tied to the ego, he experiences the supreme state."[69]

---

[67] Aurobindo, 2014, Vol 30, p. 333
[68] Idel, 2000, p. 109
[69] Odier, 2004, p. 6

In Buddhist practice, as another example, the purification of the ego is accomplished by training the mind to relinquish conceptualization in all its manifestations and complexity. The underlying theme of removing ego conceptualization is expressed in this Tibetan Buddhist 14th-century statement: "May the self suffer downfall; may the 'self' and 'real entities' become no more and be lost forever."[70]

The "self" in this particular Buddhist context is the self-referential ego, the coherence of memory and experience. It is not, however, the obliteration of the conscious mind that is being sought, but it is the replacement of its ideas and egoism with one that can see the truth of existence. It is explained in this Zen text: "No mind means there is no deluded, foolish mind; it does not mean there is no mind to discern false from true."[71] It is a mind that does not search intellectually for enlightenment, that is not interested in honor, fame, profit, reputation, thus creating a mindless wayfarer, so, "a mindless man unites with the way."[72]

The substance of a purified ego needed for the process of individuation and Eastern practices cannot be expressed perfectly but may be best explained in the concluding line of the Book of Job. When Job asks God for an explanation of why he was treated so horrifically, God, in "The Voice of the Whirlwind" section, does not answer the question directly but expounds His majesty over creation and his infallibility. This leads Job to finally answer, the very end of the tale: "Therefore I will be quiet, comforted that I am dust" (Job 42:6). Job first declares, as a prelude, that "I can understand nothing. It is beyond me. I shall never know." (Job 42:1)

There are many interpretations of these passages, and one convincing translation is "… [having met God and being reassured that I am not alone and abandoned in this world] I am comforted,

---

[70] Gyalchok & Gyaltsen, 2006, p. 261
[71] Cleary, 2005, p. 422
[72] Ibid.

vulnerable human being that I am."[73] It is, in another translation, conveying the meaning: "All of this was worthwhile – despite the fact that I failed his test – because God finally appeared to me."[74]

The entire Book of Job is crystalized in this ending: It is the understanding — bringing to the foreground — that God is there, present in all things, whether we are acting consciously or unconsciously, that is not capable of ever being known. The realization is that no concept, no search, no ideas, no conclusions can ever understand. The place of humanity is quiet humility in the face of that divine will. This is explained more clearly in a biblical interpretation of the Book of Job that this occurred because Job had *"undevious simplicity,* a willingness to accept things, unquestionably as they are."[75]

There is a more refined idea introduced by Maimonides that explains the error and hubris of Job: "While he had known God only through traditional stories and not by way of speculation, Job imagined that the things thought to be happiness, such as health, wealth, and children, are the ultimate goal. For this reason, he fell into such perplexity as he did."[76] In this context, Job realizes that he had held the importance of his body and his thoughts in too high esteem "having equated life with God's kindness."[77] He understands at the end that he now must revile the worldly life and even give up the attachment to tranquility upon which he had based his life. This is why in Rinzai Zen liberation depends on "undefiled knowledge" and "uncreated virtue," the latter being that which flows from making no effort.[78]

The refinement of ego to remove egoism and its desires is not within the purpose of psychoanalysis or psychological theory.

---

[73] Kusher, 2012, p. 160

[74] Schwab, 2005, p. 431

[75] Eisenmann, 2006, p. 4, emphasis supplied.

[76] Maimonides, Guide III:23, p. 497

[77] Ibid.

[78] Cleary, 2005, p. 487

This loss of egoism is, however, the precondition of a transformation beyond that offered by psychoanalysis that is the basis for Eastern practices. In terms of the Book of Job, the teaching is "An uncompromising refusal to become a pandering hypocrite — even in search of some assumed theological verity — will in the end yield a reward."[79] No process, no concepts, *no search*, no opinions, no proof needed.

It means in the consulting room that the work of purification can begin by exposing the unconscious forces that drive desire in a particular form and for an unsaid goal. In this orientation, engagement with the shadow, wrestling with the opposites, start to create an underlay that loosens some of the ego's grasping. However, something more is promised in Eastern practices that can establish a conscious mind that has surrendered to the unknown, that has given up the search, and can rest in the presence of God or the nothingness.

To explore how this may appear, I can only offer a final anecdote that indicates the nature of the realization of conjunctio and an ego without a conceptual point of view. Some years ago, I was walking near a cremation ground in Pushkar, Rajasthan, and was told by a villager that I should speak with a wandering sadhu who just arrived in that town and was sitting on a low wall that surrounded the ground. He appeared to me filthy, smelly, with tattered ochre robes. I was told, which darkened my desire to speak with him even more, that he had just been released after 40 years in the vicious Tihar jail in Delhi for committing a double murder. Out of curiosity, I walked over to him with hesitation, and he rose and smiled, and all I saw in his mouth was one front shiny tooth. I gave him the Indian greeting of clasped hands and said to him in my rudimentary Hindi "Namaskar Baba, kya sab theek hai?" (Greetings sadhu, is everything good?). He continued to look in my eyes and at least five minutes passed, so I had a very awkward feeling, leading me to be confused as to what I was to do and why he was just staring. He then replied in perfect

---

[79] Eisemann, 2006, p. 364

English: "There is no good and there is no bad." Here was the unity, the conjunctio in vivo, the unabated end of a search as there were no longer opposites.

Can this be the result of Eastern practices conducted in a Western environment? Is this the goal of individuation? Can we become like dust, stopping the constant egoism, ideas, concepts, hopes, desires, self-promotion, to rest in what is already there? I don't think so. Yet, I can hear the longing as I write, the glorious mist of higher consciousness, that calls us all, Western and Eastern, to the questions that can never be fully answered.

To approximate or approach calling off the search in a Western context is to approach our Eastern and psychoanalytic practices with a fragile but trusting open heart and allowing a shift in consciousness away from the ego's hopes and desires to a deep, softened acceptance of our humble nature in the face of the mystery, and an understanding that there is no gulf between what we seek and who we are.

References

1 Enoch (1913). In *The Apocrypha and Pseudepigrapha of the Old Testament in English.* R.H. Charles, Ed. Oxford: Oxford at the Clarendon Press. Pp. 163-277

Alston, A.J., Trans. (1959). *Realization of the Absolute: the 'Naiskarmya Siddhi' of Sri Suresvara.* London: Shanti Sadan

Aurobindo, Sri. (1958). *On Yoga II Tome Two.* Pondicherry, India: Sri Aurobindo Ashram

___. (2005). The Life Divine 1. Vol. 21. In *The Complete Works of Sri Aurobindo.* Pondicherry, India: Sri Aurobindo Ashram Publication Department

___. (2010). Record on Yoga. Vol. 10. In *The Complete Works of Sri Aurobindo.* Pondicherry, India: Sri Aurobindo Ashram Publication Department

___. (2012). Letters on Yoga 1. Vol. 28. In *The Complete Works of Sri Aurobindo.* Pondicherry, India: Sri Aurobindo Ashram Publication Department

___. (2014). Letters on Yoga 3. Vol. 30. In *The Complete Works of Sri Aurobindo.* Pondicherry, India: Sri Aurobindo Ashram Publication Department

Balsekar, R. (1998). *Your Head in the Lion's Mouth: Talks in Bombay with Ramesh S. Balsekar.* B. Bardo, Ed. Redondo Beach, CA: Advaita Press

Borup, J., Qvortrup Fibiger, M. (2017). Pizza, curry and whirlpool effects – Religious circulations between East and West. In *Eastspirit: Transnational Spirituality and Religious Circulation in East and West.* J. Borup & M.Q. Fibiger, Eds. Leiden, The Netherlands: Brill

Cleary, T., Trans. (2005). Zen Master Daikaku's Treatise on Sitting Meditation. In *Classics of Buddhism and Zen.* Vol. Four. Boston & London: Shambhala

Dalai, A. S., Ed. (1999). *The Psychic Being: Selections from the Works of Sri Aurobindo and the Mother.* Pondicherry, India: Sri Aurobindo Ashram

Eiseman, Rabbi M. (2006). *Job: A New Translation with a Commentary Anthologized from Talmudic, Midrashic, and Rabbinic Sources.* M. Eisemann, Trans. New York: Mesorah Publications

Gyalchok, S. & Gyaltsen, K. (Compilers). (2006) *Mind Training: The Great Collection.* T. Junpa, Ed., Trans. Boston: Wisdom Publications

Harding, E. (1973). *Psychic Energy: Its Source and its Transformation.* Princeton: Princeton University Press

Hogg, M.A., Adelman, J.R., & Blagg, R.D. (2009). Religion in the face of uncertainty: A Uncertainty-Identity theory account of religiousness. *Personality and Social Psychology Review, 14*(1), 72-83

Hunt, H. T. (2020). Intimations of a spiritual New Age: IV. Carl Jung's archetypal imagination as futural planetary neo-shamanism. *International Journal of Transpersonal Studies, 39*(1-2), 1-31

Idel, M. (2000) The Kabbalah in Morocco. In *Morocco: Jews and Art in a Muslim Land.* V.B. Mann, Ed. London: Merrell Publishers

Johnston, D. (2016). *Jung's Global Vision: Western Psyche Eastern Mind.* Victoria, Canada: Agio

Jung, C.G. (1973). *C.G. Jung Letters.* G. Adler & A. Jaffe, Eds. Princeton: Princeton University Press

____. (1989). *Memories, Dreams, Reflections.* A. Jaffe, Ed., R. & C. Winston, Trans. New York: Vintage Books

Knibb, M. (2009). *Essays on the Book of Enoch and other Jewish Texts and Traditions.* London: Brill

Kushner, H.S. (2012). *The Book of Job: When Bad Things Happened to a Good Person.* New York: Schoken

Latteri, N.E. (2015). Jewish Apocalypticism: An historiography. In *A Companion to the Premodern Apocalypse.* M.A. Ryan, Ed. Leiden. The Netherlands: Brill

Loy, D. (1982). Enlightenment in Buddhism and Advaita Vedanta. *International Philosophical Quarterly, 22,* 65-74

____. (1988). The Path of No-Path: Sankara and Dogen on the Paradox of Practice. *Philosophy East and West, 38,* 127-146

Maimonides. (1963). *The Guide of the Perplexed.* S. Pines, Trans. Chicago: University of Chicago Press

Merchant, J. (2012). *Shamans and Analysts: New Insights on the Wounded Healer.* London: Routledge

Murken, S., & Namini, S. (2006). Choosing a religion as an aspect of religious identity formation in modern societies. In *Religious Harmony.* M. Pye, E. Franke, A. T. Wasim, & A Masud (Eds). Berlin: Walter de Gruyter

Nickelsburg, G.W.E., & VanderKam, J.C. (2004). *1 Enoch: A New Translation.* Minneapolis: Fortress

Odier, D. (2004). *Yoga Spandakarika: The Sacred Texts at the Origins of Tantra*. Rochester, Vermont: Inner Traditions

Satprem. (1978). *By the Body of the Earth or the Sannyasin Unending History.* M. Fitzpatrick, Ed. New York: Harper & Row

Sayadaw, M. (1950/1965) *The Progress of Insight through the Stages of Purification.* Nyanaponika Thera, Trans. (trans.). Kandy, Sri Lanka: The Forest Hermitage

Schwab, Rav. (2005). *Rav Schwab on IYOV: The Teachings of Rabbi Shimon Schwab on the Book of Job*. New York: Mesorah Publications

Sopa, Geshe L. (2004). *Steps on the Path to Enlightenment: A Commentary on Tsongkhapa's Lamrim Chemmo.* Somerville, MA: Wisdom Publications

Spika, B., Shaver, P., & Kirkpatrick, L.A. (1985). A general attribution theory for the psychology of religion. *Journal for the Scientific Study of Religion, 24*(1), 1-20

Werline, R.A. (2015). Ritual, order and the construction of an audience in 1 Enoch 1-36. *Dead Sea Discoveries, 22,* 325-341

Whicher, I. 1998. The final stages of purification in classical yoga. *Asian Philosophy, 8*(2), 85-101

Wilber, K., Engler, J., & Brown, D.P. *Transformations of Consciousness.* Boston: Shambhala

Eastern Spiritual Practices and the Process of Individuation: Exploring Lived Experience

Patricia Katsky

C. G. Jung believed that those living in the West would not be able to fruitfully explore Eastern spiritual practices due to unspecified differences existing between these two cultural groups. However, in our contemporary world, many Western individuals have become deeply engaged with Eastern spiritual practices as the cultures of the world continue to interpenetrate and influence each other ever more deeply. This chapter examines the lived experience of eight Western individuals who have been immersed in Eastern spiritual theories and practices for decades. In their lives, the integration of these practices and their individuation journeys are interwoven in unique ways. Their stories explore the intersection of two worlds: the world of consensual, everyday reality, and the world that contains ineffable mystery and beauty: the world that allows glimpses into the nondual level of reality. Murray Stein has found experiences similar to those of the participants to be characteristic of late-stage individuation. The chapter offers a brief description of the individuals in the study and includes several thematic categories describing their experiences.

C. G. Jung held complex and contradictory views about the potential of those living in the West to meaningfully relate to Eastern spiritual practices. Hypothesizing that a large psychological gap existed between those living in the East and the West, he warned repeatedly that fruitful exploration of Eastern truths would be difficult if not impossible for Westerners.[1] However, during the time of his own inner struggles, as the events recorded in the *Black Books* (2020) and the *Red Book* (2009) were unfolding, Jung revealed, "I was frequently so wrought up that I had to do certain yoga exercises to hold my emotions in check."[2] Using these techniques, he calmed himself sufficiently to continue exploring his "images and inner voices."[3]

Jung claimed that he used these techniques differently from how they were used in the East, but, in fact, what he described is directly comparable to *vipassana* meditation in which, with a stilled and focused awareness, one notices sensations, emotions, and images as they become conscious. He proposed, "We must get at the Eastern values from within and not from without, seeking them in ourselves, in the unconscious,"[4] suggesting that he assumed Westerners would produce something different from what had previously arisen in the East. This belief is perhaps reflective of an unconscious Western cultural complex of assumed superiority and uniqueness.[5]

In Jung's time, many Eastern spiritual texts were just being translated into Western languages. In our contemporary world, the interpenetration of cultures worldwide is unprecedented — powerful, inevitable, and, in many instances, problematic. Today, many individuals in the West are pulled to Eastern spiritual wisdom and find that exploration of these traditions contributes to their individuation process. This chapter examines the lived experience of eight such Western individuals who have engaged deeply in Eastern spiritual practices, exploring the ways in which the integration of Eastern spiritual approaches and the process of individuation are interwoven in unique ways in their lives. My hope is that sharing the participants' lived experiences will prove helpful for others who are drawn to

---

[1] Jung, CW 13, § 2; CW 11, §§ 772, 773
[2] Jung, 1961/1963, p. 175
[3] Ibid.
[4] Jung, CW 11, § 773
[5] Singer & Kimbles, 2004

pursue both paths. My own involvement with this topic is grounded in a lifelong interest in nondual experience along with several decades of involvement with Eastern spiritual ideas and practices.[6]

With one exception, the participants in this study are from an exclusively Western background. In conversations and written accounts, they describe how they were drawn to engage with the unseen world, finding their way to experiences of the ineffable. They report that Eastern spiritual practices facilitate access to sources of inner knowing that have brought and continue to bring profound meaning into their lives. They have been fascinated with glimpses of the world of nonduality, experiences in which their awareness of themselves as separate individual beings fell away.

The participants' stories explore the intersection of two worlds — that of consensual, everyday reality, and another world that we might describe as the space of our inner experiences. Together, these two realities comprise the profound polarity that exists at the core of human experience. Donald Kalsched speaks of his own struggle to hold conscious awareness of both these worlds:

> These [two] worlds seem incommensurable, and I struggle as I try to hold them together. The first feels "profane," filled with human tragedy and the mind-numbing suffering that comes with mortal, embodied existence in a violent, polarized world. ... The second world feels sacred, beautiful, boundless, and eternal, opening into an ineffable mystery that soothes the soul – into what Rudolf Otto (1917) called the *numinous* dimension of human experience.[7]

In a similar vein, in *The Red Book*, Jung describes the intense inner conflict he experienced between what he called the "spirit of the times," a tendency that drew him into engagement with the world around

---

[6] Katsky, 2021
[7] Kalsched, 2013, pp. 1-2

him, and the "spirit of the depths,"[8] a markedly different tendency that turned his world upside down after the break with Freud, leading him to discover the ordering function of the Self and its role in the individuation process. Affirming his sense of the importance of this second world, Jung describes himself in his autobiography as "a splinter of the infinite deity" and professes, "The only events in my life worth telling are those when the imperishable world irrupted into this transitory one."[9]

Jeffrey Moulton Benevedes offers a beautiful description of such an irruption of the imperishable world into his own life in his *Jung Journal* review of the book, *The Spiritual Psyche in Psychotherapy: Mysticism, Intersubjectivity, and Psychoanalysis.*[10] As a prologue to his review, Benevedes shares his experiences of a Roman Catholic boyhood and his later interest in Jewish authors and liberation theology, followed by his exploration of Zen and Tibetan Buddhism. He then writes,

> Recently, while hiking in the Southern California desert on a brilliant, chilly winter morning, I was overcome by the beauty of the surrounding snowcapped mountains, the crystalline air, and the rocky barren topography. Suddenly, and quite unexpectedly, I was surrounded by what I can only call a "cloud of Jesus." Impossible to put such a numinous experience into words, I would have to call it a felt experience of a loving God presence filling me with awe and gratitude. ... This was not the first time I had experienced the presence of the divine in my conscious life, but it was the first time I had experienced the surrounding presence of Jesus himself as he radiated from the natural setting of the desert, which, for me, has always been deeply imbued with the mystical. In that unique moment, he

---

[8] Jung, 2009, p. 11
[9] Jung, 1961/1963, p. 4
[10] Pearson & Marol, 2020

created a psychic environment of love, peace,
protection, and a sureness of the rightness of all
things.[11]

His experience draws together many of the themes found in
the participants' stories: an early interest in the "world [that] feels
sacred, beautiful, boundless, and eternal …,"[12] a commitment to
studying a variety of spiritual pathways; numinous experiences,
dreams, meditative awareness, and synchronicities as moments
offering guidance; encounters with nonword-based states of
consciousness; experiences of transcendence; and the gradual
unfolding of a unique, personal integration of both Eastern and
Western ways of deep knowing.

Before exploring the participants' stories, an introductory
section will present some concepts and ideas important for this
study: numinous experience, the religious or spiritual function of the
psyche, nondual awareness, and the Self.

Numinous Experience

Numinous experience plays a significant role both in the
process of individuation and in the Eastern wisdom traditions.
Rudolph Otto, in his study of religions around the world, observes
the importance of what he describes as "numinous experience,"
moments of awareness characterized as being "tremendous,
fascinating, and awe inspiring."[13] In these moments, the individual
ego finds itself in the presence of something larger than itself,
something powerful and mysterious that exerts a compelling and
fascinating energy, leading to a feeling of being humbled by the
presence of a transcendent force.

---

[11] Benevedes, 2021, p. 126
[12] Kalsched, 2013, p. 2
[13] Otto, 1917/1958, p. 2

Jung found encountering the numinous to be crucially important in the individuation process. In a letter written in 1945, he notes that his work can be understood best as an effort to enhance the ability to contact numinous experience, the ultimate source of deep human healing. He writes:

> The main interest of my work is not concerned with the treatment of neurosis but rather with the approach to the numinous. But the fact is that the approach to the numinous is the real therapy and inasmuch as you attain to the numinous experiences you are released from the curse of pathology.[14]

Numinous experiences can arise in a variety of ways, including meaningful dreams, synchronicities, visions, participation in rituals, experiences in nature, in relationship, and in meditation, to name just a few. Such transcendent moments can be life defining, offering a sense of meaning and clarity. The individuation process is characterized by dwelling on these experiences, searching out their meaning, sometimes elaborating them in art making and journaling, and tracking their reflections in further dreams, active imaginations, and synchronicities. Ultimately, these experiences become integrated into a personal narrative focused on an ever-deepening relationship between the ego and the Self. Numinous experiences are significant markers along the paths of spiritual and psychological growth. Many such experiences are characterized by an awareness of nonduality, of the oneness of all in a moment of transcendence.

Lionel Corbett, who has written extensively about the religious function of the psyche,[15] sees the process of individuation as a spiritual journey and, as such, comparable to the quest for enlightenment in Eastern traditions. He observes, "For Jung, healing in psychotherapy

---

[14] Jung, 1975, p. 377
[15] Corbett, 1996, 2007, 2011

requires a religious attitude but not necessarily adherence to a particular tradition. This attitude means paying attention to spontaneous numinous experience."[16] The participants' reports are living examples of this attitude and offer insights into the gifts that can flow from committing to this personal path.

Religious Function or Spiritual Function of the Psyche, Dual and Nondual Awareness, and the Self

The individuation process, through its exploration of the inner world of the personal and collective unconscious, initiates a radical restructuring of one's understanding of reality. As the ego comes into increasing contact with the Self, the center of gravity of the personality shifts, and the ordering and guiding functions of the Self take on greater importance. The individuation process can be considered as an example of what Jung refers to as the "religious function of the psyche."[17] Jung uses this term to refer to the search for meaning that characterizes the individuation process. However, today, the word "religion" is often associated with particular creeds or defined belief systems. The phrase "the spiritual function of the psyche" would be more accurate given the modern usage of these two terms.

In the process of individuation and in other manifestations of the religious or spiritual function of the psyche, experiences of nonduality play an important role. Examples of nondual awareness can be found in the writings of Western mystics, and Eastern spiritual traditions characterize the essence of enlightenment as an experience of nonduality.

Different traditions offer varying perspectives on how to hold such experiences in awareness and speak of the pitfalls such encounters can bring. From a Jungian perspective, at a particular point in the individuation process, the identification of the ego with the numinous manifestation of the Self can lead to an inflated ego

---

[16] Corbett, 2007, p. 66
[17] Jung, CW 7, § 150; CW 11, § 3; CW 12, § 14

state. Jung calls this state the "mana-personality,"[18] and he believes that this inauthentic inflation needs to be dismantled before additional psychological growth could occur. Similarly, in many Eastern spiritual traditions, the profound effects of the experience of enlightenment are seen as something to "get over," although this is not always a quick process. Publicly, the Buddhist tradition does not place much attention on the numinous dimensions of individual enlightenment experiences, but their numinous quality is acknowledged privately. Remaining in a state of attachment to these feelings is reluctantly tolerated for the length of time necessary for the energy to dissipate. After that, returning from what is seen as an inflated state (which could be described as being possessed by a complex) is the requisite next step in spiritual development.[19] The Zen Ox-Herding Pictures, created in the 12th century by the Chinese Buddhist monk Kuo-an Shih-yuan, offer a depiction of the experience of enlightenment and the return to the world of consensual reality that inevitably follows.[20]

Erich Neumann offers the interesting observation that through the gradual transformation of the relationship between the ego and the Self in the individuation process, the ego is brought to an awareness of the world of formlessness. In *The Psyche and the Transformation of the Reality Planes: A Metapsychological Essay*, Neumann notes that under hypnosis, the ego can remember things previously unknown or unremembered. He calls this the phenomenon of "extraneous knowing,"[21] and he states that such knowledge is best understood to be field-based or field-sourced. In order to access this other level of knowing, the normal state of ego consciousness must undergo an *abaissement du niveau mental*, a letting go, in which the tight focus of regular conscious awareness is temporarily softened or relaxed.[22] As a result of this shift, ego consciousness may become

---

[18] Jung, CW 7, § 388
[19] Kapleau, 1980; Kornfield, 2000
[20] Miyuki, 1992
[21] Neumann, 1952/1989, p. 4
[22] Ibid., pp. 61–62

able to access knowledge that exists outside of what it has discovered through its own efforts. Neumann argues that Western consciousness overwhelmingly privileges the knowing that comes directly through the efforts of the ego, whereas other cultures and times are more open to the information (and wisdom) available through extraneous knowing. He proposes that as the individuation process unfolds, the *ordering function of the Self* comes to play a significant role in presenting to the ego important and carefully selected and timed experiences of extraneous knowing,[23] revealed to ego consciousness through events such as meaningful dreams, synchronicities, visions, meditation experiences, and active imagination. He suggests that through these powerful and often numinous experiences, the ego gradually becomes aware of the ordering energy of the Self as well as its own inseparability from an inclusive inner unity. Such moments of extraneous knowing bring ego consciousness to an awareness of nonduality and to experiences of transcendence. Murray Stein observes:

> Erich Neumann argues that everyone is a mystic, potentially, for the simple reason that everyone's consciousness rests upon archetypal layers of the psyche, and when these are exposed or when they spontaneously express themselves in consciousness, the individual falls into the grip of mystical experience.[24]

Turning to research in the field of neuroscience, recent studies suggest the need for revisions to the currently accepted psychological models of separated, individually based human consciousness. These new studies demonstrate the existence of brain synchronization occurring between individuals that occur under certain social circumstances, particularly during experiences of meaningful

---

[23] Ibid., p. 17
[24] Stein, 2019, p. 15

interaction, and these studies draw our attention to a new way of describing field-based or field-sourced consciousness. In their article, *What Binds Us?* Ana Lucía Valencia and Tom Froese, researchers in the interdisciplinary field of embodied cognitive science, suggest that neuroscience today needs to move to a two-person model.[25] As an example, they cite a study that examined the neural activity of pilots and copilots during landings and takeoffs and in the middle of flights. During the time when the two pilots needed to collaborate most closely, at takeoffs and landings, their brains showed synchronizing patterns, whereas this was not true in the middle of the flight. Valencia and Froese point to recent research grounded in complex systems theory, which postulates that consciousness emerges from multiple interacting brain networks, another way of describing field-based or field-sourced consciousness. They draw attention to the fact that "findings of brain-to-brain synchronization during cooperative social interaction … [reveal] that this phenomenon is not a general effect of a shared environment, but an emergent property of specifically social dynamics,"[26] and they conclude that some aspects of our experience of consciousness, such as our sense of social connectedness, cannot be adequately explained using the previous model of the individual brain or mind existing in isolation.

The proposed "second-person" model of human consciousness[27] suggests that moments of extraneous knowing might occur through deeply shared experiences with others as well as through the directing agency of the Self as described above by Neumann. (Some Eastern spiritual teachings have a tradition of "direct transmission," which may be related to experiences of brain synchronization.)

Murray Stein has developed the concept of "late-stage individuation," a phase when the search for meaning and transcendence becomes ever more prominent.[28] After their lifelong

---

[25] Valencia & Froese, 2020
[26] Ibid., p. 2
[27] Ibid., p. 1
[28] Stein, 2019, p. 6

commitment to the individuation process, the study participants' experiences repeatedly show the meaningful effects of moments when archetypal energies arise in connection with their Eastern spiritual practices, demonstrating how such moments offer wisdom that transforms one's life path.

The Research Study

With one exception, the individuals in this study are from an exclusively Western background and have been committed to Eastern spiritual practices (or interested in Eastern spiritual concepts) for decades. The participants are five men and three women, ranging in age from the 40s to the 80s. Most have experienced Jungian analysis or other forms of depth psychological therapy. Many have become teachers and mentors in the traditions they follow, and some are Jungian therapists or analysts. The exception mentioned is an individual of Japanese-European ancestry, who practices one of the Eastern healing arts and lives in the West.

The research methods of organic and intuitive inquiry were used in this study.[29] Accordingly, participants were encouraged to reflect on their experiences by selecting what was most meaningful to them in their process of individuation and in their exploration of Eastern spiritual traditions. The participants have reviewed this chapter and authorized the inclusion of their material.

Because their individual paths are quite different, brief descriptions of key aspects of each participant's spiritual pathway are offered. The names given are pseudonyms, except for Michael A. Franklin. Michael has written a book, *Art as Contemplative Practice: Expressive Pathways to the Self,*[30] in which he describes some of the experiences he expanded on during his interview. He has given his permission to be mentioned by name.

---

[29] Anderson, 1998; Clements, 2004
[30] Franklin, 2017

Participants in the Study

Drawn to the numinous since childhood, *Christopher* stresses the importance of time spent in nature, experiencing "soul-in-earth." He entered a contemplative Western religious order in his early 20s. Living in a rural setting, he continued to have strong mystical experiences of "God-in-nature." Then, in his late 20s, he came to feel that he had "little emotional foundation" for his spiritual life and had become "disincarnate — a spirit in a shell of a body." *Christopher* left the order and moved to a rural yoga center and began practicing "karma yoga." His exploration of Eastern spiritual practices has increased in his experience of embodiment.

Arthur's interest in meditation began in high school but became more focused in his early 20s, when he was suffering from ulcerlike stomach pains. He found that meditating with one hand on his stomach brought relief from the pain. Now in his 60s, he has practiced meditation all his life as a "preventative treatment" when he has felt himself "getting into trouble, physical or mental."

Bicultural and biracial, *Hayao* has "spent a lifetime trying to reconcile East and West" in his own person. He was raised in Japan and has lived mostly in the United States since college. He remembers becoming interested in mystical experience around age 13. For him, nature is sacred. He works as an acupuncturist and herbalist and experiences the "creative process and the physical act of art-making" to be spiritual activities.

Willow was curious about Eastern spirituality in college but lost this interest after marrying. Years later, after a painful divorce, she had a radical experience of nonduality while helping to crew a boat caught in a fierce storm. Afterward, she was drawn to meditation. She values the effects of meditation and feels gratitude for her inner experiences because of "how they cause you to be in the world." *Willow* views numinous experiences as moments of "the psyche saying, 'Yes,'" and, along with dreams and synchronicities, she finds these experiences to be "signposts along the way."

As a child, *Michael* experienced the passing of several members of his extended family, leaving him with a desire to learn more about death. He became interested in yoga and meditation at around age 16 and practiced Transcendental Meditation in college. On a whim, he went to India for a monthlong silent retreat, which led to an intense awakening experience. He has traveled to India several additional times to work with this teacher and occasionally dreams of her. He has also explored the Jewish Renewal Movement, led by Rabbi Zalman. Twice, *Michael* has had experiences of profound bodily knowing, a kind of direct awareness inward, once related to cancer and another time to heart disease. These experiences saved his life. The clarity of mind and the capacity to focus attention are important aspects of meditation for him. He considers making art as a meditation and teaches art as contemplative practice in a graduate program.

As a child, *Sophia* was interested in esoteric experiences and felt a deep connection with nature. In a high school class on world religions, she found that the material being taught already felt familiar to her. She was drawn to spending time at sacred sites and explored different Eastern spiritual traditions, eventually finding that *vipassana* and *metta bhavana* meditations drew her most deeply. Dreams are important to *Sophia*, and she composes music and song-poems that arise from her meditation, dreams, and inner images.

Elijah, a poet and physician, spent many years studying Buddhism, yoga, and Advaita Vedanta with different teachers in several Asian countries. He has been drawn to the study of nonduality for most of his adult life and is committed to attempting to articulate in words his experiences of nonduality.

Penelope was religious as a child and became interested in mystical experience in her adolescence, when she considered joining a cloistered convent. A near-death experience in a car accident strengthened her curiosity about life beyond the physical body. Synchronicities and dreams during and after a trip to India led to years of studying yoga and Tibetan Buddhist meditation practices. The experience of stilling the mind is an important part of meditation for *Penelope*, and her dreams continue to comment on the relationship between the process of individuation and the search for enlightenment.

Most of the participants in this study became interested in Eastern spiritual practices over journeys comprising decades. Some were touched by experiences in meditation, others by unlikely synchronicities or dreams, and yet others by experiences arising during long years of studying various Eastern spiritual traditions. A number had strong spiritual interests as children, sometimes outside of any of the mainstream Western traditions, whereas others were significantly involved in Western spiritual practices when young. Some look back at the influence of life traumas on their journey. Our conversations clarified that Eastern spiritual practices sometimes led to states of consciousness that move beyond verbally based consciousness and to experiences of nonduality. Although it is difficult to describe such experiences in words, several of the participants attempted to do so. The participants' experiences have been grouped into the following six themes.

Developing Advanced States of Consciousness Including Nondual Awareness

Sophia shared that she has had experiences of nonduality in meditation where there is "no front or back" and she has been "in the vastness," although simultaneously feeling anchored and experiencing compassion for human suffering. She described these experiences as being "almost like a sound." Meditation has led her to see the spark of the nondual in everyone and in nature.

Hayao reported that in adolescence he "became consumed with the notion of mystical experience: the thought that one could merge with the Absolute in ecstatic union." Reflecting on his understanding of nonduality, he stated:

> In addition to the Chinese view of *Qi* as the connector of all things, another version of

this idea comes from Buddhism, where it is called *pratityasamutpada,* or "dependent origination." If we conceive of things not in terms of individual causes and effects but rather as ONE THING in which every part is intimately connected to and "caused" by every other part, it's hard not to care, not only about our fellow humans but about other beings and all things.

At the level of practice, commenting on the contrast between focusing on a form-based divinity versus an awareness of nonduality, *Christopher* shared:

Currently, anchoring or rooting in an *Ishtadeva* ("form-based" or personal divinity) is extremely important to me. It is an integral component of my personal, daily practice (most recently, the Tantric-inspired Goddesses, or *Mahavidyas*), as well as guidance and protection. However, while maintaining form is important, these visualizations often do lead to a type of nondual awareness where "I" and "not-I" do dissolve or merge. Then even 'meditation' disappears and there is only ____.

A dramatic encounter with the nondual world occurred for *Willow*, when, as a young woman, she found herself on a boat caught in a storm. She recalled:

It was not the lark I had expected it to be. We got caught in a storm lasting several days. We were being tossed about by waves that towered over us and had difficulty keeping the boat from being swamped. It seemed clear that the storm was so powerful we were not going to make it to a port, and I decided that I needed to face Death.

I found a place to directly confront the water that was going to swallow me. I was terrified. And then everything changed. I saw in the water that there was no difference between me and the water. I saw that everything is interconnected. Everything is connected to everything else, and it was like I could see it. And it was so beautiful. All fear vanished. I went into an altered state that was totally fearless. Later I thought that maybe what I saw is what's sometimes referred to as "Indra's net." It's like I had a visual of all of the interconnections of the universe. There's no fear there. It's incredibly freeing.

Willow reported other experiences of nonduality in meditation:

These experiences defy being described in words. There are times in retreat when the body/mind takes over and perceptions of the world change. Sometimes objects are seen without names or labels, and they shimmer with luminescence. Sometimes joy arises and boundaries blur, making it clear that the individual self is not actually an entity in itself — we are just flow.

A similar sensation occurred for *Penelope*, who shared:

Sometimes I have experiences in meditation of hearing a sound, like a low hum, coming into my right ear. The sound is absolutely compelling, and it feels like my whole being is trying to connect with it. Ultimately, it feels like I merge with the sound. A teacher told me this is called *Nada Yoga,* the yoga that everything in the universe consists of vibrations.

Gaining access to nondual awareness is a theme that runs through the participants' stories. Such experiences, which from a Jungian perspective might be viewed as encountering the transpersonal level of the Self, were essential grounding and orienting containers in their lives. Several participants commented that although it seems paradoxical, they found their experiences in deep meditation to be more "real" than their experiences in normal waking consciousness. Acknowledging the power of these engagements with the unseen world and committing to this dimension of their experience became a lifelong project. For some, commitment to individuation and Eastern spiritual practices existed in a "side-by-side" way, whereas for others, the balance was different, with significantly more life energy being centered in Eastern spiritual practices. Returning to this theme later, I explore how the participants hold the two traditions in relationship with each other. For some participants, engaging with nonworded experiences led to creativity, an occurrence that is explored in the section on meditative states of consciousness and creativity.

Meditation and Dreams

The connection between dreaming and meditation varied among the participants. For some, dreams offered images that enriched their understanding of meditative states as well as commenting on other areas of their lives. For others, dreams supported the meditation practice more directly by providing images that symbolically describe the essence of these experiences.

Penelope recalled:

> Many years ago, I had a dream that connects to my experience of the intense stilling of the mind in meditation. In the dream, I'm looking down at the ocean from a high cliff, watching the waves come in and go out. After I watch

75

for a while, I begin to see that there may be something hidden beneath the waves, at the bottom of the ocean. I realize I can only catch glimpses of it during the split second when the sea is completely still in between the coming and going of the waves. I concentrate my attention strongly and focus on those fleeting moments of stillness in the water. Finally, I succeed, and I am able to see that there is a beautiful round garden growing at the bottom of the sea. I awoke overwhelmed by the beauty and mystery of the image.

Willow revealed, "I often dream of initiations or something that's going on in my meditation practice" and gave an example:

The other day, I had a dream about a test of my meditative efficacy ... I was asked a question by a teacher, and I laughed at an image that came into my head about digging a hole, something about thinking one is digging out when one is digging oneself deeper in, and the foibles of human nature. The teacher sees I understand, but this is just one step of many in the test.
So, it's the practice that comes into the dream.

Michael has had dreams in which his teacher appears to him that feel like *darshan*, the Hindi term for beholding a deity or a holy person in image form. These experiences, he said, "feel like a deep prayer" and follow him into waking life.

According to *Hayao:*

One of the ideas coming from the East that can inform one's spiritual life is ... that nonordinary states such as dream, deep contemplation, possession, and revelation are as real as the

76

"real world" and are a source of wisdom and useful information.

He mentioned his connection to the Chinese character *zheng,* which he said is usually translated as "right," "upright," "righteous," "correct," "authentic," or "straight." *Hayao* explained:

> Zheng is the enactment of the idea that humans are the connector between Heaven [another word for the immensity of the Universe, or Nature] and Earth. For me, this means that when one "is zheng," upright in posture and attitude, one's own integrity facilitates the integrity of the cosmos. ... This is something I learned through judo as a child, ... but one could learn it through seated meditation or tea ceremony just as well.

The idea of *zheng* was present for *Hayao* in a powerful dream:

> About a year ago, I had a dream that I now believe is about *zheng.* In the dream, I woke up in my bed and saw a coil of thick copper wire suspended from the ceiling by a string. The coil began swinging around erratically, as if by some kind of poltergeist activity. I looked on in alarm, and suddenly the copper wire went from being coiled to being perfectly straight and vertical. It was held in this position by what I sensed to be an immensely powerful force field. I felt as if I would die if I were to reach for the copper. I have wondered many times since about that dream, about what it signified. Though I still can't say with any certainty, I now believe that the coil represents me, and that in its straightening, it embodies *zheng* and the power that results when one joins Heaven

77

and Earth. I made a sculpture of the coil and hung it in a sacred place where I live.

A number of years ago, a deeply meaningful dream occurred for *Christopher* that spoke to long-term inner tensions that are still alive for him:

> I am in my parent's backyard (a regular dreamscape for me). There is an underground tunnel, and in it is a black panther facing outwards, toward the entrance of the tunnel. I am both behind the panther, and I am the panther. I can sense, see, feel its soft, yet bristly black fur. I am one with this magnificent animal. And yet there is a conflict. Each time the black panther attempts to emerge from the tunnel, it is sideswiped by a golden-yellow lion. Another magnificent, fierce, powerful, yet beautiful creature. This happens three times. Each time the panther/I emerge from the underground tunnel the lion comes and knocks me/us back underground.
>
> The "resolution" comes in the following scene where there appears a young boy (myself) standing under a large oak tree in my parents' side yard. The lion appears next to me. It lifts its paw. We shake hands.

Christopher commented:

> This dream has been with me now for over a decade. I am emotional as I share it here. The integration foreshadowed in the dream is still incomplete; a tension I still feel living in me — solar vs. lunar; above vs. below; inner vs. outer; intimacy, vulnerability vs. power, a general struggle between "light" and "dark." The incarnation still feels incomplete,

and I experience an interior longing for
reconciliation as I write this now.

All the participants spoke of their connection with the world of
dreams, although dreams were more significant for some participants
than others. For one participant, dreams became mostly subsumed
into Eastern spiritual practice, whereas for others, dreams commented
both on the practice and on other aspects of their lives, examples of
the unique ways in which the religious or spiritual function of the
psyche manifests. A further exploration of *Christopher's* experience
of the inner conflict between embodiment and transcendence occurs in
the discussion of psyche and body below, where there are additional
reports of dreams.

Meditative States of Consciousness and Creativity

The role of creativity in providing a space for psyche to engage
with emerging material is evidenced in these comments of Jung:
"Anytime in my life [that] I came up against a blank wall, I painted
a picture or hewed stone. Each such experience proved to be a *rite
d'entrée* for the ideas and works that followed hard upon it."[31]
For some participants, absorption in meditative states led to
creative acts, such as *Hayao's* experience of creating an object based
on a dream image. For other participants, creativity occurred in several
different forms, most specifically in art and music.
Michael described his experience of meditation in relation
to creativity: "Meditation teaches me to become the witness of my
thoughts, and art allows me to see the content of those thoughts. ...
Thoughts such as fear, love, and rage are translatable into art."
In describing his experiences with art making after receiving
a cancer diagnosis, *Michael* said:

During the cancer, I made a lot of pots, of
clay work. ... I made 80 pots during the cancer

---

[31] Jung, 1961/1963, p. 175

experience. As is often the case, the implicit content in terms of the symbolic depth was twenty steps ahead of my conscious orientation at that moment. The art was revealing prophecies to me about myself. One pot took me six years to make, and it still talks to me.

He reflected:

[Art is] like a synthetic or symbolic presenta-tion of nonduality. There are the parts — the background, the middle ground, the fore-ground; warm, cool colors; rough textures or smooth. All of these simultaneous components unify into one painting. They are the dualities of the parts that cohere and exist within the uni-fied one. ... Art [presents] the things we know before we cognize and think them. That is what art is — the preconscious, nonconceptual realm where you are manifesting very accurate sym-bolic content, but it is still not in your conscious awareness. ... Meaning arrives in stages, not right away.

Sophia composes music and the song-poems she creates come to her from meditation, dreams, and inner images. In her description of this process, one can see the seamlessness of her inner consciousness as it moves from dream to meditation to creation:

Melodies have come through dreams and have emerged out of meditative states. Sometimes a phrase will accompany the melody as well, but usually it starts with just the melody first, and I put words to it by repeating the melody over and over again until words start to form. In one case, [I had a dream in which] an Erik Satie melody was sung to me by a little girl in a pram. This dream occurred the night before I had an ovary removed because of a benign cyst. I worked with this dream in active imagination and let it guide me before and after surgery, speaking to my ovary and letting it go with compassion.

I did not recognize the music as a Satie melody until months later, although I knew I had heard it somewhere before. I put in a music CD, and the Satie piece was on it. I looked up the title of the haunting piece. He entitled it "Gnossiennes No. 1." It was part of his Gnossiennes series composed while he was involved with a Rosicrucian sect. I created a poem to accompany the music.

Hayao's description of the meditative and spiritual aspects in artmaking involves a sense of nonduality:

In my experience, the creative process and the physical act of artmaking is itself spiritual. When I am woodworking or metalworking, I find that my perception of time is altered; many hours pass but it feels like no time has passed at all. ... I am absorbed by the work and the material; the rasping and polishing of wood or metal becomes a metaphorical polishing of my own soul. The production of the artwork in its final form is less creation than it is revelation.

For some participants, creative activity occurs in a meditative state, perhaps comparable to the state of "flow."[32] For others, the connection to the creative is more on a global level and manifests in a quality of wholeness and balance in their lives.

---

[32] Csikszentmihalyi & Csikszentmihalyi, 1992, pp. 15-35

Psyche and Body

The relationship between meditation, dreaming, and the body is prominent for most of the participants in richly divergent ways. In terms of the physical body, in meditation and in dreams, several participants had experiences of their consciousness being separated from their bodies. All those having this experience found them to be transformative of their sense of who they were, bringing an awareness of a reality beyond that found with normal sensory-based consciousness and offering a powerful teaching in terms of personal growth. This separation of consciousness from their physical being left them with an awareness of mystery — an intimation of the realms of existence beyond ordinary reality.

Arthur recalled that, in his 20s, while meditating, he had an experience of leaving his body and "going up in the air about 3-4 feet and looking down on myself meditating." Although this was not unpleasant, after several minutes, he began to feel, "If I didn't get back down and into my body, I might not be able to get back in. And so I went back." He concluded:

> I think what all this has meant to me is that I am open to life and ways of being beyond our temporal/physical world. I've had enough of these beneficial experiences that it is easy to be open to the spiritual realm.

Sophia had a powerful dream several years ago in which she felt as if she were dying, perhaps from a heart attack. She said that at that moment, she was unclear if she was in reality or a dream. She described leaving her body and flying through black holes and caves on earth and in the sky. She said she felt calm and joyful, as though she were being given a glimpse of not being in her physical body.

Michael reported that about 20 years ago, he had a dream in which two presences "from the other side" visited. Each took hold of him under one of his armpits and "pulled him out of his body," taking him to the "other side." He awakened feeling this dream to have been a great privilege in his life, but without any direct memories of what he saw.

Penelope had a dream in which she became a point of light and was able to enter the cells of a red rose. This dream initiated a series of dreams of becoming a point of light, often rising toward high ceilings. In these dreams, she would sometimes become afraid that she was becoming too separated from her body and might not be reunited with it. At last, one night, she decided in a dream to let the experience continue and lead where it may. She floated high above, among ancient statues and artifacts in an upper realm, and then returned. After this culminating dream, the dreams of becoming a point of light came to an end.

The participants reported the importance of connecting with the body in new ways. Looking back on the period of his life around age 29, *Christopher* commented:

> As I reflect on this tumultuous period, I notice a pattern between trauma and spirituality. On the one hand, the intense desire to connect with the numinous — a deeply felt transpersonal source of meaning, connection, and containment; on the other, the desire to further incarnate, to heal, to "integrate the shadow" aspects of my psyche — the body, eros, a conscious, loving relationship to the feminine. This "more integrated" (and more difficult) path was preceded by a desire for transcendence that was often split off from those very same aspects — as if my personal trauma was fueling my desire to escape ("transcend") the difficult work of incarnation. [For the last 10 or so years] my journey has been one of descent, oriented *toward* earth, nature, body, eros, feeling, connection, intimacy, even as my more monastic and "younger" parts still seek a perhaps immature transcendence, disembodiment, and release from suffering through spiritualist escape. "Holding the tension" of what I

(still) experience as "opposites" continues to be my work as I enter midlife.

He continued:

> Meditation has always served as a psycho-spiritual tool. Whereas for many it is an opportunity to transcend or leave the body, I have, at least since 2008-09 used meditation as a tool (mostly) to more deeply enter into my body. "Praying with the body" was a mantra for me for many years, and something I utilized when teaching yoga classes. Meditation is an opportunity for me to enter into nondual awareness with my body. ... [Meditation allows me] to enter into a state of deep receptivity, to allow images and symbols to emerge from the psyche-soma. To unite spirit and flesh. This, to me, is a lived experience of non-dual awareness, as well as a taste of integration or "wholeness."

Hayao emphasized, "Whether you are learning meditation, yoga, sword fighting, or the tea ceremony, part and parcel of the tradition is learning how to be in your body." He explained, "Holding your body with integrity affects not only your physical ability to maintain balance and composure, but your ethics, your health, and ultimately your surroundings and the entire universe itself."

An experience of the symbolic relationship with one's body is reflected in *Penelope's* account of a dream:

> During a period when I was intensively practicing yoga, I had a dream that I was river rafting. In the distance, I could see strangely shaped mountains, and a companion commented that they were the "Kundalini mountains." As I looked more closely at them in

the dream, I realized the tops of the mountains
were the shapes of the human spine. It seemed
as if we were "river rafting" somewhere inside
my body. It felt like an experience of knowing
myself internally at a cellular level.

Arthur referred to an experience of adopting a meditative
perspective that united psyche and soma in relation to the physical world:

When I was younger, for a while I commuted
to work in a subway that went underwater for
part of the trip. At first, the screeching sound the
train made when it went underwater interrupted
my focus. I was frustrated by this, but then
sometime later I decided to go with it, and just
focus on my breath and the sound. ... It became
my regular practice.

The variety of these reported experiences shows how the
relationship between the body and the psyche, influenced by dreams
and meditation, is a uniquely personal experience and an important
part of the spiritual path of most of the participants. It is likely that
the ability to achieve and maintain heightened states of focused
attention is important in these experiences.

The Sacredness of Nature

Most of the participants shared the importance of nature
in their lives. Jung's own experiences of mystical connection with
nature are described in these two passages from his autobiography:
"At times I feel as if I am spread out over the landscape and inside
things, and am myself living in every tree, in the plashing of the
waves, in the clouds and the animals that come and go, in the
procession of the seasons."[33] And: "There is so much that fills me:

---

[33] Jung, 1961/1963, pp. 225–226

plants, animals, clouds, day and night, the eternal in man. The more uncertain I have felt about myself, the more there has grown up in me a feeling of kinship with all things."[34]

Hayao expressed the spiritual relationship with nature that developed in his childhood:

> Growing up in Japan, I was constantly reminded of the sanctity of nature. Shinto, the indigenous Japanese religion, is very much a "nature religion," a religion of place, of mountains and rivers and natural forces. Whether hiking in the forest or exploring the alleyways of a large city, it was not unusual to stumble upon shrines and temples built around things and places of unusual natural beauty and power: extraordinary trees, strangely shaped boulders, springs and waterfalls gushing with pure sweet water were often demarcated as holy sites where we would stop, clap our hands together, and offer a prayer.

Christopher reported a similar developmental path:

> I have been drawn toward — or into — numinous experiences or relationship with psychic and natural forces since childhood. I was a deeply "shamanic" child. Time in nature was both soothing and a haven for me. These early experiences with soul-in-earth imprinted a lasting impression on my psyche.

The experience of a "deep silence" in nature has had a transformative effect for *Penelope,* who said, "hiking is a moving meditation." She related:

---

[34] Ibid., p. 359

> Since I was a child, I've been deeply affected
> by being in the natural world, particularly
> mountains, forests, and the seashore. When
> I'm in nature I can become overwhelmed
> with intense joy, seeing light through leaves
> or smelling the forest on a summer's day.
> Sometimes when I'm in nature, I become aware
> of a deep silence behind the sounds around me.
> This deep silence seems to pervade and unite
> everything into a seamless whole.

The sense of a mystical connection with nature was a theme
for several of the participants. These meditative experiences in nature
point to an awareness of a unity underlying the natural world, with
immersion in the beauty of nature being part of nondual awareness.

Synchronicity

Occurrences of synchronicity were highlighted by some
participants in connection to Eastern spiritual practices, including
meditation. *Christopher* stated:

> I think what is most profound as I look back
> are the synchronicities that happened around
> Eastern spiritual practices: the Jungian analyst
> who first suggested, on a whim, that I visit
> the yoga center where I later lived, then
> worked at for a number of years, as well as
> where I completed my yoga teacher training.
> It was a tremendously generative place and
> period — seven years total. ... Always there
> was this ongoing drive, desire, hunger, thirst
> for wholeness, with these longings projected
> onto some sort of monastic establishment or
> retreat center; a fully human life, with one foot
> firmly rooted in the natural world, while ever
> seeking to more fully impregnate myself with
> the divine.

Regarding a Jungian technique that incorporates a meditative state of awareness, *Willow* recalled:

> A while back, I was working with a lot of active imagination. A woman came into my active imagination and told me her name was Sadha. She became a guide for me, wonderful, so comforting. I could go to her, and she would always comfort me. She was one of two. The other was male, masculine, and he was more intellectual. ... I found out (I don't know if it is Pali or Sanskrit), that Sadha means conviction or faith. It's the word used for "faith" in my Buddhist tradition. When I first read about that, I noticed the synchronicity, and that kept me going.

Sophia related this occurrence: "After my father's death, both my sister and I had a long series of synchronicities around dragonflies that were connected to him in significant ways."

Penelope also remembered a synchronicity:

> On a trip to India, while I was very sick, I had the following dream. I see a very old person sitting cross-legged on the ground wrapped in a shawl, deep in meditation. He or she is approached by a helper who offers a bowl of water. The person meditating brushes the bowl away and then reaches down with one hand and touches the ground with a finger. Immediately water emerges from a spring. When I returned to the US, by chance I met a Tibetan Buddhist monk from the Gelugpa order who became a significant teacher for me. It turns out this dream tells the story of one of the protector holy men of his tradition.

Experiences of synchronicity are numinous in their mystery and power. They strengthen the awareness of the nondual basis of experience, pointing at the unseen, unitive world beyond our conscious knowing.

Metaphysical Ponderings

The participants struggled to different degrees with how to understand the place of these two streams of experience, dual and nondual, in their lives. For *Elijah* in particular, articulating his experiences has been a lifelong quest. He shared:

> As I see it, nonduality isn't an experience, numinous or otherwise, that is insinuated in ordinary living. It is rather a "way of experiencing" (everything) in a continual stream and not hooked to a particular event. Ironically, seeing one undivided process rather than many different ones renders "the ordinary" extraordinary, even numinous.
>
> "Stream of experience" doesn't quite capture what I am getting at though. If I were to say that the apparent stream is perfectly still, that is to say, that motion and stasis are "not-two," it gets closer. How can this be? I don't know, except to say that motion seems to be an appearance while stasis seems to be the empirical fact. It is like the actual mirror stays still while the insubstantial, shadow-like, reflections move.
>
> Let me try saying it differently: the instantiation of "now," the undeniable felt sense of being, doesn't change. It is like the mirror. In other words, sentience, or presence, or awareness, or "is," feels and "looks" identical at all times. On the other hand, objects or events or experiences are always in flux, unstable, and don't carry the imprimatur of unchanging actuality.

Further, when talking about "my experience," it is generally assumed that it is something that I have undergone or partaken in. But the referent of the word "I" is ultimately what is being investigated (as I would understand individuation) and so "my experience" presupposes or assumes, on some level, that we all know and agree what this "I" is that is doing the experiencing. It is like the cart before the horse. The unaddressed question lingers, to whom does "my experience" occur? The nondualist would say that "my experience" is not mine — that there is no bifurcation between identity and experience.

I look around the room. Are there many things happening? Is the light shining, the heater fan blowing, my hands typing, the candle burning, the music playing or is that segmentation inferential? Or is there really just one process happening? I am inclined to think the latter — one process (even the description is unhelpfully divisive). ...

I suppose, in the end, if I were to try and link individuation and nonduality, I would have to say that individuation culminates in the nondual vision. It is the ultimate integration. It is a vision where there are no longer pieces or parts, conscious and unconscious, numinous and ordinary, just one radically inclusive whole that seems to see itself and can't believe it!

Continuing this line of thought, *Michael* reflected:

Images emerge from the nondual essence core of us. The pure essence consciousness that we are. We're the universe contemplating itself. ... We are embodied infinity. We are embodied consciousness. Consciousness is the essence aspects of our animating force

90

that survive or migrate to maybe incarnate again.

I don't have a problem with the multi-plicities of dualities that are in this realm. But I know that behind that, behind the behind, behind and behind that, and yes, behind that, is the nondual essence core of what we are. I hold awareness of both, but by no means am I established in a nondual unity consciousness. I have touched moments of that, but I don't live anchored in that state.

Reflecting on the combination of different perspectives and practices, *Hayao* stated:

Instead of operating on the faith that somebody got it right and we just have to find out who so we can follow them, I think we should instead just agree that the search for meaning, and for a connection to something greater than us, are universal human urges, and that it is only natural that different people fulfill these urges in different ways. It is from this perspective that I think we should approach the question of how to best integrate Eastern and Western spirituality. ... I think that what you think or do privately in the service of your spiritual well-being can and should be a highly personal affair, and there is no harm in borrowing from other cultures as long as you are not portraying yourself as an emissary ... of those cultures. ... The various cultural and spiritual traditions of East and South Asia offer much to the Westerner trying to forge his or her own spiritual path.

In a similar vein, *Christopher* offered:

> It was (and is) for me the integration of Eastern, embodied contemplation practices, with "Western" psychotherapy, particularly Jungian psychology, that has and continues to forge the crucible my psyche lives with, in, and through today.

Penelope related the benefits of meditative practice and a nondual perspective in her life:

> My experience has been of being led forward on my path by forces beyond my control. Some events in my life have been hard to survive, such as the loss of a child, but even that experience was softened by dreams, premonitions, and indications about what is unknown — the mystery — that provided something to hold onto through the storm. My dreams have been important, and also the stilling of the mind coming from meditative practice.

Although some of the participants experienced a pressing need to articulate in words their experience of deeply connecting with Eastern spiritual traditions, others were more focused on their direct experience of meditative states and felt less inclined to attempt to find words to describe them. In all cases, the exploration of Eastern spiritual traditions played a significant role in what held the most meaning in their lives.

Conclusion

Looking at the ways these eight individuals describe their engagement with Eastern spiritual traditions and their understanding of how these experiences related to their individuation journeys offers us a glimpse into their rich and unique inner worlds. Through this study, several common themes emerge, reflecting the development of advanced states of consciousness and drawing close to the experience of nonduality, as well as identifying the themes of the relationship between meditation and dreaming, and between meditation and the body, art, nature, and synchronicity. The participants' stories show a process of seamless interweaving of Eastern and Western approaches in their lives. Leslie Stein in his book, *The Self in Jungian Psychology: Theory and Clinical Practice*, explored in detail the aspect of the Self as agency, leading the individual forward in the individuation process.[35] Similar to Neumann's ideas in *The Psyche and the Transformation of the Reality Planes*,[36] Stein examined the ordering function of the Self and the role it plays in presenting to the ego important and carefully selected components of extraneous knowing as the individuation process unfolds. These other forms of knowing are revealed to ego consciousness through events such as powerful and meaningful dreams, synchronicities, visions, meditation experiences, and active imagination. Such moments bring ego consciousness to an awareness of nonduality and to numinous experiences of transcendence. This study offers a deeper understanding of how the search for enlightenment and the individuation process can intersect in the lived experience of individuals who pursue both paths simultaneously.

---

[35] Stein, 2021
[36] Neumann, 1952/1989

References

Anderson, R. (1998). Intuitive inquiry: A transpersonal approach. In W. Broad & R. Anderson, Eds. *Transpersonal Research Methods for the Social Sciences: Honoring Human Experience.* 69–74. Thousand Oaks, CA: Sage

Benevedes, J. M. (2021). God dwells within me as me. Review of the book *The Spiritual Psyche in Psychotherapy: Mysticism, Intersubjectivity, and Psychoanalysis.* W. Pearson and H. Marol, Eds. *Jung Journal, 15*(2), 126–134

Clements, J. (2004). Organic inquiry: Toward research in partnership with spirit. *Journal of Transpersonal Psychology, 36*(1), 26–49

Corbett, L. (1996). *The Religious Function of the Psyche.* London: Routledge

____. (2007). *Psyche and the Sacred: Spirituality beyond Religion.* Asheville, NC: Chiron Publications

____. (2011). *The Sacred Cauldron: Psychotherapy as a Spiritual Practice.* Asheville, NC: Chiron Publications

Csikszentmihalyi, M., & Csikszentmihalyi, I. (1992). *Optimal Experience: Psychological Studies of Flow in Consciousness.* Cambridge: Cambridge University Press

Franklin, M. (2017). *Art as contemplative practice: Expressive pathways to the Self.* Albany, NY: State University of New York Press

Jung, C.G. (1963). *Memories, dreams, reflections* (Rev. ed.). A. Jaffé, Ed. R. Winston & C. Winston, Trans. New York: Vintage Books

____. (1975). *C. G. Jung letters. Vol. 2: 1951–1961.* G. Adler & A. Jaffé, Eds. R. F. C. Hull, Trans. Princeton: Princeton University Press

____. (2009). *The Red Book: Liber Novus.* S. Shamdasani, Ed. S. Shamdasani, M. Kyburz, & J. Peck, Trans. New York: W. W. Norton

____. (2020). *The Black Books, 1913-1932: Notebooks of transformation.* Vols. 1-7. S. Shamdasani, Ed. M. Liebscher, J. Peck, & S. Shamdasani, Trans. New York: W. W. Norton

Kalsched, D. (2013). *Trauma and the Soul: A Psycho-spiritual Approach to Human Development and its Interruption.* London: Routledge

Kapleau, P. Compiler & Ed. (1980). *The Three Pillars of Zen: Teaching, Practice, and Enlightenment.* New York: Anchor Books

Katsky, P. (2021). Enlightenment, individuation, and nonduality. *Jung Journal, 15*(1), 104–128

Kornfield, J. (2000). *After the Ecstasy, the Laundry: How the Heart Grows Wise in the Spiritual Path.* New York: Bantam Books

Miyuki, M. (1992). Self-Realization in the Ten Oxherding Pictures. In *Self and Liberation: The Jung/Buddhist Dialogue,* D.J. Meckel & R. L. Moore. Mahwah, N.J.: Paulist Press

Neumann, E. (1989). The Psyche and the Transformation of the Reality Planes: A Metapsychological Essay. H. Nagel, I. Roberts, & W. Goodheart, Trans. In W. McGuire (Ed.), *The Essays of Erich Neumann.* Vol. 3. Princeton: Princeton University Press

Otto, R. (1958). *The Idea of the Holy: An inquiry into the Non-rational Factor in the Idea of the Holy: The Divine and its Relation to the Rational.* J. W. Harvey Trans. Oxford: Oxford University Press

Pearson, W., & Marlo, H. (2021). *The Spiritual Psyche in Psychotherapy: Mysticism, Intersubjectivity, and Psychoanalysis.* London: Routledge

Singer, T., & Kimbles, S. (2004). The emerging theory of cultural complexes. J. Cambray & L. Carter, Eds. In *Analytical Psychology: Contemporary Perspectives in Jungian Analysis.* East Sussex: Brunner-Routledge

Stein, L. (2021). *The Self in Jungian Psychology: Theory and Clinical Practice.* Asheville, NC: Chiron Publications

Stein, M. (2019). Psychological individuation and spiritual enlightenment: Some comparisons and points of contact. *Journal of Analytical Psychology, 64*(1), 6–22

Valencia, A., & Froese, T. (2020). What binds us? Inter-brain neural synchronization and its implications for theories of human consciousness. *Neuroscience of Consciousness, 6*(1)

HINDUISM AND
THE ATMAN

4

Individuation to Transcendence – The Hindu Perspective on the Concept of the Self – The Self/Spirit Axis

Ashok Bedi

The sweet fruit of Jung's Analytical Psychology is the concept of the Ego/Self axis as the Jacob's ladder to the Individuation process to become the most evolved version of one's latent potential. The Hindu paradigm is that the first half of life must accomplish this task by midlife guided by the Vedic map of a Dharmic life and then this Dharmic or Individuated psyche must embark on the core purpose of human incarnation to ascend to the Self/Spirit axis. Each of the four Vedas is divided into four quadrants. The first two of these four quadrants give us a road map for the Ego/Self axis and the last two of these four sections are a GPS for the Self/Spirit axis.[1]

Introduction

Jung defines Self as an empirical concept and designating the whole range of psychic phenomena. It encompasses the experienceable and inexperienceable or not yet experienced. It is a transcendent concept that can be described only in part but, for

---

[1] Acknowledgement: My deep gratitude to my friend and colleague Dr. Robert "BJ" Jakala for editing the paper and Leslie Stein for his guidance in clarifying my ideas and to meet the publication guidelines.

the other part, remains at present unknowable and illimitable. The Upanishads offer a detailed anatomy of the concept of Self in the Vedic scriptures and lay out the portals for this Self to align itself with the Spirit or the Brahman consciousness.

The Upanishads are a mystical tradition and merged into the later flowering, ritual sacrifice-based Vedic thought. Some of this mystical tradition can be traced to the pre-Aryan Indus Valley civilization. The sages of Upanishads studied the states of consciousness. They observed the dreams and the witnessing consciousness in wakefulness and dreams, but who is the witness in the dreamless sleep? The question remains as to why we crave this adventure to the core of our consciousness.

The Upanishad implies that this is part of our evolutionary heritage to discover who we are, what is our place in the Universe and the meaning of our transient life against the backdrop of eternity. Carl Jung postulated five human instincts: hunger, sex, action, reflection, and creativity. This essay adds the transcendent instinct — the search for our core and its place in the Universe. These Janus aspects of the human quest for individuation as preparation for transcendence is the basic tenet of Hinduism. Individuation is considered a necessary first step to optimize our terrestrial self in its quest for transcendence to claim its celestial core. The anatomy of this portal to establish the Ego/Self/Spirit axis is explored in the backdrop of Vedas, Upanishads, Patanjali's Yoga Sutras, emerging neuroscience and analytical psychology.

When the Aryans migrated to India around 2000 B.C.E, they found a 1,000-year-old advanced Indus valley civilization. The Aryans brought their gods and religion, which honored nature, environment, and sacrificial rites. These form the foundation of the pyramid of the Vedas. Subsequently, these Vedas became the four collections: Rig, Sama, Yajur, and Atharva Vedas. The first and the largest part of each Vedas is "Karma Kanda," which preserves the hymns and philosophical interpretations of rituals used in Hindu worship to this day.

The second part of each Veda, called "Jnana Kanda" does not concern the rituals but contains wisdom about the existential issues that confront human consciousness. This wisdom text of the Vedas is the Upanishads. This wisdom is a derivative of the pre-Aryan Indus valley civilization. The word Upanishad means "sitting down near": at the feet of a teacher who is retired from the tangles of life and established in the forest as an anchorite, Rishi, or wise old person.

A brief overview of the Hindu canon and the location of Upanishad within it may orient the reader to a road map by which to navigate this ancient wisdom tradition. The Hindu tradition and philosophy evolved in several stages.[2]

    1.   Indus Valley Civilization — c. 2500-1750 B.C.E.
The urban societies along the Indus River, which formed the first cohesive civilization along the Indus river in the third and the second millennium B.C.E.

    2.   A Vedic age — c. 1200-200 B.C.E.
The appearance of the Vedas, a period of the great oral tradition with dominant paradigms and unchallenged sacred utterances of Hindu philosophy.

    3.   An Epic age — c. 400 BCE-800 BCE through 200 C.E.
The post-Vedic oral tradition of the great Epics of Hinduism, including the Mahabharata and Ramayana; thus, the Epic period.

    4.   The Sutra period — c. 750-1750 C.E.
The fourth medieval age between the classical and modern age when several masters crystallized the philosophical, theological and devotional bases of Hinduism, e.g., Vedanta and commentaries by Shankara and Ramanuja.

    5.   Modern India — C.E 1750-present
Modern Hinduism is impacted by the interface with the British and the West.

---

[2] Knipe, 1991, pp. 1-46

Structure of each Veda[3]

Each Veda has four parts (Figure 1):

Samhitas — Mantras or hymns are the beginning of the Hindu philosophy and are the creation of poets.

Brahmanas — The Brahmanas are religious documents that include rituals and sacrificial rites and are the creation of priests. They provide the rituals for the householder, and when the householder retreats into the forest in old age, provide new rituals for the forest dweller.

Aranyakas — Aranyakas encourage meditative life and transition to the introduction of the tenets of Upanishad.

Upanishads — The creation of philosophers. It has a thesis of spiritual monism and emphasizes intuition rather than logic as the path to the source.

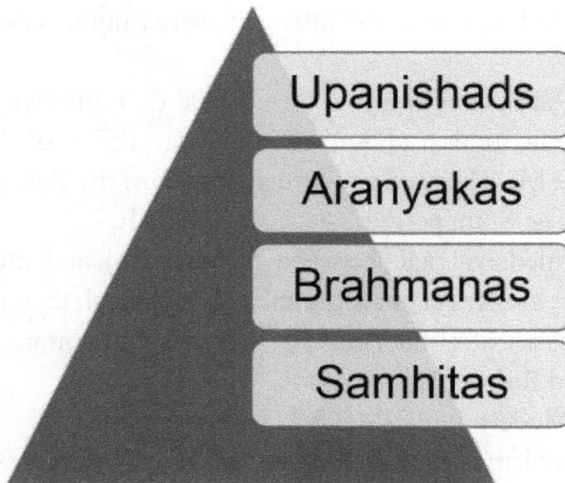

Figure 1

---

[3] S. Radhakrishnan & Moore, 1957, p. xviii

According to Eknath Easwaran,[4] their purpose is not to instruct but to inspire. Each essay is complete, a snapshot of the transcendent reality. While embedded in the Vedas, the Upanishads are a stand-alone system and make little reference to the rituals in the Vedas, though the gods and goddesses overlap. While the Vedas look outward to nature and God/Goddess archetypes projected onto the phenomenal world, the Upanishads look inward at the study of human consciousness. The Vedas focus on the objective reality, while the Upanishads study the observer itself and the process of observation, i.e., the subject is the focus of study.

The mystical tradition of the Upanishads can be traced to the pre-Aryan Indus Valley civilization. Archaeologists have uncovered a stone image identifiable as Shiva in a meditative posture.[5] (Figure 2)

Figure 2[6]

[4] Eknath & Nagler, 1988, p. 20

[5] Ibid., pp. 20-22

[6] https://www.harappa.com/indus/33.html. Seal, Mohenjo-daro 33. (Last accessed 02/24/2022). Square seal depicting a nude male deity with three faces, seated in yogic position on a throne, wearing bangles on both arms and an elaborate headdress.

The sages of Upanishads studied states of consciousness. They observed dreams and the witnessing consciousness in wakefulness and dreams, but who is the witness in the dreamless sleep? This witness in the dreamless sleep, medically the non-REM (NREM) sleep, is the Self — the Antar Yamin, the spark of the divine within. The study of this consciousness is called Brahmavidya — the science of the supreme.[7] They explored different strata of consciousness: waking, dreaming and the dreamless sleep, now substantiated by EEG studies. What is the constant in these states of consciousness? They found a key; in the dreamless sleep, we are detached from the body, senses and mind or cognitive apparatus. They equate this to a bird (Self-Soul), which is flying (in the outer world, in the inner world, in waking, sleeping, and dreaming) and, when tired, it "settles down to rest" in the dreamless sleep.[8] This is the deepest level of our unconscious, the diamond body, a state of deep autonomic healing — the relaxation response.[9]

This still world is always present in the deepest core of the psyche. When we wake up to this still core, we are truest to our essence, uncorrupted by time, space and causality, i.e., to our samskaras, our complexes or psychic Vriti or turbulence: the push and pull of these competing forces of the unconscious. Patanjali's yoga sutras offer a spiritual paradigm to establish this stillness to reach our diamond body. The Vedanta path is a major culmination of the Vedic wisdom to establish a connection with our still core. In the Vedanta thesis, when we stabilize the turbulence in the layers or Koshas of consciousness, then we establish such stillness — our diamond body. This is accomplished via contemplative practices, e.g., Meditation and Mindfulness.[10]

---

[7] Eknath & Nagler, 1988, p. 26
[8] Ibid., pp. 29-30
[9] Benson, 1975
[10] Bedi, 2013, pp. 122-141

The question remains as to why we crave this adventure
to the core of our consciousness. The Brihadaranyka Upanishad[11]
implies that this is part of our evolutionary heritage to discover who
we are, what is our place in the Universe, and the meaning of our
transient life against the backdrop of eternity. [12] Carl Jung postulated
five human instincts: hunger, sex, action, reflection, and creativity.[13]
I would add the transcendent instinct — the search for our core and
its place in the Universe. (Figure 3)

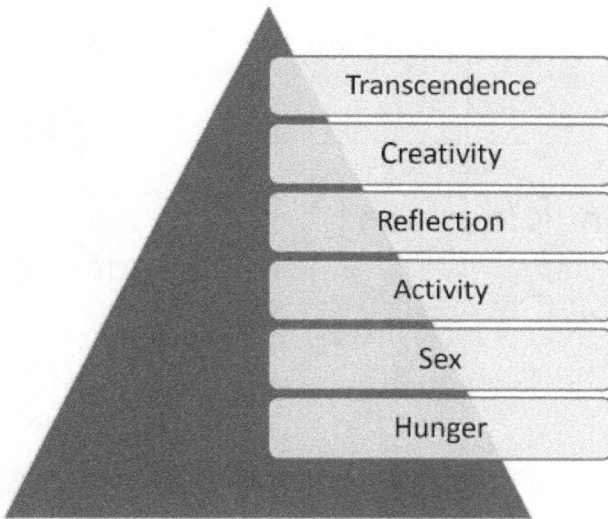

Figure 3

The Taittiriya Upanishad postulates that the body is one of
several layers of human consciousness, each more subtle till we reach
the Annadmayakosha, the blissful core of our diamond body — the
bliss body. All that divides us from the infinite Brahman consciousness
is a thin layer of personality, "I." When we transcend the I, we
experience and merge with the primal consciousness, the Brahman.

---

[11] Eknath & Nagler, 1988, pp. 29-30
[12] Ibid., paraphrased from pp. 33-34
[13] Jung, CW 8, § 232-262

Such a state is called "Turiya," the fourth state of consciousness beyond awake, sleep and dream states. Turiya is the equivalent of waking up in this Turiya state — experienced in Samadhi as outlined in Patanjali's yoga sutra.[14] If we can sustain such a Samadhi, we experience Moksha, or freedom from the constraints of I, time, space and transience. Here, our innermost core, the Self, merges into the Brahman, or the collective consciousness of the Universe. Thus, the great formula: Mahavakyas is "Tat tvam asi, that are thou."

The Janus of the Human Quest

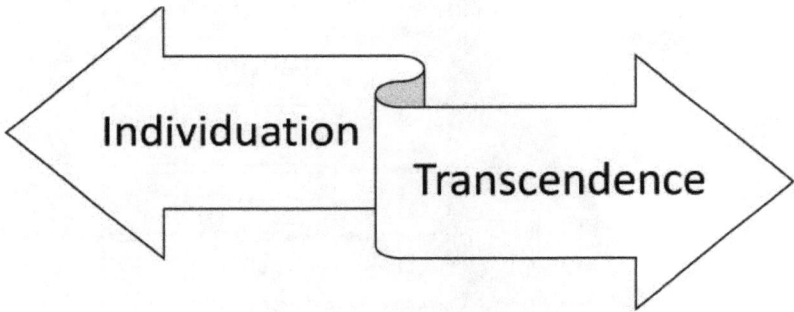

Figure 4

These Janus aspects of the human quest for individuation as a preparation for transcendence is the basic tenet of Hinduism (Figure 4). While individuation is considered a necessary preparation for the quest for transcendence, it is no less important. Patanjali's Yoga Sutra prescribes the eight limbs of this process. The first four limbs or steps pertain to individuation, living a spiritually aligned life; the fifth step is about optimal detachment from the outer life to prepare for the journey of transcendence; and the last three prescriptions are a gradual merger with the transcendent. Let us now explore these eight steps, or Ashtanga (Ashtha= eight, Anga= limbs).

---

[14] Satchidanada, 1978

The 8 Limbs of Yoga[15]

2.29 The eight limbs of Union are self-restraint in actions, fixed observance, posture, regulation of energy, mind control in sense engagements, concentration, meditation, and realization. (Figure 5)

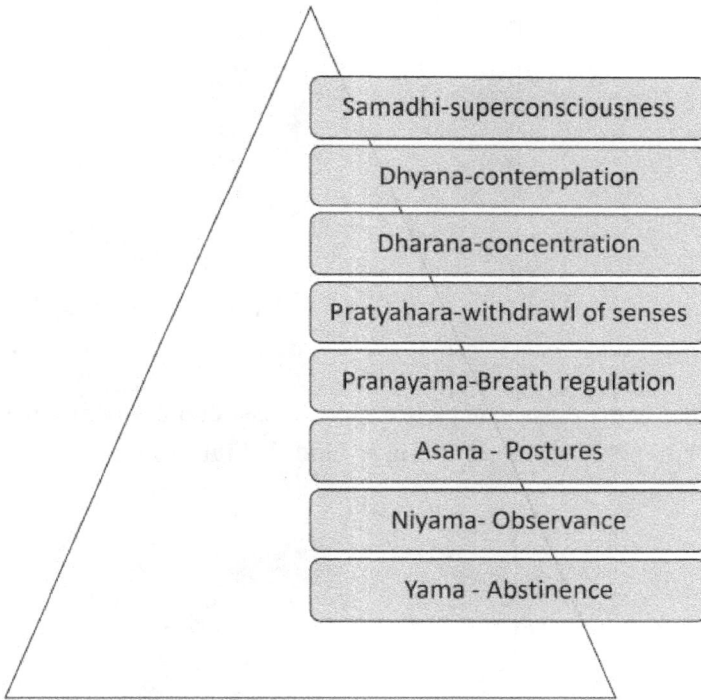

Samadhi-superconsciousness

Dhyana-contemplation

Dharana-concentration

Pratyahara-withdrawl of senses

Pranayama-Breath regulation

Asana - Postures

Niyama- Observance

Yama - Abstinence

Figure 5

Yama[16]

2.30 Self-restraint in actions includes abstention from violence, from falsehoods, from stealing, from sexual engagements, and from acceptance of gifts.[17] (Figure 6)

---

[15] Ibid., p. 117

[16] Ibid., 1978, p. 118

[17] Patanjali, 2001, p. 4 (paragraph numbers from the sutras)

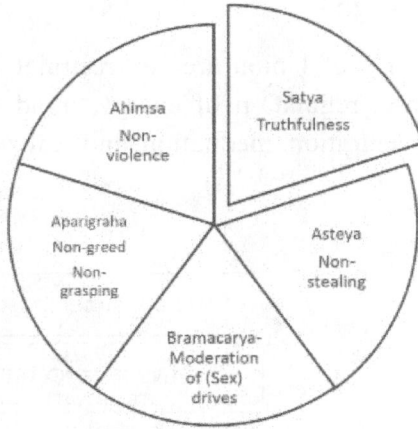

Figure 6

Niyama

2.32 The fixed observances are cleanliness, contentment, austerity, study, and persevering devotion to God.[18] (Figure 7)

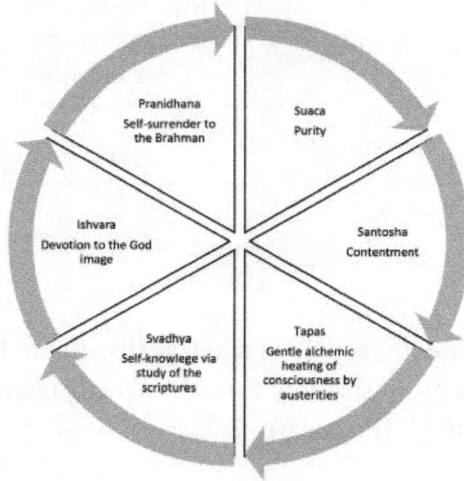

Figure 7

---

[18] Ibid., p. 5

Asana[19]

2.46 The posture should be steady and comfortable.[20]

The Hatha Yoga.

Pranayama[21]

2.48 From that there is no disturbance from the dualities.
2.49 When that exists, control of incoming and outgoing energies is next.
2.50 It may be external, internal, or midway, regulated by time, place, or number, and of brief or long duration.[22]

Pratyahara[23]

2.54 When the mind maintains awareness, yet does not mingle with the senses, nor the senses with sense impressions, then self-awareness blossoms.
2.55 In this way comes mastery over the senses.[24]

The ninth image from the Rosarium Philosophorum is a prototype of the concept of Pratyahara from an analytical perspective as discussed by Jung in his treatise of the process of psychotherapy.[25]

The image is divided into three parts: The lower third is the inner work of the individual; the middle third is the current consciousness; and the upper third is the teleological potential for individuals to reclaim their connection with their guiding angel — the Self and the Brahman.

---

[19] Satchidanada, 1978, pp. 42-43
[20] Patanjali, 2001, p. 5
[21] Satchidanansa, 1978, pp. 148-149
[22] Patanjali, 2001, pp. 5-6
[23] Satchidanada, 1978, pp. 154-157
[24] Patanjali, 2001, p.6
[25] Jung, CW 16, § 494-524

In the lower third of this image is an inner dialogue between the winged bird and the wingless bird. The winged bird is the emerging consciousness, while the wingless bird is the old adaptation, including the complexes. Individuals must now make a choice to fly away from the wingless bird to claim a reconnection with their guiding angel or perish with the wingless bird. For codependent individuals, this calls for establishing an attitude of compassionate detachment with an individual with whom they are locked into an enmeshed matrix of their codependent complex.

While this unconscious negotiation is occurring, the current life, as depicted in the middle third of the image, has a static, deathlike quality. For the king and the queen, a vibrant connection with the contrasexual archetype: the anima and the animus, are frozen without the infusion of the vitality from the Self — the returning angel from the heavens, the transcendent principle.

The upper third of this Rosarium image is the symbol of hope, the potential for a vital connection with the guiding angel — the Self. The Self is a continuum of the Collective consciousness, the Pleroma, the Psychoid, the Brahman awareness, the Quantum, the mind/matter continuum, the Purusha/Prakriti = Consciousness/ matter interface, the residing place of the healing archetypes prepared to offer a new GPS for a spiritually purposeful life.

Dharana[26]

3.1 One-pointedness is steadfastness of the mind.[27]

Dharana is the binding of mind to one place, object, or idea.

---

[26] Satchidanada, 1978, pp. 161-163
[27] Patanjali, 2001, p. 6

Dhyana[28]

3.2 Unbroken continuation of that mental ability is meditation.[29]

This is meditation-contemplation upon one single cognition (idea, object).

Samadhi[30]

3.3 That same meditation when there is only consciousness of the object of meditation and not of the mind is realization.[31]

This is participation mystique with the Brahman. Neuroscience studies consider this a move from the Alpha to Gamma consciousness.[32]

Jung's Concept of the Self

While consolidation of the Ego is the central theme of Freud's approach to the unconscious, the agency of the Self and Ego's relationship with it is the core tenet of Jung's analytical psychology. Here is how Jung summarizes the anatomy of the Self:

> "an empirical concept, the self designates the range of psychic phenomenon in man. … It encompasses both the experienceable and the inexperience able (or the not yet experienced). … It is a transcendental concept … that can only be described in part but, for the other part,

---

[28] Satchidanada, 1978, pp. 163-164
[29] Patanjali, 2001, p. 6
[30] Satchidanada, 1978, pp. 164-166
[31] Patanjali, 2001, p. 6
[32] A. Lutz, Greischar, Rawlings, Ricard, & Davidson, 2004. In an EEG, the Alpha waves of 8-12 Hertz per second are correlated with relaxed states of consciousness, while the Gamma waves of 24-80 Hertz per second are indicative of deep states of consciousness akin to Samadhi in experienced meditators. They are considered to be related to the creation of new consciousness.

remains at present unknowable and illimitable. Empirically, the Self appears in dreams, myths, and fairytales in the figure of the "supraordinate personality" (vs Ego), such as a king, hero, prophet, savior, etc., or in the form of totality symbol, such as a circle, square, *quadrature circuli,* cross, etc. When it represents a *complex oppositorum,* a union of the opposites, it can also appear as a united duality, in the form, for instance, of *Tao* as the interplay of *yin* and *yang,* or the hostile brothers, or the hero and his adversary (arch-enemy, dragon), Faust and Mephistopheles, etc. ... These empirical symbols often possess a distinct *numinosity.* ... It thus proves to be an *archetypal idea,* (v. *Idea; Image*) which differs from other ideas of the kind in that it occupies a central position befitting the significance of its content and its numinosity.[33]

The establishment of the Ego-Self axis is the royal road to the individuation process. The goal of this collaboration is to live a life informed by the Self and the collective unconscious. Its outcome is moving beyond adaptation to the demands of the outer world to honoring the call of the Self. This balance of outer and inner adaptation thus leads to wholeness of personality. Such an individuating individual is in sync with the flow of the collective and lives not just the spirit of the time but the spirit of the depths.[34] Thus, one lives out not just the No. 1 ego personality on the horizontal ego existence but the No. 2 Self personality,[35] adding verticality, interiority, and a vocational calling to one's life trajectory, or teleos.

Jung's focus is the development of the personality toward its potential for wholeness and balance between ego's striving and

---

[33] Jung, CW 6 § 780-791
[34] Jung & Shamdasani, 2009, p. 229
[35] Jung & Jaffé, 1963, pp. 35-45

soul's calling. Its goal is a higher degree of adaptation, not just to the outer demands but inner guidance. However, from a Hindu perspective, this amounts to getting all dressed up with nowhere to go! What is the purpose of this preparation? What is the ultimate destination of the Self? How does this Self manifest and be cultivated for its final destination? The goal of a Hindu is not just individuation, but transcendence. The Upanishads of the Vedic tradition give us a treasure map to this mystery. Let us explore this next.

Upanishad's profiles in the Self

Most European scholars are agreed in deriving upa-ni-shad from the root "sad," to sit down, preceded by the two prepositions "ni," down, and "upa," near, so that it would express the idea of a session, or assembly of pupils sitting down near their teacher to listen to his instruction.[36]

The first germs of Upanishad doctrines go back at least as far as the Mantra period, which provisionally has been fixed between 1000 and 800 B.C.E. Conceptions corresponding to the general teaching of the Upanishads occur in certain hymns of the Rig-Veda Samhita; they must have existed therefore before that collection was finally closed. The recognized place for the ancient Upanishads is in the Aranyakas, or forest-books, which, as a rule, form an appendix to the Brahmanas. At all events the Upanishads, like the Aranyakas, belong to what Hindu theologians call Shruti, or revealed literature, in opposition to Smriti, or traditional literature, which is supposed to be founded on the former and allowed to claim a secondary authority only. The earliest of these philosophical treatises will always, I believe, maintain a place in the literature of the world, among the most astounding productions of the human mind in any age and in any country.[37]

The ancient Vedic literature, the foundation of the whole literature of India that has been handed down in that country in an

---

[36] Müller, 1879
[37] Ibid.

unbroken succession from the earliest times within the recollection of man to the present day, became known for the first time beyond the frontiers of India through the Upanishads. The Upanishads were translated from Sanskrit into Persian by, or, it may be, for Dara Shukoh, the eldest son of Shah Jehan, an enlightened prince who openly professed the liberal religious tenets of the great Emperor Akbar and even wrote a book intended to reconcile the religious doctrines of Hindus and Mohammedans. He seems first to have heard of the Upanishads during his stay in Kashmir in 1640. He afterward invited several Pandits from Benares to Delhi, who were to assist him in the work of translation. The translation was finished in 1657. Two years after the accomplishment of this work, in 1659, the prince was put to death by his brother Aurangzeb 1, in reality, no doubt because he was the eldest son and legitimate successor of Shah Jehan, but under the pretext that he was an infidel, and dangerous to the established religion of the empire.

When the Upanishads had been translated from Sanskrit into Persian, at that time the most widely read language of the East and understood likewise by many European scholars, they became generally accessible to all who took an interest in the religious literature of India. In 1775, Anquetil Duperron, the famous traveler and discoverer of the Zend-Avesta, received one manuscript of the Persian translation of the Upanishads, sent to him by M. Gentil, the French resident at the court of Shuja ud daula, and brought to France by M. Bernier. After receiving another manuscript, Anquetil Duperron collated the two and translated the second Persian translation into French (not published) and into Latin. That Latin translation was published in 1801 and 1802.

This translation, though it attracted considerable interest among scholars, was written in an utterly unintelligible style, which required the lynxlike perspicacity of an intrepid philosopher such as Schopenhauer to discover a thread through such a labyrinth. Schopenhauer, however, not only found and followed such a thread, but he had the courage to proclaim to an incredulous age the vast treasures of thought which were lying buried beneath that fearful jargon.

114

Schopenhauer not only read this translation carefully, but he made no secret of it that his own philosophy is powerfully impregnated by the fundamental doctrines of the Upanishads. He dwelt on it again and again, and it seems both fair to Schopenhauer's memory and incredibly important for a true appreciation of the philosophical value of the Upanishads, to put together what that vigorous thinker has written on those ancient rhapsodies of truth.[38]

The number of Upanishads translated by Dara Shukoh amounts to 50; their number, as given in the Mahâvâkyamuktâvalî and in the Muktikâ-upanishad, is 108. Professor Weber thinks that their number, so far as we know at present, may be reckoned at 235. In order, however, to arrive at so high a number, every title of an Upanishad would have to be counted separately, while in several cases, it is clearly the same Upanishad that is quoted under different names.[39]

When these texts were composed, or who composed them, no one knows. The sages who gave them to us did not care to leave their names, but the truths they set down were eternal and the identity of those who arranged the words irrelevant. We do not even know how many once existed. For the last thousand years, however, 10 have been considered the "principal Upanishads" on the authority of Shankara, a towering eighth-century mystic who reawakened India to its spiritual heritage. These 10 Upanishads are discussed in this chapter along with one other of equal importance and great beauty, the Shvetashvatara.

These Ten Upanishads (Dashopanishads) are:[40]

1. Isha Upanishad (White Yajurveda): Isha=Lord/ God
2. Kena Upanishad (Samaveda)
3. Katha Upanishad (Black Yajurveda)
4. Prashna Upanishad (Atharvaveda): Prashna=Question.
5. Mundaka Upanishad (Atharvaveda)

---

[38] Ibid.
[39] Ibid.
[40] Ibid.

6.   Mandukya Upanishad (Atharvaveda)
7.   Taittiriya Upanishad (Black Yajurveda)
8.   Aitareya Upanishad (Rigveda)
9.   Chandogya Upanishad (Samaveda)
10. Brihadaranyka Upanishad (White Yajurveda)

The other two commented on by Shankara are Shvetashva-tara Upanishad and Narasimha Tapaniya Upanishad. We will now explore the profiles in Self and its transcendent instinct as amplified in these sacred texts of the East.

Self as Immanent and Transcendent — Isha Upanishad
The Inner Ruler as a Source of Abundance

Each Upanishad comes with an invocation drawn from a traditional set. Consistent with the condensed meaning of the Upanishad itself, it proposes that the inexhaustible reality, the infinite of "that" world, the unseen, sends forth "this" world of infinite variety in which we live, without ever being diminished.

> All this is full. All that is full.
> From fullness, fullness comes.
> When fullness is taken from fullness,
> Fullness still remains.
> OM shanti shanti shanti[41]

The Isha Upanishad amplifies the Self as immanent and transcendent, the inexhaustible reality, projected onto the objective reality. Those who live in abundance and fullness of the Self do not experience the distortion of material deprivation. As Mahatma Gandhi famously said, "There is enough in the world for everyone's need but not enough for everyone's greed."

The following quote from Isha Upanishad captures this essence of the fullness of the Self:

---

[41] Eknath & Nagler, 1988, p. 56

In the dark night live those for whom the Lord
Is transcendent only, in night darker still,
For whom he is immanent only.
But those for whom he is transcendent.
And Immanent cross the sea of death
With and immanent and enter into
Immortality with the transcendent.[42]

The Deathless Self — Katha Upanishad — Death as Teacher[43]

When a person dies, there arises this doubt:
"He still exists," say some; "he does not."
Say others. I want you to teach me the truth.
1.1.20

In Katha Upanishad, a teenager, Nachiketa, has an encounter with Yama, the god of death. He is granted three boons by the god of death. The first boon is to restore Nachiketa's loving relationship with his father; the second boon is to learn the mystery of the fire sacrifice rite that leads to heaven. In the third boon, Nachiketa asks for clarification as to what exists for an individual beyond death. In lieu of this mystery, Yama offers Nachiketa the fulfillment of all worldly desires, power to dominate the earth, celestial delights gained through religious rites, miraculous powers beyond time and space. However, this was a test, and Nachiketa renounces all these gifts for the pursuit of the truth of existence beyond death. What follows in Yama's amplification is the most profound elaboration of the phenomenology of Self as differentiated from the ego, concluding with these remarks on the deathless Self:

The supreme Self is beyond name and form,
Beyond the senses, inexhaustible,
Without beginning, without end, beyond

---

[42] Ibid., pp. 53-59
[43] Ibid., pp. 63-92

Time, space and causality, eternal,
Immutable. Those who realize the Self,
Are forever free from the jaws of death.
1.1.15

Hindus believe that death is the end of our ego consciousness, but our essence lives on in merger with the Brahman awareness. If we have not completed the tasks of Self maturation in this lifetime, however, we must reincarnate in lower life forms to retire our Karma till we become worthy of this merger with the Brahman — a state of Moksha, or freedom from the opposites. This is akin to Jung's rendering of the alchemic opus "solve et coagula."[44] For a Hindu, one must die many deaths before one graduates to eternity. In one life, it may reflect the process of working through the shadow, complexes, contrasexual archetypes, relativization of the superior and auxiliary functions, and reworking of our personal myth. David Rosen proposes the concept of "egocide" for the authentic Self to emerge.[45]

The Subjective Self — the Inner Witness and Experiencer- The Dweller in the Dreamless Sleep — Brihadaranyka Upanishad — The Forest of Wisdom

As a caterpillar, having come to the end of one blade of grass, draws itself together and reaches out for the next, so the Self, having come to the end of one life and dispelled all ignorance, gathers in his faculties and reaches out from the old body to a new.
4.4.3

Brihadaranyka means "of the great forest," and that is an apt name for this Upanishad, which is like walking through a great forest with paths leading off in unpredictable but somehow meaningful directions; we keep coming across gems of wisdom.

---

[44] Jung, 1970, p. xiv
[45] Rosen, 2002, pp. 61-84

The opening is a dialogue between a great sage, Yajnavalkya, and his wife, Maitreyi. Yajnavalkya has just reached a critical juncture in his life: He is about to leave home in the pursuit of truth, or Self-realization. Maitreyi shares his yearning for immortality, and so the parting dialogue between them turns into a deep session of "spiritual instruction" — one of the meanings of the word Upanishad.

This section amplifies the Self as a subjective entity experienced via projection onto the objective world. It is the inner experiencer and the cause of outer existence just as a drummer of the drum, the blower of the conch, the music as created not by the veena but by the musician who plays it, and all of creation as an objective projection of the subjective supreme (Self).

In the concluding reflections of chapter 2 of this Upanishad is the amplification of the inner witness, the cause, and the experiencer of the objective world.

> Just as a lump of salt thrown in water dissolves and cannot be taken out again, even so, beloved, the separate Self dissolves in the sea of pure consciousness, infinite and immortal. Separateness arises from identifying the Self with the body. 2.4.12.

> "Those who know the Imperishable (Self) attain immortality when the body is shed at death."

> The Imperishable is the seer, though unseen, the hearer, though unheard, the thinker, though unthought, the knower, though unknown. Nothing other than the Imperishable can see, hear, think, or know. It is in the Imperishable that space is woven, warp and woof. 3.1.10-12

> The human being has two states of consciousness: one in this world, the other in the next.

119

But there is third state between them, not unlike the world of dreams, in which we are aware of both worlds, with their sorrows and joys. When a person dies, it is only the physical body that dies; the Self lives on in nonphysical body, which carries the impressions of the past life. It is these impressions that determine the next life. 4.9

It is said of these states of consciousness that in the dreaming state, the Self who never dreams, watches by its own light the dreams woven out of past deeds and present desires. As an eagle weary after soaring in the sky, folds its wings and flies down to rest in its nest, so does the Self enter the state of dreamless sleep, where one is freed from all desires. 4.11-29

The Brihadaranyka Upanishad emphasizes the dreamless sleep: the NREM sleep as the abode of the Self. If one can wake up in a dreamless sleep, one is in the Self. The meditative practices strive to attain this state of consciousness to experience the Self. Neuroscience pioneers like Richard Davidson and Antoine Lutz have studied advanced meditators and established the neuropsychology of these dreamless, meditative states with a preponderance of Gamma waves.[46] Interestingly, the Gamma waves are also the frequency of the cosmic background radiation in physics echoing the process of creation of our Universe.[47]

Self as the Inner Experiencer — the imperishable — resides in the dreamless sleep — is Brahman. Chandogya Upanishad

Those who depart from this world without knowing who they are or what they truly desire have no freedom here or hereafter.

---

[46] A. Lutz et al., 2004
[47] Bedi, 2013, Appendix: Physics and the Psyche, pp. 213-215

But those who leave here knowing who they
are and what they truly desire have freedom
everywhere, both in this world and in the next.
8.1.6

Svetaketu went to a teacher and studied all the
Vedas for 12 years. Proud of his education,
he returned home where his father Uddalaka
asked him if his teacher taught him the
spiritual wisdom which enables you to hear
the unheard, think the unthought and know the
unknown. Now the father instructs the son into
the sacred knowledge. 4.1.2

As by knowing one lump of clay, we come to
know all things made out of clay, so through
the spiritual wisdom, we come to know that all
of life is one (manifestation of the Self). 4.1.4
In the beginning was only Being,
One without a second.
Out of himself he brought forth the cosmos.
And entered into everything in it.
There is nothing that does not come from him.
Of everything he is the inmost Self.
He is the truth; he is the Self supreme. 4.2.2-3

Chandogya amplifies that Self is the innermost essence of all beings
but made of the same Brahman essence.

In sleep, it that does not sleep is the Self. 4.8.1
Self is the honey sucked by the bees from
many flowers, it does not identify with one
flower or the other. 4.9.1

As many rivers merge into the ocean, so all
creatures lose their separateness when they
merge into the Self -Brahman. 4.10.1

Self is the root that nourishes the trunk, the
branches and the leaves. They may shed but
the roots live on as the innermost Self. 4.11.1

The infinite is above and below, before and behind, to the right and to the left. The Self is above and below, before is behind, to the right and the left. One who meditates upon the Self and realizes the Self everywhere and rejoices in the Self. Such a one lives in freedom and is at home wherever he goes, but those who pursue the finite are blind to the Self and live-in bondage. 4.25.1

One who meditates upon and realizes the Self discovers that everything in the cosmos-energy and space, fire and water, name and form, birth and death, mind and will, word and deed, mantra and meditation – all come from the (projection of) the Self. 4.26.1

The Self is one, though it appears to be many (projections). Control the senses and purify the mind (withdraw the projections). In a pure (subjective) mind there is constant awareness of the Self. Where is there is constant awareness of the Self, freedom ends bondage and joy ends sorrow. 4.26.2

The Many Projections of Self — Shvetashvatara Upanishad[48]

The Lord (Self) dwells in the womb of the cosmos, the creator who is in all creatures (projections).
He is that which is born and to be born (teleos);
His face is everywhere.
II.16

The Shvetashvatara Upanishad is a classic rendering of the unity of Self in its many projections that our ego experiences as the

[48] Eknath & Nagler, 1988, pp. 155-178

objective reality — a mere hologram of the projections of the aspects of the subjective Self. This theme is amplified in myriad ways and manifestations, establishing the unity of Self in its outer projections onto the objective reality and inner continuity with Brahman or ultimate awareness. This theme is also reflected in chapters 10 and 11 of the Bhagwad Gita.[49]

Here are some excerpts from the Shvetashvatara amplifying this theme of projections of the unity of the Self.

> What is the cause of the cosmos? 1.1
> Time, nature, necessity, accidents,
> Elements, energy, intelligence-
> None of these can be First Cause.
> They are effects, whose only purpose is
> To help the Self rise above pain and pleasure.
> 1. 2
>
> He is the inner Self of all,
> Hidden like a little flame in the heart.
> Only by the stilled mind he be known.
> Those who realize him become immortal. 3.13
>
> He (Self) resides in the city of nine gates (senses),
> Which is the body. 3.18
>
> He (Self) runs without feet and holds without hands.
> He sees without eyes and hears without ears.
> He knows everyone, but no one knows him.
> He is called the First, the Great, the Supreme.
> 3.19
>
> He (Self) has no beginning, he has no end.
> He is the source from whom the worlds

---

[49] Miller, 2004, pp. 89-109

(objective projections of the subjective Self)
evolve. 4.4

He (Self) is pure consciousness, omnipresent,
Omnipotent, omniscient, creator
Of time and master of the three Gunas (Tamas
– inertia, Rajas – activity and Sattva – balance
and lucidity).
Evolution (individuation) takes place at his
command. 4.2

The Lord (Self) is hidden in the hearts of all
(projections).
The eternal witness, pure consciousness,
He watches our work from within, beyond
The reach of the Gunas. 4.11

Contemporary neuroscience research by eminent neuro-scientist V.S. Ramachandran provides evidence for the concept of unity of the Self in its many projections. He proposes the concept of the "Gandhi Neurons."[50] He amplifies the discovery of Mirror neurons by Rizzolatti's group.[51] Ramachandran observed that individuals will mimic the behaviors of other circuits of the Mirror neurons. These include motor and sensory Mirror neurons, which set up the motor and sensory resonance between the individual and their observed behaviors. These Gandhi Neurons literally blur the boundary between Self and the others. Further brain imaging experiments by Christian Keysers have substantiated these observations.[52]

Ramachandran further elaborates that we do not reflexively act or feel based on these neurons because of the null neurons that help us distinguish between self-experience and observed experience via a sort of virtual reality. These null neurons signal, "Empathize by all means, but don't literally feel the other person's sensations." These

---

[50] Ramachandran, 2011, pp. 120-135
[51] Rizzolatti & Craighero, 2004
[52] Keysers, 2009

are frontal brain inhibitory circuits. However, during anesthesia, stroke, phantom limb, and echopraxia, patients' observations, where these null neurons are absent or temporarily paralyzed, this boundary between self and the other is suspended. It is theoretically possible to use the meditative states of consciousness to suspend these null neurons, whereupon one may establish unity between the Self and the observed world — the unity that Shvetashvatara Upanishad postulates. Dr. Ramachandran presented this formulation to His Holiness the Dalai Lama at a conference.[53] It may be interesting for neuroscientists to research the brain imaging studies of deep meditators to discern the specific location of null neurons activated during contemplative practices leading to states of Samadhi.

Through the lens of analytical psychology, we may postulate that the Self is initially experienced via projections onto the objective world, but when we become conscious of the subjective dimension of the objective world, it enhances our consciousness, relationships are decontaminated from the projective sludge, which then becomes the gold of the individuation opus. The most succinct description of this process is Michael Fordham's concept of the "de-integration of the Self," which must then be made conscious and reintegrated into the personality.[54]

The Ego and the Self — Two Modes of Knowing. Self the Source of Higher Knowledge — Mundaka Upanishad[55]

> As the web issues out of the spider and is
> withdrawn, as plants sprout from the earth,
> As hair grows from the body, even so, the sages
> say, this universe springs from the deathless
> Self, the source of life. 1.7

---

[53] Visit: http://www.uctv.tv/dalai-lama for more video where His Holiness the Dalai Lama engages with Larry Hinman of the University of San Diego, V.S. Ramachandran of UC San Diego, and Jennifer Thomas of San Diego State University in a scientific and philosophical discussion of human consciousness. [Show ID: 23653]
[54] Fordham, 1985, pp. 31-33
[55] Eknath & Nagler, 1988, pp. 181-196

The Mundaka Upanishad is the prequel to the Jungian concept of the ego and the Soul.

> Like two golden birds perched on the selfsame tree,
> Intimate friends, the ego and the Self
> Dwell in the same body. The former eats
> The sweet and sour fruits of the tree of life.
> While the latter looks on with detachment. 3.1
>
> As long as we think we are the ego,
> We feel attached and fall into sorrow.
> But realize that you are the Self, the Lord.
> Of life, and you will be freed from sorrow.3.2
>
> When you realize that you are the Self,
> Supreme source of light, supreme source of love,
> You transcend the duality of life,
> And enter into the unitive state. 3.3

Here are the two modes of knowing: via the ego and the Self.

> What is that by knowing which all is known?
> The illuminated sage replied.
> The knowledge is twofold, higher and lower.
> 1.3
>
> The study of Vedas, linguistics,
> Rituals, astronomy, and all the arts,
> Can be called the lower knowledge (of the Ego).
> The Higher knowledge
> Is that which leads to Self-realization. 1.5

The Mundaka Upanishad offers a transcendent rendering of the Self and a path to the transcendence.

The shining Self dwells in the heart,
Everything in the cosmos, great and small,
Lives in the Self. It is the source of life,
It is the goal of life. Attain this goal. 2.2

Take the great bow of the sacred scriptures,
Place on it the arrow of devotion.
Then draw the bowstring of meditation.
And aim at the target, the Lore of Love (Self
as Eros). 2.3

The mantra is the bow, the aspirant.
Is the arrow, and the Lord (Self) the target.
Now draw the bowstring of meditation,
And hitting the target be one with it (Ego/Self
axis). 2.4

The Self Dwells in the Fourth State of Consciousness — The Mandukya Upanishad[56]

This Upanishad is the precursor to the contemporary neuroscience research into states of consciousness.[57] Here are some excerpts from the Mandukya Upanishad amplifying these four states of consciousness and the dwelling of the Self in the fourth state. One may connect with this fourth state symbolically by reciting the sacred syllable OM.

The Self has four states of consciousness. 1.2

The first is called Vasihvarana (awake), in which,
One lives with all the senses turned outward,
Aware only of the external world. 1.3

---

[56] Ibid., pp.199-205
[57] Thompson, 2015

Taijasa (dream state) is the name of the second,
The dreaming state in which, with the senses,
Turned inward, one enacts the Impressions,
Of the past deeds and the present desires (wish
fulfillment). 1.4

The third state is called Prajna, the deep sleep,
In which one neither dreams nor desires.
There is no mind in Prajna, there is no
separateness; but the sleeper is not conscious
of this. Let him become conscious in Prajna
and it will open the door to the state of abiding
joy. 1.5

Prajna, all-powerful and all knowing, dwells
in the hearts of all as the ruler (Self). Prajna is
the source and end of all.1.5-6.

The fourth is the superconscious state called
Turiya, neither inward nor outward, beyond
the senses and the intellect, in which there is
none other than the Lord (Self and Brahman
-Collective). It is the supreme goal of life. It is
infinite peace and love. Realize it. 1.7

Turiya is represented by AUM. Though
indivisible, it has three sounds. 1.8
A stands for Vasihvarana (wakefulness). 1.9
U indicates Taijasa. Those who know this
by mastering even their dreams, become
established in wisdom. 1.10
M corresponds to Prajna. Those who know this
by stilling their mind, find their true stature
and inspire everyone to grow. 1.11

The mantra AUM stands for supreme state of
Turiya, without parts, beyond birth and death,
symbol of everlasting joy. Those who know
AUM as the Self become the Self. 1.12

Self — the Source of Consciousness — Kena Upanishad[58]

Who Moves the World?

> The light of Brahman flashes in lightning;
> The light of Brahman flashes in our eyes. It
> is the power of Brahman that makes the mind
> to think, desire, and will. Therefore, use this
> power to meditate on Brahman. 4.4-6

Kena Upanishad constellates Self as the inner mover, the primal source of consciousness. It is the inner mover, the inner witness, and the inner consciousness that underlies the ripples of cognitive processes that we equate as consciousness. The center of this inner consciousness is the Self. Jung referenced the Kena Upanishad to amplify the innermost center of the consciousness in explaining the workings of the psyche of the "Seeress of Prevorst."[59] Here is the dialogue between a student and his teacher in the Upadishad.

> Student:
> Who makes the mind think? Who fills my
> body with vitality? Who causes my tongue
> to speak? What is that Invisible one who sees
> through my eyes and hears through my ears?
> 1.1
>
> Teacher:
> The Self is the ear of the ear, the eye of the
> eye, the mind of the mind, the word of words,
> and the life of life. Rising above the senses
> and the mind, the wise realize the deathless
> (transcendent) Self. 1.2
>
> The ignorant think the Self can be known
> by the intellect, but the illumined know it is

---

[58] Eknath & Nagler, 1988, pp. 209-218
[59] Jung, Falzeder, & Hoerni, 2019, pp. 83-84

beyond duality of the knower and the known. 2.3

The Self is realized in the higher state of consciousness when you have broken through the wrong identification that you are the body, subject to birth and death (of ego and the complexes). To be the Self is to go beyond death (of identification with the body and the ego complex). 2.4

Self as Prana — The Breath of Life — Prashna Upanishad[60]

Prana is the breath — pneuma-spirit-numinous. Prashna Upanishad is the foundation of the science of Pranayama or breath meditation, a central feature of all the contemplative practices of Vedic tradition.[61] It has now been studied extensively from a neuroscience lens as the key feature of the relaxation response.[62] Here are some excerpts from the Prashna Upanishad amplifying the phenomenology of Pranayama.

Prana burns as fire; he shines as the sun; He rains as the cloud; he blows as the wind; He crashes as the thunder in the sky. He is the earth; he has form and no form; Prana is immortality. 2.5

This is Prashna, or inquiry by six seekers to the sage Pippalada, about the nature of the reality. We will amplify the third inquiry wherein Prana, or breath and energy infused by breath, is the Self and its manifestations. Here are some excerpts to illustrate this thesis.

---

[60] Eknath & Nagler, 1988, pp. 221-237
[61] Iyengar, Evans, & Arava, 2005
[62] Benson, 1975

130

The second inquiry explores the source of this power of breath.

> The student Bhargava approached the sage
> and asked, "Master, what powers support the
> body? Which of them are manifested in it?
> And among them all, which is the greatest?"
> 2.1

> The sage replied: "The powers are space, air,
> fire, water, earth, speech, mind, vision and
> hearing. All these boasted, 'We support the
> body.' 2.2
> But prana, vital energy, supreme over them
> all, said,' Don't deceive yourselves. It is I,
> dividing myself fourfold, who hold this body
> together." 2.3

> But they would not believe these words of
> Prana. To demonstrate the truth, prana arose
> and left the body, and all the powers knew they
> had to leave as well. When Prana returned to
> the body, they too were back. 2. 4

> Prana burns as fire, it shines as the sun; it rains
> as the cloud, it blows as the wind; It crashes
> as the thunder in the sky. It is the earth; it has
> form and no form; Prana is immortality. 2.5

Now the third inquiry highlights the manifestation of Prana as the
five breaths of human energy metabolism. Let us explore!

> Then student Kausalya approached the sage
> and asked: "Master, from what source does
> this prana come? How does it enter the body,
> how live after dividing into five, how leave the
> body at the time of death? How does it support
> all that is without and all that is within?" 3.1

The sage replied. "Prana is born of the Self.
As a man casts a shadow, The Self casts Prana
into the body at the time of birth." 3.3

As a king appoints officers to do his work
in all the villages, so prana works with four
other pranas, each a part of Self, to carry out
different functions in the body. 3.4

The main prana dwells in eye, ear, mouth
and nose; Apana, the downward force, in
the organs of sex and excretion. Samana, the
equalizing force in the middle, digest food and
kindles the seven fires. 2.5

Vyana, distributor of energy, moves through
myriad vital currents, radiation from the heart,
where lives the Self. 3.6
At the time of death, through the subtle track,
Udana, the fifth forced, leads the selfless up
the long ladder of evolution, and the selfish
down. 3.7

Self — Encased in Five Sheaths of Consciousness and the Source of Ananda — Joy and Bliss — Taittiriya Upanishad — Ascent to Joy[63]

The Self is the source of abiding joy.
Our hearts are filled with joy in seeing him
Enshrined in the depths of our consciousness.
If he were not there, who would breathe, who
live?
He it is who fills every heart with joy. 2.7.1

Taittiriya Upanishad offers the anatomy of the Self as
embedded in five sheaths of consciousness. When we stabilize these

---

[63] Eknath & Nagler, 1988, pp.241-261

five layers of consciousness, we are in the Self and experience Ananda
— joy and bliss that radiates from the Brahman, via the Self into our
experience. This is to be differentiated from pleasure, which is an
experience of our senses. These five sheaths of consciousness may be
stabilized using meditation and mindfulness practices.[64]

Here is an exploration of these five sheaths of consciousness.
(Figure 8)

The physical sheath is made up of food, within it is contained
the vital sheath. 2.2.1 This is akin to the physical or gross body —
the Annadmayakosha.

> Men and women, beast and bird live by breath.
> Breath is therefore called the true sign of life.
> It is the vital force in everyone that determines
> how long we are to live. 2.3.1

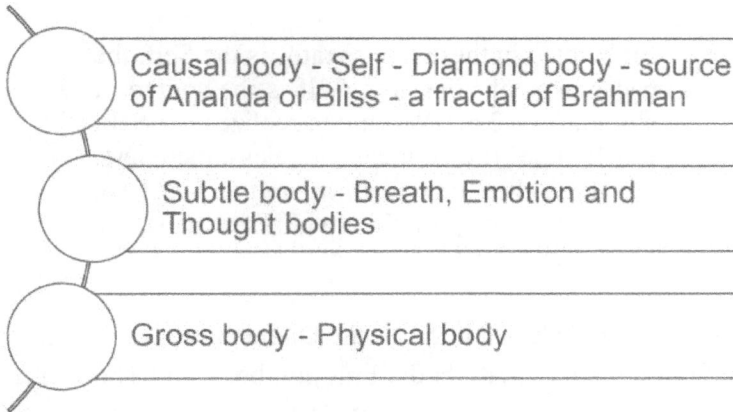

Causal body - Self - Diamond body - source
of Ananda or Bliss - a fractal of Brahman

Subtle body - Breath, Emotion and
Thought bodies

Gross body - Physical body

Figure 8

This is our breath body or energy body. In Sanskrit, it is called the
Pranamayakosha, or the breath body. It is regulated by the autonomic
nervous system.

---

[64] Bedi, 2013. The meditation and mindfulness practices are explored in detail including
practical exercise, pp. 122-141

The vital sheath is made of living breath. Within it is contained the mental sheath. 2.3.1 This is the emotional body. It is regulated by the limbic nervous system — the center for memory, emotions, and the archetypal memory of our ancestors. This would be the site of the 2-million-years-old Self.[65]

Within the mental sheath, made up of waves of thought, there is contained the sheath of wisdom. 2.4.1 Wisdom means a life of selfless service. The wisdom sheath is made of detachment. 2.5.1

This is the thinking body — in Sanskrit, the Vignanmayako-sha. The center for this thinking body is the neocortex.

Within the thinking body is contained the sheath of bliss. This is the Annadmayakosha — the Bliss body generated by the integration of our three brains: the reptilian autonomic nervous system, the limbic brain, and the neocortex. This concept of our three brains — the Triune brain has been well established in the neuroscience research.[66]

> Embedded in these five sheaths is the Self, the pacemaker of bliss. The Self is the source of abiding joy. 2.6.1 When one realizes the Self, in whom all life is one, changeless, nameless, formless, then one fears no more. Until we realize the unity of life (with Brahman), we live in fear. 2.7.1

This is the Causal body, or the Diamond body. It is the cause of the Subtle body (Breath body, Emotion body and Thought body) and the Gross body (Physical body). The Diamond body or the Self is a manifestation of the Brahman. Brahman existed as unmanifest.

Brahman brought the Lord (Self) out of himself; therefore, he is called the Self-existent. 2.7.1

---

[65] Stevens, 2005
[66] MacLean, 1990

Self as the Creation Myth of Consciousness — Aitareya Upanishad — The Unity of Life[67]

> The Self is in all. Earth, air, fire, water, and
> space; all creatures, Great or small, born of
> eggs, of wombs, of heat, of shoots, horses,
> cows, elephants, men, and women; and all that
> neither walk nor fly. 3.1. 2-3

Aitareya Upanishad is the creation myth of the Self. Since the Self is a manifestation of Brahman and is projected onto the objective world, at core, there is unity of all life and reality. This is embodied in one of the four Mahavakyas — great truths of the Upanishads: Prajna (Self) is Brahman. 3.1.3 Let us now explore the creation myth of the Self.

> Before the world was created, the Self alone
> existed; nothing whatever stirred. Then the Self
> thought: "Let me create the world." 1.1.1
>
> He brought forth all the worlds out of himself.
> Marichi – the sky, Mara – the middle region that
> is earth and Apa – the realm below of water.
> Ambhas – ether, high above the sky, 1.1.2
>
> The Self thought: "I have created these worlds.
> Let me now create guardians for these worlds."
> From the waters, he drew forth Purusha and
> gave him a form. 1.1. 3
> As the Self brooded over the form, a mouth
> opened, as does an egg, giving forth the speech
> and fire; nostrils opened with power of breathing
> the air; Eyes opened, giving rise to sight and
> sun; And ears opened to hear the sound in space.
> Skin appeared and from it hair; from hair came
> plants and trees. The heart gushed forth; from
> the heart came the mind, and from the mind

---

[67] Eknath & Nagler, 1988, pp. 265-275

came the moon. The navel appeared with the downward force, Apana, which gave rise death. The sex organs rose with the living water which gave rise to birth. 1.1.4

The Self thought, "How can this be without me? If speaking is done by speech, breathing by the breath, seeing by the eyes, hearing by the ears, smelling by the nose, and meditation by the mind, then who am?"1.1.11

Then entering the body through the gateway at the crown of the head, he passed into the three states of consciousness in which the Self resides. 1.1.12 (Awake, Dream state and Deep dreamless sleep)

Filled with wonder, we sing: "I see the Lord." 1.1.13 So his name is Idamdra (Self), "He who sees." 1.1.15.

Who is the Self on whom we meditate? It is the Self by which we see, hear, smell, and taste. 3.1.1.
Through which we speak in words? Is Self the mind by which we perceive, direct, understand, know, remember, think, will, desire and love? These are but servants of the Self, who is pure consciousness. This Self is in all. He is all the gods, the five elements, 3.1.2.

Earth, air, fire, water, and space; all creatures, great or small, born of eggs, wombs, of heat, of shoots, horses, cows, elephants, men and women; all being that walk, all beings that fly, all that neither walk nor fly. Prajna (Self) is pure consciousness, guiding all. The world rests on Prajna, and Prajna is Brahman. 3.1. 3.

And those who realize the Brahman live in joy and go beyond death. 3.1.4.

The following image summarizes the profiles in Self from an Upanishad perspective. (Figure 9)

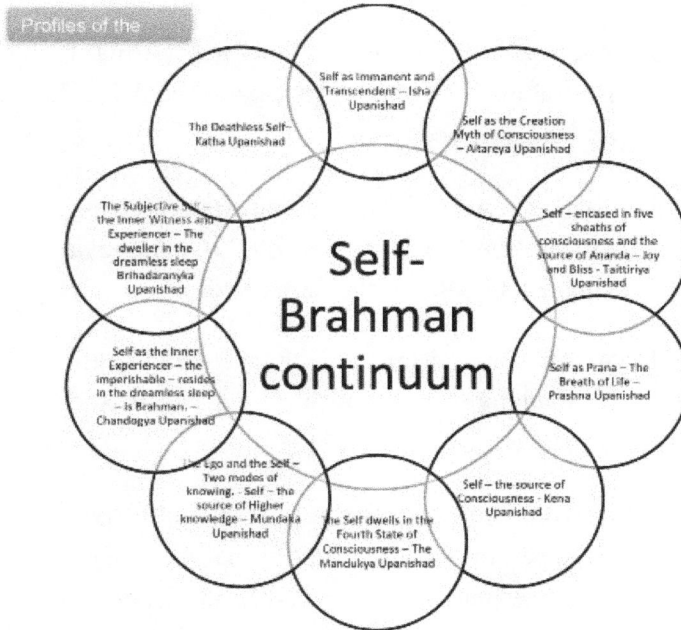

Figure 9

Self and Brahman — The Four Mahavakyas

The Upanishads assert the continuity of Self, or Atman, with the Collective consciousness, or Brahman. This theme is encapsulated in the four great sayings or Mahavakyas of the Upanishads. These four were commented upon by Adi Shankara.[68]

There are four principal statements in the Upanishadic part of the four Vedas. Shankara considers it necessary to understand the real meaning of at least one of them for enlightenment. These statements or Mahavakyas are:

---

[68] Chaturvedi, 2017, pp. 44-48

1. Prajñānam Brahma "Insight is Brahman," or "Brahman is insight." (Aitareya Upanishad 3.3 of the Rig Veda)[69]

2. Ayam Ātmā Brahma — "This Self (Atman) is Brahman." (Mandukya Upanishad 1.2 of the Atharva Veda)[70]

3. Tat Tvam Asi — "That essence (tat, referring to sat) 'the Existent' are you." (Chandogya Upanishad 6.8.7 of the Sama Veda)[71]

4. Aham Brahmāsmi — "I am Brahman." (Brihadaranyka Upanishad 1.4.10 of the Yajur Veda)[72]

The interrelatedness of the Self to the collective consciousness is one of the central tenets of Jung's analytical psychology and corresponds to the Atman-Brahman axis in the Upanishads. Let us explore some of Jung's thoughts in this context.

From the outset of his working career, Jung was investigating the unconscious dynamics in personal complexes and addressing the relationships of psyche to soma and between different individuals, when psychic facts and physiological facts are combined. Already, he was demonstrating a monistic view of body and mind, and a profound connection between certain people in results consistent with his later understanding of the psychoid.[73]

The following quote foreshadows Jung's later account, in which he attributes a role to psychoid processes in meaning-making

---

[69] S.-E. Radhakrishnan, 2019, pp. 523-524
[70] Ibid., p. 695
[71] Ibid., p. 458
[72] Ibid., p.168
[73] Addison, 2017, p. 4

through the embodied elaboration of unconscious imagery, the practice that he himself developed in *The Red Book*:

> Just as the effects of archetypal processes manifest in embodied images within the psyche-soma continuum, so also may embodied experience feed back into the archetypal organizing process. The result enriches and vitalizes the personality, bringing to conscious realization the personalized effects of the archetype, and setting in train the coming-to-be or purposive unfolding of the Self, which Jung called individuation.[74]

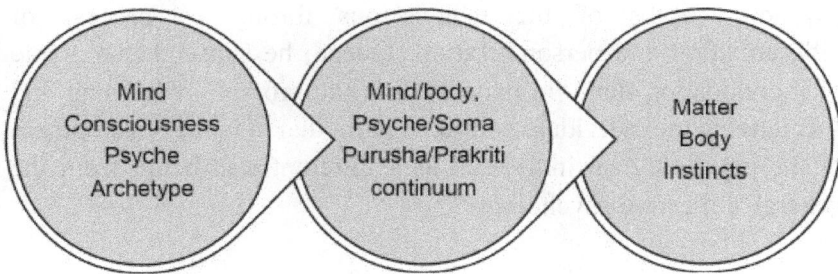

Figure 12

In the *Seven Sermons to the Dead*, Jung elaborates the themes above from his Mysterium encounter in terms of Pleroma[75] and Creatura. The Pleroma is described as nothingness or fullness, both differentiation and undifferentiation, whose qualities are undifferentiated pairs of opposites, such as living and dead, light, and dark, time and space, good and evil.

---

[74] Ibid., pp. 6-7

[75] Pleroma in Gnosticism is the spiritual universe as the abode of God and of the totality of the divine powers and emanations; in Christian theology, it is the totality or fullness of the Godhead which dwells in Christ.

Jung has borrowed a well-known Gnostic term, which he later designates the Unus mundus, or unknowable psychoid substratum of the collective unconscious[76]. Man's nature is distinctiveness, and the danger for man is to fall into the Pleroma, or undifferentiated state, and become submerged in nothingness. His fight to achieve differentiation leads to the "Principium individuationis." Ribi[77] considers that Creatura should be regarded as the universal principle of individuation, which emerges from the Self and is the cause of individual consciousness, stating that something can only become conscious when it is separated out of the Pleroma. He notes that the Gnostics see the Pleroma as the origin of the individual.[78] In the *Seven Sermons*, therefore, Jung is describing the emergence of the individual human being out of the unknowable and undifferentiated psychoid depths of the unconscious through a process of differentiation and personalization. Indeed, he subsequently wrote of individuation that, "in general, it is the process of forming and specializing the individual nature; in particular, it is the development of the psychological individual as a differentiated being from the general, collective psychology."[79]

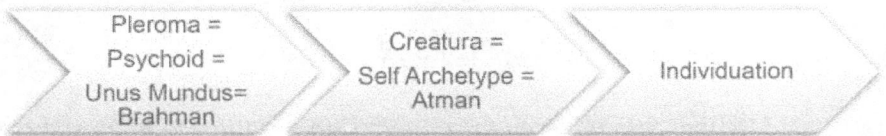

Pleroma = Psychoid = Unus Mundus = Brahman → Creatura = Self Archetype = Atman → Individuation

Figure 9

The concepts of Pleroma and Creatura correspond to the structure of Brahman and Atman in the Hindu metapsychology. The

---

[76] Cambray, 2009, p.xii. In the series forward, editor David Rosen terms this as a Psychoid archetype. This would be in juxtaposition to the Self archetype; the Pleroma and the Creatura respectively. The concept of the Psychoid archetype was evolved by Pauli/Jung collaboration.

[77] Ribi, 2013, pp. 196-197

[78] Ibid., p.180

[79] Addison, 2017, pp. 7-8

goal of transcendence, as outlined in Patanjali's Yoga Sutra, is the conscious religation of the Atman/Self with the Brahman awareness via the process of Yoga culminating in Samadhi.[80]

The Self-Collective and Atman-Brahman continuity is further amplified by the synchronicity phenomenon. Let us explore this further. Synchronicity is the phenomenon of falling together in time, a kind of simultaneity. Jung chose to term synchronicity as a hypothetical factor equal in rank to the causal principle. It relativizes space and time.

> The possibility exists that the psyche observes not the external bodies but itself. In Rhine experiments, the subject's answer is not the result of physically observing the cards but is product of pure imagination of "chance" ideas which reveal the structure of that which produces them, i.e., the unconscious. It is the decisive factors in the unconscious psyche, the archetypes which constitute the structure of the collective unconscious. It is identical in all individuals. It is irrepresentable – and Jung calls it the "psychoid."[81]

In summary — from Self to the Collective

The primary focus in Jung's analytical psychology has been the Ego/Self axis. The central thrust of the Hindu tradition as embodied in the Upanishads is the Self/Spirit axis. This Spirit-Brahman drive is the teleological vector of the Self. This Self/Spirit axis is navigated by the Patanjali's Yoga Sutra as a GPS. The alchemical process of gradual alignment and union between the Self and the Brahman is phenomenologically manifest in the Upanishads along several dimensions as outlined in this brief overview. The path between the Self and the Brahman is traversed by the contemplative traditions of the East. It has now become a subject of study in the emerging field of

---

[80] Bryant, Patañjali, & Patañjali, 2018; Satchidananda, 1978
[81] CW 8, § 840-841

Contemplative Neuroscience[82] and the study of contemplative states, as in Lutz's research[83] of experienced meditators demonstrating high-intensity and -frequency gamma waves, perhaps a most promising indicator of the Self/Spirit axis.[84] The emerging field of Contemplative Neuroscience[85] has been inspired by His Holiness the Dalai Lama.[86]

The teleology of the Hindu path is for an individual who is well differentiated from the collective to reclaim a conscious continuity with the collective Brahman consciousness without losing their own ground of individuation. For Hindus, the goal of individuation is their spiritual purpose, or Dharma. The concept of Dharma aligns each one of us with our unique role in the matrix of the Brahman. The path back to our origins, the Uroboric process of return to the source, is the essence of the Hindu path. The purpose of our journey back to the source is to optimize our Dharma in the overall unfolding of the Brahman. In this, we contribute to the ongoing manifestation of Brahman in our sector of the multiverse. This conscious return to the source — transcendence, is accomplished via the algorithms outlined in the Upanishads and the Patanjali's Yoga Sutras. Such a state is called Samadhi, where we are both uniquely individual and yet in a seamless continuum with the collective or Brahman consciousness. We thus crystallize our place in the Indra's net[87] of Brahman consciousness.

---

[82] Thompson, 2015, p. 70

[83] A. Lutz et al., 2004. Practitioners understand "meditation," or mental training, to be a process of familiarization with one's own mental life leading to long-lasting changes in cognition and emotion. Here we find that long-term Buddhist practitioners self-induce sustained electroencephalographic high-amplitude gamma-band oscillations and phase-synchrony during meditation.

[84] Verela, 2001: An exploration of the concept of Brainweb: Phase Synchronization and Large Scale Integration of the Gamma Activity of the Brain during contemplative practices. (Juergen, 2010), explores Alpha and Gamma EEG Brain Activity as a measure of contemplative depth. (Real Cahn, 2010), explores Gamma activation during Vipassana Meditation

[85] A. Lutz, et al, 2007: an exploration of Meditation and Neuroscience of Consciousness.

[86] Dalai, 2006

[87] "Indra's net" is an infinitely large net of cords owned by the Vedic deva Indra, which hangs over his palace on Mount Meru, the axis mundi of Buddhist and Hindu cosmology. In this metaphor, Indra's net has a multifaceted jewel at each vertex, and each jewel is reflected in all of the other jewels: Cook, 1977, para. 8.8.6-8.8.8

Other eminent neuroscientists are on this quest. This chapter is not the place to discuss the exciting frontiers of Contemplative Neuroscience, Quantum Physics and Genomics and their correlation with the Self/Brahman axis and Jung's Collective Unconscious and its scientific validation. For instance, the meditation and mindfulness practices have a measurable impact on neural, epigenetic structures, and Telomeres.[88] It is my intuition that Jung would have pursued this exciting frontier of the Contemplative Neuroscience based on his beginnings in experimental psychology with the word association test and culmination of his work with Wolfgang Pauli.[89]

Just as dreams, imagination, synchronicities, complexes, medical and psychiatric symptoms, relationships, creative products, and active imagination give us a glimpse of the Self, similarly, in the foreseeable future, it may be feasible to study the Self states via the lens of neuroscience with techniques like EEG, neuroimaging studies, and psychedelic-assisted psychotherapies.[90] I hope to explore this further in future explorations of the matter, but this is a frontier that neo-Jungians may consider a subject of inquiry. It will be a fruitful area of research for scholars, seekers, and sufferers alike. This brief overview of the Hindu view of Transcendent Individuation is not meant as a summary of the immense metapsychology of the East but as a glimpse into this kaleidoscopic matrix at this point in time with the limited knowledge we have to understand this rendering of eternity from my slit of discernment.

---

[88] Carlson et al., 2015; Hoge et al., 2013; Lengacher et al., 2014; Mendioroz et al., 2020; Schutte & Malouff, 2014; Schutte, Malouff, & Keng, 2020. A telomere is the end of a chromosome. Telomeres are made of repetitive sequences of non-coding DNA that protect the chromosome from damage. Each time a cell divides, the telomeres become shorter. Eventually, the telomeres become so short that the cell can no longer divide. https://www.genome.gov/genetics-glossary/Telomere (Last accessed – 2/20/22)
[89] Shamdasani, 2003
[90] These studies explore the emerging frontier of the psychedelic assisted psychotherapies and mystical states of consciousness: Schatzberg, 2020; Holoyda, 2020, Carhart-Harris & Nutt, 2014; Griffiths, 2006

References

Addison, A. (2017). Jung's psychoid concept: An hermeneutic understanding. *International Journal of Jungian Studies*, *9* (1), 1-16

Bedi, A. (2013). *Crossing the healing zone: from illness to wellness*. Lake Worth, FL: Ibis Press

Benson, H. (1975). *The Relaxation Response*. New York, NY: William Morrow and Company, Inc.

Bryant, E. F. (2018). *The Yoga Sūtras of Patañjali: a New Edition, Translation, and Commentary: with Insights from the Traditional Commentators.* New Delhi: Macmillan

Cambray, J. (2009). *Synchronicity - Nature and Psyche in an Interconnected Universe*. College Station: Texas A&M University Press

Carhart-Harris, R., & Nutt, D. (2014). Was it a vision or a waking dream? *Front Psychol, 5*, 255

Carlson, L. E., Beattie, T. L., Giese-Davis, J., Faris, P., Tamagawa, R., Fick, L. J., Degelman, E.S., Speca, M. (2015). Mindfulness-based cancer recovery and supportive-expressive therapy maintain telomere length relative to controls in distressed breast cancer survivors. *Cancer, 121*(3), 476-484

Chaturvedi, S. (2017). *Seven Works of Shankaracharya - With Original Sanskrit text and Consice Commentary*. India: Vedic Scriptures Publishing

Cook, F. H. (1977). *Hua-Yen Buddhism: The Jewel Net of Indra*. New York: Penn State Press

Dalai Lama (2006). *The Universe in a Single Atom: How Science and Spirituality Can Serve Our World*. London: Abacus

Eknath, E., & Nagler, M. N. (1988). *The Upanishads*. London: Arkana

Fordham, M. (1985). *Exploration into the Self.* London: Karnac Books

Griffiths, R. R., Richards, W. A., McCain, U., and Jesse, R. (2006). Psilocybin can occasion mystical-type experiences having substantial and sustained personal meaning and spiritual significance. *Psychopharmacology, 187*(3), 268-283

Hoge, E. A., Chen, M. M., Orr, E., Metcalf, C. A., Fischer, L. E., Pollack, M. H., De Vivo, I., Simon, N. M. (2013). Loving-Kindness Meditation practice associated with longer telomeres in women. *Brain, behavior, and immunity, 32*, 159-163

Holoyda, B., (2020). "Psychedelic psychiatry: Preparing for novel treatments involving altered states of consciousness. *Psychiatric Services, 71*(12), 1297-1299

Iyengar, B. K. S., Evans, J. J., & Abrams, D. (2005). *Light on Life: the Journey to Wholeness, Inner Peace and Ultimate Freedom.* London: Rodale

Juergen, P., et al. (2010). From Alpha to Gamma: Electrophysiological Correlates of Meditation Related States of Consciousness. *Medical hypotheses, 75*

Jung, C.G., Falzeder, E., & Hoerni, U. (2019). *History of Modern Psychology: Lectures Delivered at the ETH Zurich.* Princeton, NJ: Princeton University Press

Jung, C.G., & Jaffé, A. (1963). *Memories, Dreams, Reflections.* London: Collins and Routledge & Kegan Paul

Jung, C.G., & Shamdasani, S. (2009). *The Red Book = Liber Novus* (1st ed.). New York: W.W. Norton & Co.

Keysers, C., Gazzola, V. (2009). Expanding the mirror: Vicarious activity for Actions, Emotions, and Sensations. *Current opinion in neurobiology* (19), 666-671

Knipe, D. M. (1991). *Hinduism: Experiments in the Sacred.* San Francisco, CA: HarperSanFrancisco

Lengacher, C. A., Reich, R. R., Kip, K. E., Barta, M., Ramesar, S., Paterson, C.L., et al. (2014). Influence of mindfulness-based stress reduction (MBSR) on telomerase activity in women with breast cancer (BC). *Biological Research for Nursing, 16*(4), 438-447

Lutz, A., Dunne, J.D., Davidson, R.J., et al. (2007). Meditation and neuroscience of consciousness: An introduction. In P.D. Zelazo, M. Moscovitch, & E. Thomson (Eds), *The Cambridge Handbook of Consciousness* (pp. 499-553). Cambridge, UK: Cambridge University Press

Lutz, A., Greischar, L. L., Rawlings, N. B., Ricard, M., Davidson, R. J. (2004). Long-term meditators self-induce high-amplitude gamma synchrony during mental practice. *Proceedings of the National Academy of Sciences of the United States of America, 101*(46), 16369-16373

MacLean, P. D. (1990). *The Triune Brain in Evolution: Role in Paleocerebral Functions.* New York: Springer

Mendioroz, M., Puebla-Guedea, M., Montero-Marín, J., Urdánoz-Casado, A., Blanco-Luquin, I., Roldán, M., Labarga, A. & Garcia-Campayo, J. (2020). Telomere length correlates with subtelomeric DNA methylation in long-term mindfulness practitioners. *Scientific Reports, 10*(1), 4564

Miller, B. S. (2004). *The Bhagavad-gita: Krishna's Counsel in Time of War.* New York: Bantam Books

Müller, M. (1879). The Upanishads, Part 1 (SBE01),. Retrieved from https://www.sacred-texts.com/hin/upan/index.htm

Radhakrishnan, S. (2019). *The Principal Upanishads* India: Indus / HarperCollins India

Radhakrishnan, S., & Moore, C. A. (1957). *A Source Book in Indian Philosophy.* Princeton, NJ: Princeton University Press

Rael Cahan, B,. Delorme, A., Polich, J. (2010). Occipital gamma activation during Vipassana meditation. *Cognitive Processing 11*, 39-56

Ramachandran, V. S. (2011). *The Tell-tale Brain : a Neuroscientist's Quest for What Makes Us Human* (1st ed.). New York: W.W. Norton

Ribi, A. (2013). *The Search for Roots: C. G. Jung and the Tradition of Gnosis.* Los Angeles, CA: Gnosis Archive Books

Rizzolatti, G., & Craighero, L. (2004). The mirror-neuron system. *Annual Review of Neuroscience, 27*, 169-192

Rosen, D. (2002). *Transforming Depression: Healing the Soul Through Creativity.* USA: Nicolas-Hays

Satchidanada, S. S. (1978). *The Yoga Sutra of Patanjali.* Buckingham, VA: Integral Yoga Publications

Schatzbert, A. (2020). Some comments on psychedelic research. *American Journal of Psychiatry, 177*(5), 368-369

Schutte, N. S., & Malouff, J. M. (2014). A meta-analytic review of the effects of mindfulness meditation on telomerase activity. *Psychoneuroendocrinology, 42*, 45-48

Schutte, N. S., Malouff, J. M., & Keng, S.-L. (2020). Meditation and telomere length: a meta-analysis. *Psychology & Health, 35*(8), 901-915

Shamdasani, S. (2003). *Jung and the Making of Modern Psychology: the Dream of a Science.* Cambridge, MA: Cambridge University Press

Stevens, A. (2005). *The Two-Million-Year-Old Self, (Carolyn and Ernest Fay Series in Analytical Psychology).* College Station: Texas A&M University Press

Thompson, E. (2015). *Waking, Dreaming, Being: Self and Consciousness in Neuroscience, Meditation, and Philosophy.* New York: Columbia University Press

Varela, F., Lachaux, J-P., Rodriguez, E., & Martinerie, J. (2001). The brainweb: Phase synchronization and large-scale integration. *Nature Reviews Neuroscience, 2*, 229-239

5

Jung's Self and the Ātman of the Upaniṣads

Lionel Corbett

This paper discusses the relationship between Jung's notion of the Self, the Ātman/Brahman of the Upaniṣads, and the Puruṣa of Saṅkhyā philosophy and the Yoga system of Patañjali. According to Jung, the Ātman forms "an exact parallel to the psychological idea of the self."[1] The paper discusses some ways in which this is a valid comparison and some ways in which it is not. The author suggests that the numinous manifestations of the Self actually correspond to a determinate level of the divine that manifests qualities, known as Saguṇa Brahman or Iśhvara. Accordingly, Jung's notion of the Self can act as a useful bridge between depth psychology and the Upaniṣadic traditions.

This paper discusses the relationship between Jung's notion of the Self, the Ātman/Brahman of the Upaniṣads, the Puruṣa of Saṅkhyā philosophy, and the Yoga system of Patañjali.[2] Jung wrote

---

[1] CW16, § 474

[2] For the sake of space, I have to ignore the major differences between various schools of Indian thought. For example, the Saṅkhyā school, which denies the existence of a creator God, says that insentient, inert Prakṛiti is the cause of material reality; it manifests itself as the objects of experience when it contacts Puruṣa, which is the sentient principle of awareness. There are an infinite number of Puruṣas. Saṅkhyā maintains a dualism between Puruṣa and Prakṛiti. In contrast, Vedanta teaches that the Atman-Brahman alone is the cause and creator of the world; it is all-pervading and the only reality; the

147

that: "What is meant by the self[3] is not only in me but in all beings, like the Ātman, like Tao."[4] According to Jung, the Self is comparable to "Puruṣa, Ātman,"[5] and the Ātman forms "an exact parallel to the psychological idea of the self."[6] On what grounds can Jung's assertion be justified?

Various authors deny any similarity between Jung's Self and the Upaniṣadic Ātman.[7] Whitney points out that Jung's Self is not entirely conscious of itself and is not self-illuminating, since it requires a human consciousness to become conscious of its dark side.[8] Furthermore, as Corbett and Whitney point out, Jung refused to relinquish the importance of the ego, so he does not develop the kind of fully nondual model found in the Upaniṣadic tradition and Advaita Vedānta.[9] However, although in some of the Upaniṣads, Brahman is seen as impersonal, indeterminate, transcendent, formless, and Absolute, devoid of qualities (Nirguṇa Brahman), the Upaniṣads also admit the existence of a determinate level of the divine that has qualities known as Saguṇa Brahman or Iśhvara. I suggest that it is this level to which Jung's Self corresponds, and accordingly, Jung's notion of the Self can act as a useful bridge between depth psychology and the Upaniṣadic traditions. I will first describe the

---

universe is the expression of Consciousness. Patañjali's Yoga school also refutes the notion of multiple Puruṣas, acknowledging only one divine Self, and recommends that the mind's activity should be suppressed or controlled in order to experience the Atman. Advaita Vedanta suggests that suppression of mental activity is not necessary, because by means of spiritual practice the mind can be transformed into its true nature, which is pure Consciousness. Yoga philosophy sees the mind as a very subtle form of matter, unlike the gross matter of the body, quite distinct from Puruṣa or spirit.

[3] In the English editions of Jung's *Collected Works*, the word "self" is written with a lowercase letter "s," to avoid the implication that Jung was writing about religion. To distinguish it from the personal self, I follow the common usage of writing the word with an uppercase "S" when it refers to the *imago dei*.

[4] CW 10, § 873

[5] CW 9i, § 248

[6] CW 16, § 474

[7] Whitfield, 2009; Whitney, 2017; Sachdeva 1978

[8] Here she is referring to Jung's idea in his *Answer to Job* that the Self was unconscious of its own dark side in his treatment of the biblical Job.

[9] Corbet & Whitney, 2016

Ātman-Brahman/Puruṣa within some of the traditions that emerged from the Upaniṣads, clarify the similarities and differences between the Ātman and Jung's account of the Self, then suggest ways that these differences may be bridged.

An Initial Note on Terminology

There is a good deal of variation in the use of words such as "consciousness." I use the word with a lowercase "c" in order to speak about the personal or individual levels of the psyche. I use "Consciousness" to refer to a transpersonal or infinite dimension of the psyche, which in some Advaitic literature is referred to as Awareness. This Consciousness is unmediated and unconditioned. (I will not enter into the debate about whether Pure Consciousness exists or not; this argument is ably discussed in Forman.[10]) In my chapter, I will take the position that consciousness and Consciousness are a unity. They cannot be divided except conceptually and for heuristic and clinical purposes. Furthermore, beginning with Jung's axiom *psyche = consciousness,*[11] I suggest that Consciousness and consciousness combined are synonymous with Jung's term "totality of the psyche," which has both personal and transpersonal dimensions. In my usage, the world "psyche" does not simply refer to its contents; psyche and its contents are like the ocean and its waves; they are inseparable.

The Ātman-Brahman of the Upaniṣadic tradition

The word Ātman has a range of meanings in the Upaniṣads. According to Radhakrishnan,[12] in the early Upaniṣads, this word referred to the sense of "I," the individual soul or individual consciousness, but eventually, the Ātman was seen to be synonymous with Brahman, the infinite, universal spirit or the transcendent Self, the divine spirit of creation (Aitareya Upaniṣad I.2.1.)

---

[10] Forman, 1990
[11] CW 8, § 380, emphasis in original.
[12] Radhakrishnan, 1953

Saguṇa Brahman, or the divine with attributes,[13] is also referred to as the Puruṣottama, or the determinate personal God of the Bhagavad Gītā. This level of Brahman is said to project the world and enter into the world, assuming the form of the world and its creatures, without undergoing any change in itself (e.g., Bṛhad-āraṇyaka Upaniṣad II.3.1). It assumes the form of the gross body and (importantly for our comparison with Jung) the dream state, among other forms of consciousness, even as it transcends them.[14] [15]

In the tradition of the Upaniṣads and Advaita Vedānta, non-dual Consciousness or Brahman is identical to all existence. This Consciousness is undivided, homogeneous, and unqualified in any way. Consciousness is reality, the divine ground, the supreme principle of the universe, and the true nature of human experience and being. In this account, apparently separate objects are modifications of Consciousness.

The Ātman is the eternal Self, the supreme soul within each individual (there are no separate selves at this level). The term jīvātman is used to refer to the individual, embodied soul, which is only empirically real, while the term Paramātman refers to the highest level of the Ātman. This situation is sometimes described metaphorically as two birds in a tree. One eats of the fruit of the tree and tastes both its sweet and bitter fruits, while the other calmly looks on without eating (Muṇḍaka Upaniṣad, III. 1.2). The active bird represents the apparent individual engaged with the world, while the other remains aloof. It is the "unseen Seer, the unheard Hearer, the unthought Thinker ... the Self." (Bṛhad-āraṇyaka Upaniṣad III.7.23)

The Ātman or Self can be spoken of as the Awareness that lies behind all layers of personality. The Ātman is not limited to our personal existence; it is the same in all existences, unlimited by

---

[13] It is difficult or impossible to reconcile the idea of an Absolute divinity with attributes such as perfection. Śaṅkara believes that this question only arises within the world of experience and logic; it does not apply to reality from the point of view of the Absolute.
[14] To say that Brahman transcends the world and the body is to imply a dualism between them. However, this linguistic formulation is almost unavoidable.
[15] Prajnananda, 1973

anything finite and unmodified by the personality. The Self is pure, undifferentiated, self-luminous Consciousness (Bṛhad-āraṇyaka Upaniṣad, IV. 3. 9). It is timeless, spaceless, and unthinkable by the mind. It was not born and does not die: "Birthless, eternal, everlasting, and ancient, it is not killed when the body is killed." (Kaṭha Upaniṣad, I. 2. 18) It is self-luminous Being. There is no experience without the Ātman; according to Śaṅkara, it is "by nature the very essence of perception itself."[16] It is that by which our conscious experience of the world is made possible. The Ātman cannot be perceived by the sense organs because it is the ultimate perceiving Subject; the senses are only the instruments through which perception happens. The Ātman is that which sees through the eyes and hears through the ears: "You cannot see that which is the witness of vision: you cannot hear that which is the hearer of hearing." (Bṛhad-āraṇyaka Upaniṣad III.4.2) The Ātman itself has no sound, taste, or other sensory quality. Whereas the empirical ego sees itself as a subject that perceives objects, transcendent Consciousness can never be known by thought as an object, because it is the ultimate knower or Subject of all experience (Bṛhad-āraṇyaka Upaniṣad I. 4. 14). It cannot become an object of thought because it is unlimited. More strictly speaking, at the nondual level, pure Consciousness is neither a subject nor an object; it only knows itself because there is only itself. Accordingly, it cannot be conceptualized, qualified, or defined. We only know the Ātman implicitly by being aware of being aware and through the felt sense of "I am."

Ātman-Brahman cannot be described with language, since the nondual cannot be described within a dualistic, verbal framework. It is sometimes said to have no attributes, but sometimes it is endowed with descriptors such as absolute existence, absolute Consciousness, and absolute bliss or fullness (Saccidānanda). Or it is described as Satya (Truth), Jñāna (Knowledge) and Ananta (Infinite). These are merely terms that express the ways in which Ātman-Brahman is ex-

---

[16] Śaṅkara, commentary on the Brahma-Sūtra, III, iii, 54

perienced by human beings and formulated by the mind; they are not adjectival in the limiting sense. Ātman-Brahman is unlimited, and within it, there are no distinctions or qualities. In the Advaitic tradition, our perception of a separate world of apparently separate objects and individuals, or whenever there is a subject-object distinction, is seen to result from māyā, which is thought of as the creative power of Brahman or Īśvara to appear as the phenomenal world of multiplicity. We mistakenly take this appearance to be real.

Because Brahman cannot be described in words or thoughts, the Upaniṣads describe it in terms of negation — it is "not this, not this" (Bṛhad-āraṇyaka Upaniṣad, II. 3. 6). Brahman is both the essence of the entire universe as well as the divine spark within human beings. Its spontaneous activity produces the appearance of the phenomenal world. From the point of view of the world, the world can be said to emerge from Brahman, but from the nondual point of view, there is no world separate from Brahman. All appearances and apparent dualities are constructed by the mind and its sensory organs; Brahman is non-dual, Pure Consciousness. According to Śaṅkara, it "has no distinguishing mark such as name, or form, or action, or heterogeneity, or species, or qualities."[17] Pure Consciousness is unaffected by anything. This Consciousness is self-revealing as the manifest universe. It is self-luminous, as if, like the sun, it is a light that illumines itself and everything else. The metaphor of Consciousness as light is used throughout the Upaniṣads. Ātman/ Brahman is also spoken of as a center of peace and happiness within us. In meditation, the ego may dissolve into this calm. Also: "The wise man beholds all beings in the Self, and the Self in all beings." (Īśha Upaniṣad VII, 6; Bhagavad-Gītā 13. 27)

Another Upaniṣadic tradition to which Jung refers is Saṅkhyā philosophy. Here, the Ātman or the indwelling spirit or pure Conscious Being is called the Puruṣa. In this system, absolute Consciousness or spirit (Puruṣa) is distinguished from Prakṛiti,

---

[17] Quoted in Indich, 1980, pp. 23-24

which includes matter, the mind, and phenomenal consciousness. That is, both body and mind spring from Prakṛiti, which consists of three qualities, or guṇas, that determine the characteristics of things. These are sattva, or purity and harmony; rajas, or activity of any kind, and tamas, or dullness and inertia. These always interact with each other, in different proportions, although one may predominate in any situation. Jung believed that the idea of rajas offers support for his idea of neutral psychic energy,[18] and he equates Prakṛiti and its guṇas with the archetypal Great Mother and her qualities of goodness, passion, and darkness.[19]

In the pure form of this system, Puruṣa is immobile, immutable, self-luminous, and a passive Witness with no active will; this description is inconsistent with Jung's notion of the Self, which has a variety of effects within the personality.

In Saṅkhyā philosophy, Prakṛiti is a mechanical, energetic process, and by being reflected in Puruṣa, it takes on the appearance of the activities of consciousness and the unconscious, action, sensory knowledge, and so on. The combination of Prakṛiti and Puruṣa is the cause of the universe. Intelligence and will are the result of the action of Buddhi, a principle of discrimination and coordination. The sense of an ego is the subjective aspect of Buddhi by which the Puruṣa identifies itself with the activity of Prakṛiti. Because Prakṛiti is reflected in Puruṣa, the consciousness of the spirit is attributed to what is really mechanical and insentient, which takes on the appearance of consciousness. In pure Saṅkhyā, there are an infinite number of Puruṣas, but in the Gita, which is a Vedantic form of Saṅkhyā, the Self or the Puruṣa is regarded as one, not many. In the traditional Saṅkhyā system, soul and nature are different entities, but in the Gita, they become two aspects of one divine Being. The Puruṣa of Patañjali's Yoga system, which is seen as a theistic branch of Saṅkhyā, is Pure Consciousness, while the Puruṣa of the Gita

---

[18] Coward, 1985
[19] CW 9i, § 158

becomes Īśvara, the Lord or the creator God of nature, or the divine with form, and the cause of the actions of Prakṛiti. Īśvara is the divine personified as an object of loving devotion, analogous to the world creator of the theistic traditions.

Jung and Nonduality

Jung asserts that the Self is the totality of consciousness, including both conscious and unconscious processes.[20] He also says "God is Reality itself and therefore — last but not least — man,"[21] that "the psyche ... is existence itself,"[22] and that "... this [s]elf is the world, if only a consciousness could see it."[23] As well, he believes it is the same Self in all of us.[24] In these ways, his work is consistent with the nondual spiritual traditions.[25] His idea of synchronistic events that emerge from an underlying *unus mundus* also suggests his belief that, at its deep level, reality is undivided: "Everything that happens, however, happens in the same 'one world' and is a part of it. For this reason, events must possess an a priori aspect of unity."[26] However, Jung is unwilling to completely embrace a nondual position, because he cannot relinquish the idea that the ego is essential for consciousness. He believes that: "If there is no ego there is nobody to be conscious of anything. The ego is therefore indispensable to the conscious process."[27] Jung believes that because the ego's functions of "selection and discrimination" are essential for consciousness, for the ego to dissolve in the universal Consciousness of the Atman would be "logically identical with unconsciousness."[28] Whereas the nondual meditative traditions see this union as a form of

---

[20] E.g., CW 7, § 274; CW 12, § 44; CW 14, n. 66, p. 107
[21] CW 11, § 631
[22] CW 1, § 18
[23] CW 9i, § 46
[24] CW 10, § 873
[25] Discussed in more detail in Corbett & Whitney, 2016.
[26] CW 14, § 662
[27] CW 11, § 774
[28] CW 9i, § 520

spiritual illumination of the highest degree, Jung felt this approach is not suited to the Western psyche; he saw it as a "psychic catastrophe"[29] for the ego to be assimilated by the Self. He was skeptical about the complete merger of subject and object described in the nondual traditions because he felt that there must always remain a residual "infinitesimal ego."[30] Jung therefore rejected the possibility of the types of higher states of consciousness such as samādhi described by Eastern meditative traditions.

Jung asserts that if there is an egoless consciousness, "Inasmuch as it exists, we do not exist."[31] (However, for the Vedāntic tradition, pure Consciousness is not something we possess; it is what we are, our true nature.) Jung believes that, even in states of samādhi, there must be a residual ego present or there would be no memory of the experience; "without ahamkāra [the ego-maker] there would be absolutely no one there to register what was happening."[32] He therefore wants to make the ego and Self two distinct centers of consciousness, whereas the nondual tradition sees the ego as not self-existent, at most a reflection of the Consciousness of the Self. Jung believes that the ego can gradually assimilate more and more awareness of the Self by paying attention to its symbolic intrapsychic manifestations such as mandalas. The Vedantic approach would be more like stripping away everything that has been mistakenly superimposed on the Self, in order to allow its direct apprehension.

Jung does not believe that consciousness is possible outside the context of subject-object duality, which is abolished in deep meditation. However, Jung believes that the Eastern meditative traditions run various risks for the Western psyche; to identify ego consciousness with the Self or to lose the ego into the Self may entail "great psychic danger" of "an inflation which threatens [ego]

---

[29] CW 9ii, § 45
[30] CW 11, § 817
[31] Jung, 1973, p. 247
[32] CW 11, § 959

consciousness with dissolution."[33] Or, these practices might lead to a repression or avoidance of unconscious contents, especially shadow material.[34]

Because of his adherence to a Kantian epistemology, Jung also rejected many Eastern metaphysical claims; he saw Eastern philosophers as "symbolic psychologists" whose claims should not be taken literally.[35] He believed that the idea that the ego can be transcended was an Eastern intuition that "overreached itself."[36] He felt that this was a metaphysical idea that is not grounded empirically; for Jung, what the yogis describe are trance states. This view has been challenged by several authors such as Schlamm,[37] who have noted that the translations of Eastern texts used by Jung were inadequate.

Jung realized that the practices described in the Yoga Sūtras produce a "remarkable extension of consciousness," but he believed that with this increased extension "the contents of consciousness lose in clarity of detail," and "consciousness becomes all-embracing but nebulous."[38] In an earlier version of this paper,[39] Jung refers to this extension of consciousness as "vast but dim." However, (from personal experience) the experience of Pure Consciousness is not dim; it can be shining, vivid, and peaceful, or sometimes shimmering and exhilarating. Samādhi is not "equivalent to a state of unconsciousness" as Jung claims;[40] Consciousness is always present. Thus, samādhi is also known as knowledge,[41] but this is not knowledge restricted to the level of concepts; it is knowledge by means of direct perception. Rather than being a regressive or unconscious state, the meditator moves beyond the limitations of the

---

[33] CW 9i, § 254
[34] CW 11, § 939
[35] CW 13, § 74
[36] CW11, § 818
[37] Schlamm, 2010
[38] CW 9i, § 520
[39] Jung, 1939, p. 26
[40] CW 9i, § 520
[41] Śaṇkarācārya, 2020

empirical personality into an expanded vision of reality. Samādhi is the achievement of a highly disciplined mind. Jung's view of this state is reductionistic.

Jung could not conceive of consciousness without an ego; he felt that even if unitary consciousness is attained, to have a memory of the event, there "must always be somebody or something left over to experience the realization, to say I know at-one-ment. ... One cannot know something that is not distinct from oneself."[42] Jung sees nondual reality or Pure Consciousness without an ego as not knowable or even a self-contradictory idea. However, Consciousness is not a thing; it is the knowing. Ultimate reality is not knowable because pure Consciousness is the ultimate Subject that knows itself. Pure Consciousness illumines personal consciousness but cannot be contained within it.

Jung's Self and the Ātman: Conceptual Similarities and Differences

Consistent with the Upaniṣadic notion of an Absolute level of Consciousness, Jung asserts that the deepest nature of the Self is unknowable; the images it produces have an "unknowable metaphysical background."[43] I suggest that this background refers to the transcendent Nirguṇa Brahman, or the noumenal level of the archetype *an sich*. This level of the Absolute is then the ontological ground of Jung's Self.

Jung is consistent with the Upaniṣadic tradition when he sees the Self as a priori, "pre-existent to [personal] consciousness," and having an "incorruptible" or "eternal" character.[44] Jung writes that his model of the Self "serves to express an unknowable essence which we cannot grasp as such, since, by definition, it transcends our

---

[42] CW 11, § 817

[43] Ibid., § 558

[44] Ibid., § 401

power of comprehension."[45] This attitude toward the Self is again consistent with the Upaniṣadic view. However, Jung believes that aspects of the Self can be experienced symbolically, for example as objects in dreams,[46] in contrast to the Advaitic view that the Self, which is Consciousness itself, can never be experienced as an object. It is the ultimate and unknowable Subject of all experience.

Although the Self at its ultimate level can never be the object of experience, Jung believes that the Self manifests itself in the form of numinous experiences[47] that have long been associated with the experience of divinity.[48] I suggest that the source of numinous experiences is the Upaniṣadic Saguṇa Brahman, and I believe that Jung's description of the phenomenology of the Self as it appears intrapsychically is consistent with this level of Brahman. Said another way, numinous experiences reveal the activity of Saguṇa Brahman within the empirical personality, or they symbolically depict glimpses of the Ātman refracted through personal levels of the psyche. The numinous manifestations of Ātman/Brahman or Īśvara within the psyche, because they are names and forms, are phenomenal manifestations of māyā.

In the Advaitic system, Īśvara is Brahman (the Absolute) veiled by ignorance. Jung's Self, or experiences of God within the psyche, can be seen as attempts to symbolize Īśvara so that personal consciousness can relate to it, as it takes on the limitations inherent in a symbol. Although Jung believes that the ego can experience the Self in symbolic forms, he agrees that none of these is the Self itself — they are all pointers to a deeper, noumenal reality. Advaita would agree that the Ātman-Brahman itself cannot be thought, because it can never become an object of consciousness; it is, at the same time,

---

[45] CW 7, § 399
[46] CW 9i, § 315
[47] CW 12, § 9; Corbett, 2006
[48] CW 11, § 757

paradoxically that which knows, the process of knowing, and also what is known.

For Jung, awareness of the Self, and the progressive embodiment of the Self in the form of the realization of its archetypal potentials within the personality, are goals to which the individuation process strives. This is a different goal from the experiential realization of the Self in the meditative traditions with the concomitant loss of the sense of a separate self. For Vedānta, liberation requires knowledge or realization of oneself as the Self; it is attained through spiritual practice, self-inquiry, or by divine grace. The Ātman reveals itself when ignorance is removed. Realization of the Self occurs "through hearing, reflection, and meditation" (Bṛhad-āraṇyaka Upaniṣad II.4.5) and through spiritual intuition, but not by means of thought. For Jung, knowledge of the Self is obtained by paying attention to its numinous manifestations. Although these "primordial experiences" are not considered to be particularly important by the Eastern meditative traditions, Jung thinks they are very important for the process of individuation, certainly for Westerners.

In *Answer to Job*, Jung suggested that the Self is unconscious of its dark side, as reflected in Yahweh's brutal treatment of the innocent Job. Jung also believed that the Self requires a human ego to reflect the antinomies within its nature.[49] However, these assertions make no sense from a Vedantic point of view, since the Self is Consciousness itself; it therefore cannot be unconscious of itself, and there is no other consciousness to reflect it. The idea of an unconscious Self is meaningless from a nondual point of view, since Consciousness cannot be unconscious. The very idea of the unconscious is only meaningful from the ego's perspective. If the Self is the totality of the psyche, and Jung's own statement that "*psyche* =

---

[49] Ibid., § 642

consciousness"[50] is correct, the Self cannot be unconscious of itself. Fire does not require heat to become hot.

Jung's notion that the Self has a dark side is inconsistent with the nondual Vedantic Self, which is beyond such opposites; good and evil are seen as the human mind's conditioned reactions to experiences that are either positive or painful. Jung did not believe that consciousness is possible outside the context of subject-object duality. He did believe in the certainty that the world "rests on a transcendental background,"[51] but this realization was probably based on numinous experiences and his spiritual intuition, rather than on experiences derived in meditation. However, Jung believed that the Eastern meditative traditions run various risks for the Western psyche; to identify ego-consciousness with the Self or to lose the ego into the Self may produce "great psychic danger" of "an inflation which threatens consciousness with dissolution."[52] Or, these practices might lead to a repression of unconscious contents. Borelli[53] and Clarke[54] have listed several other possible motivations for Jung's rejection of Eastern spiritual practices.

Jung does seem to intuit a level of the Self that is not affected by descriptions such as good and evil; he talks about a "higher consciousness" that looks on while we are affected by emotional storms. This would be the Vedāntic Self at the level of Pure Awareness, which is not affected by psychological storms and has no qualities.

Stein has suggested that the attainment of enlightenment in the East and the individuation process in analytical psychology both share the goal of the transformation of consciousness.[55] However, for the nondual traditions, only what seem to be personal levels of consciousness could be transformed; Pure Consciousness is

---

[50] CW 8, § 380, emphasis in original.
[51] CW 14, § 787
[52] CW 9i, § 254
[53] Borelli, 1985
[54] Clarke, 1994
[55] Stein, 2019

unchanging and self-illuminating. Jung speaks of the realization of the Self as the goal of the individuation process, which is fostered by becoming conscious of symbols of the Self. It is possible that the full individuation of the personal self may lead to the Upaniṣadic Self, or the realization: "Thou art That."[56] Katsky has reported a dream image that suggests that there may be a continuum between the individuation process and enlightenment achieved by meditation practice.[57] However, for strict nonduality, liberation cannot be attained by any kind of willful activity. For Jung, the Self is realized by paying attention to its manifestations; for Advaita, the Self is realized when nothing is superimposed upon it. Direct knowledge of oneself as Brahman may occur as a result of self-inquiry and by means of valid mediate knowledge such as the Vedas. There is a debate between various schools of Vedanta about whether one can arrive at enlightenment through intrapsychic means, or by grace alone, or whether meditation and mediation by means of the scriptures are essential.

The tradition of the Vedānta attaches no special importance to the kind of symbolic material on which Jung focuses. Eastern traditions primarily rely on meditative techniques to realize the Self; meditation leads to direct knowledge that erases the distinction between knower and known. During meditation, imagery is allowed to simply flow through the mind without paying attention to it. Jung saw this kind of approach as a potential avoidance of the need to dialogue with the unconscious, a relationship he regarded as essential for the West. Rather than simply observing the mind, Jung preferred that Westerners use attention to dreams and active imagination as a form of meditation and connection to the Self. Jung believed that the Self must be translated into psychological terms "in order to make it perceptible at all,"[58] which is why attention to its imagery is important. For the Vedantic system, Self-knowledge is a matter of recognition of Awareness, which

---

[56] Chāndogya Upaniṣad VI.8.7
[57] Katsky, 2021
[58] CW 18, § 1538

is the ground of experience. This requires that we stop superimposing personal material, conditioned thoughts and feelings, on our true nature. It is arguable that psychotherapeutic work assists in this process by reducing the intensity of such conditioning. However, constant attention to intrapsychic material runs the risk of intensifying our identification with our personal history, complexes, memories, and so on, whereas the attainment of Pure Consciousness requires that we entirely relinquish the importance of such conditioned material, realizing that it is not our true Self. Pure Consciousness has no content, quality, attributes, or limits. Dream imagery, for instance, can be seen as nothing more important than any other *vṛitti*, or modification of the mind that must be stilled to experience the Puruṣa.

The main focus of Jung's clinical work is on the contents of consciousness, rather than on Consciousness itself, whereas Yoga philosophy is concerned with the cessation of fluctuations within the mind rather than the detailed analysis of its contents. Jung believes that attention to these contents leads to the emergence of transpersonal material, which is a manifestation of the Self. In this process, the empirical personality is strengthened and made more comfortable, broadened, and deepened. Not surprisingly, therefore, these traditions have different aims and methods. From the Yogic or Advaitic point of view, one might be relatively well-balanced psychologically but still be enveloped in ignorance. The notion of liberation, or *mokṣha,* in Yoga and Advaita is quite different from the Western notion of psychological health. It is clear from the behavior of some Eastern spiritual teachers who have exploited their students that spiritual realization does not necessarily improve mental health or lead to personality integration. Clinical experience also confirms that years of meditation do not necessarily lead to the softening of painful complexes.

In the Upaniṣadic tradition, the Self is always already present, like the sun behind the clouds. Even the attempt at detachment from phenomenal activity by means of discrimination and spiritual practice is an activity grounded in ignorance, since it involves an apparent subject trying to achieve a goal that is already present. In Śaṅkara's metaphor, it is like searching for the necklace that is around one's neck.[59] The only true liberation occurs with the transcendence of all forms of duality in nirvikalpa samādhi, a state of total absorption in Brahman. (Śaṅkara does not believe that the attainment of samādhi is enough to eradicate false knowledge and superimposition, which is the real cause of bondage, so samādhi is not enough for liberation.[60]) Jung, however, believes that liberation from the tension of the opposites can only be partial because the complete overcoming of this tension would require abolition of the ego, which is responsible for separating the opposites. Accordingly: "Complete liberation means death."[61] In the Vedantic tradition, another form of liberation occurs in the form of a liberated sage, a jīvanmukta, a person who realizes that he is actually the Self and who sees all beings as the Self. That is, unlike the uniquely personal individuation process, for Advaita Self-realization is impersonal, beyond individuality and personal will; it transcends any modified form of consciousness.

Jung is sometimes criticized for conflating the unconscious with what Indian philosophy sees as a "superconscious" level of the psyche; in most systems of Indian thought, the ultimate can only be realized by attaining this level. Accordingly, Satchdeva suggests that Assagioli's concept of a higher consciousness came closer to the notion of the Atman than did Jung's notion of the collective unconscious.[62] However, for Jung, the collective unconscious *is* the spiritual dimension or the Universal Mind of Hindu philosophy,[63] and, like that Mind, the unconscious is the "birthplace of thought-

---

[59] Indich, 1980, p. 107
[60] https://realization.org/p/misc/comans.samadhi-advaita.html (Last accessed 3/10/22).
[61] Jung, 1973, p. 274
[62] Satchdeva, 1978
[63] Jung, 1939, p. 15

forms."[64] The unconscious is of "indefinite extent with no assignable limits."[65] Jung noted that as we descend into the unconscious, we experience what feels like an "illumination from above," referring to the numinous manifestations of transpersonal levels of the psyche, which for Jung are its spiritual level.[66] The mistake here is taking the notion of "higher" and "lower" too literally; the psyche is not spatial. Terms like "depth" and "height" are only metaphors. Jung notes that the psyche is not only "the condition of all metaphysical reality, it is that reality."[67] Here Jung is consistent with the Upaniṣadic notion of Consciousness as identical with Brahman, the ultimate reality.

There are various areas in which Jung's work is incompatible with the nondual traditions. For instance, Jung seems to have believed that consciousness arose and evolved. In a letter, he says that "warm-bloodedness and a differentiated brain were necessary for the inception of consciousness."[68] Also, "the psychic structure must, like the anatomical, show traces of the earlier stages of evolution it has passed through."[69] In the Upaniṣadic view, Consciousness did not evolve; it is eternal, with no beginning or end. However, Jung might be referring to the contents of the psyche, or its personal levels, rather than the psyche itself. In his early work, Jung speaks of the collective unconscious as the repository of human experience that took eons to form,[70] but later he says that we do not know the origin of the psyche or its archetypal level. He believes that the question of whether the psyche "originated" is a metaphysical problem that cannot be answered;[71] he suggests that the psyche arose "with life itself."[72] This latter opinion is consistent with the Advaitic belief

---

[64] CW11, § 782
[65] Ibid., § 390
[66] CW 16, § 493
[67] CW 11, § 836
[68] Jung, 1975, p. 494
[69] CW 15, § 152
[70] E.g., CW 7, §. 151
[71] CW 9i, § 187
[72] CW 11, p. 149, n. 2

that absolute Consciousness transcends evolution. Indich makes the further point that Jung's theory of the collective unconscious or the Self includes its teleological function, guiding the individual through the process of individuation.[73]

A further important difference between Jung and the nondual traditions is that these traditions offer the possibility of transcendence of suffering, whereas Jung believed that: "Complete redemption from the suffering of this world is and must remain an illusion."[74] For Jung, the only way to deal with suffering is to endure it[75] or outgrow it.

The Ego

Jung thinks of the ego as revolving around the Self in a way that is analogous to the earth's revolution around the sun,[76] or "the ego stands to the self as the moved to the mover."[77] The Self "dwarfs the ego in scope and intensity."[78] However, speaking of the ego in these ways tends to implicitly concretize it or turn it into an entity. Jung does not deconstruct the ego in the manner of the Upaniṣadic traditions, which say that the ego merely reflects and seems to appropriate or own the Consciousness of the Ātman. The word ego at best can only refer to an illusory attempt to objectify infinite awareness. By maintaining the importance of the ego, Jung never fully abandons his Western dualistic bias, although his insistence on a distinction between ego and Self raises the question of how they can truly be different if he also insists that they are part of the same totality of the psyche.

In Jung's model of the psyche, the ego is the center of the field of consciousness or the sense of "I," which we feel as a primary

---

[73] Indich, 1990, p. 94
[74] CW16, § 400
[75] Jung, 1973, p. 236
[76] CW 7, § 405
[77] CW 11, § 391
[78] CW 8, § 430

reality. In the Vedāntic approach, that core sense of "I" or the feeling of "I am" is, in fact, produced by the Ātman, but we attribute this awareness to an illusory entity we call the ego. Jung reifies the ego by saying that the ego emerges out of the Self, which for him is "an a priori existent out of which the ego evolves. It is, so to speak, an unconscious prefiguration of the ego."[79] His view is therefore inconsistent with the Vedāntic insistence that the ego is not an entity, but it is consistent with the Vedāntic idea that the Consciousness of the Ātman is the real substrate of the subjective self of the individual. However, paradoxically, the Ātman is said to experience no changes or emotions.[80] Here we meet the eternal question of how the Absolute becomes the phenomenal, or how the infinite Ātman is related to the limitations of body and personality; this remains a mystery, but one that is only a problem for the realm of duality.

In *Memories, Dreams, Reflections*, Jung describes two dreams that led him to believe that the Self "is the generator of the empirical personality."[81] One is the dream of a UFO that literally projects Jung's existence, suggesting that the ego emerges as an emanation of the Self. The other is the dream of a Yogi (with Jung's face) who is meditating or dreaming Jung's existence; Jung then is a content of the Yogi's mind, and the Yogi and Jung are a unity even though the dream ego seems to be separate. As Jung says about this dream, "in the opinion of the 'other side,' our unconscious existence is the real one and our conscious world is a kind of illusion."[82] That is, Jung's waking life is the dream, and the transpersonal dimension is the reality from which it emerges. If the Yogi and the UFO represent the Self, out of which the ego emerges, the projection from the UFO and the dream of the Yogi suggest that the Self is conscious of the ego, or the ego is a content of the Self. The dreams are pointing out a Consciousness other than the ego and that the ego is illuminated or

---

[79] CW 11, § 391
[80] Radhakrishnan, 2008/1923
[81] Jung, 1965, p. 324
[82] Ibid.

created by that Consciousness. Just as in a dream, everything seems entirely solid and real, so the waking world is a manifestation of the Consciousness of the Self. The metaphor of the dream is often used in the Advaitic literature, which suggests that empirical reality is a manifestation or "dream" of the larger Consciousness, just as the individual's dream is a manifestation of the local mind. In his essay on synchronicity, Jung quotes with approval the idea that such events are "arranged as if they were the dream of a 'greater and more comprehensive consciousness, which is unknowable.'"[83] The notion that solidity might be only an appearance of an underlying spiritual essence is also well-known in Western philosophy.[84] Consciousness might well be that essence. Certainly, for Jung, "Spirit and matter may well be forms of one and the same transcendental being."[85]

The nondual spiritual traditions all stress that the personal sense of self is not a discrete entity separate from the totality of Consciousness. What we refer to as the personal self, or the empirical personality, is a combination of the Consciousness of the Self with conditioned levels of consciousness based on factors such as personal identity, memory, bodily sensations, information from the sense organs, complexes, and individual circumstances. The operations of body, mind, and senses combine to produce what is referred to as an ego. There is an inherent tendency for these limiting factors to be superimposed on the Self, or they become apparent colorings of the Consciousness of the Self. When these factors are removed or seen though, what is left is Pure Consciousness.

Jung believed that a human being cannot be conscious without an ego. He insists that ego functions such as "exclusion, selection, and discrimination are the root and essence of everything that lays claim to the name consciousness."[86] Or, "an ego-less mental

---

[83] CW 8, § 831

[84] For example, Plato's Ideas, Schopenhauer's will and representation, Kant's noumena and phenomena.

[85] CW 9i, § 392

[86] CW 9i, § 520

condition can only be unconscious to us, for the simple reason that there would be nobody to witness it."[87]

Importantly, because he wants to maintain the importance of an ego, Jung would not accede to the Upaniṣadic insistence that the personal self is inseparable from the Supreme Self. In many ways, the purpose of the Upaniṣads is to demonstrate this unity, whose realization is considered to be liberation. The Upaniṣadic tradition would argue that Jung errs in assuming that consciousness has to be identified with ego-consciousness, since the Self is Consciousness itself. Furthermore, the Self is conscious of itself, and it is the only Consciousness that exists. Ego-functions such as discrimination and selection, or the everyday working mind, are simply the result of conditioned differences and preferences illuminated by the totality of Consciousness.

There is an almost invariable tendency in the psychoanalytic and Jungian literature to reify the ego. However, even though the ego is not an entity, it is convenient to use the word "ego" for clinical and heuristic purposes as a shorthand term for what *seems to be* the field of individual consciousness that belongs to an empirical personality. Although from the nondual point of view there is really only one Agent and one ultimate Subject — the Self — at the everyday empirical level, and for the sake of clarity, we may talk about the ego and Self *as if* they were different, and *as if* the ego were an agent. However, in the Vedāntic tradition, the ego has no consciousness of its own; the Self is the source of the ego's consciousness. Just as the moon reflects the light of the sun, so the ego reflects the consciousness of the Self; the core sense of "I" that seems to be personal is actually rooted in the Ātman. The sense of "I" is mistakenly assumed to be an independent consciousness. Śaṅkara believes that we superimpose the idea of personal identity or an ego on to our intuitive sense of existing. In Śaṅkara's metaphor, when an iron ball is heated to red

---

[87] CW 11, § 774

heat, the qualities of redness and heat are mistakenly superimposed on the iron as if they were the same as the iron.[88]

Jung believes that the Self is the totality of consciousness and the unconscious; within his usage, the ego is related to the Self as part to the whole,[89] and the part cannot know the whole. If the Self is the totality of the psyche, the ego must be one of its constituents. However, the Jungian literature often uses the term "ego-self axis" in a manner that treats ego and Self as if they were different, but if the Self is the totality of the psyche, this cannot be the case. It is also a mistake to think of the Self as "an" archetype among others; the Self is superordinate to any of its individual constituents or symbolic manifestations. What seem to be symbols of the Self are personified fragments of the totality, not the Self itself. Because intrapsychic symbols of the Self are partial and come and go, they cannot be the Self itself; in Vedantic terms, they are aspects of māyā, which is the principle that allows the One to appear as the many.

Attempts at Bridging

There are some immediately obvious similarities between the Ātman and Jung's Self; for example, Jung describes the Self as the "God within," which is certainly consistent with the Upaniṣadic understanding of the Ātman. Although the symbolic, intrapsychic manifestations of the Self that Jung describes are not discussed in the Upaniṣads, I suggest that Jung's Self-symbols are manifestations or personifications of the Ātman. The Ātman is the undifferentiated or noumenal level of Jung's Self, prior to its intrapsychic manifestations. Jung realized that this level existed, but he felt it could not be known until it manifests itself symbolically, in contrast to the meditative traditions that teach the direct realization of the Self. One could think of the numinous experiences of the Self as manifestations of what the tradition calls Saguṇa Brahman, or God with

---

[88] Prabhavananda, 1975
[89] CW 9i, § 341

attributes, also referred to as Īśvara, which can be understood to be the Self as it expresses itself within māyā, conditioned by illusion.

According to the Upaniṣads, we cannot know that which knows. However, numinous experiences can be seen as pointers to the deeper reality of the Ātman. Although it may be useful for devotional and psychological purposes to see the Ātman in these symbolic forms, symbols are by their nature limited, and we cannot attribute limitations to the unlimited. We certainly cannot use language to talk about the nature of the Self, since language always requires a subject and object, and the Self transcends the subject-object differentiation, so language would always misrepresent the situation. As Jung put it, the Self produces "symbolism which has always characterized and expressed the Deity,"[90] so that, "For psychology the [S]elf is an *imago dei* and cannot be distinguished from it empirically."[91]

The Upaniṣads do not discuss the psychology of the Ātman with anything like the level of detail in which Jung describes symbols of the Self. The Upaniṣads assert the presence of the Ātman based on the testimony of seers, *ṛṣis,* or spiritually advanced sages who realized this truth in meditation. Jung is trying to provide empirical evidence for the existence of the Self by describing its images and other manifestations within the psyche, which are often related to personal material. The Upaniṣadic tradition does not describe these kinds of images, and it sees the Self as entirely impersonal. However, in the Upaniṣads, Consciousness is said to be self-revealing, and it is entirely possible that the Self symbols that Jung describes are part of this process of self-revelation. Part of the value of paying attention to the numinous manifestations of the Self is that while we are immersed in māyā, these experiences remind us of our relationship to the divine, or to our original unity with it.

According to the Vedāntic tradition, personal psychological material obscures our recognition of the pure Consciousness at

---

[90] CW 11, § 757
[91] CW 5, § 612

the center of the personality — the theory of superimposition. The psychotherapeutic clarification of this material is like clearing the dust off a mirror so that we can see a reflection of the true Self more clearly. In psychotherapeutic terms, this clearing process involves seeing through one's personal material during the individuation process. Jung pointed out that, during this process, the ego "senses itself as the object of an unknown and supraordinate subject,"[92] obviously referring to the Self. Another way of saying this is that the empirical personality intuitively senses the presence of the Self. Because the notion of the Ātman-Brahman may lead to a rather impersonal spirituality since it may feel subjectively difficult to relate to the Absolute, a focus on the individuation process and the psychological appearances of the Self are important reminders of the human dimension. The individuation process involves increasing consciousness of the objective psyche, which Jung believes contains the saṁskāras, a term that traditionally refers to latent impressions or imprints on the mind from previous lives. For Jung, saṁskāras would refer to the individual's archetypal endowment.[93] These are not incompatible views if one's archetypal endowment is acquired by karma. Jung suggested that karma "is essential to a deeper understanding of the nature of an archetype."[94] Coward makes the point that Jungian scholars have downplayed the importance of karma in Jung's thought, apparently because acknowledging it would make his psychology even less acceptable to mainstream Western psychology.[95]

Jung often speaks of psychological work, such as attention to dreams and synchronicities, as ways to experience the Self, but Advaita suggests that knowledge of the Self is not the result of any ego-driven activity. In the Advaitic tradition, realization of the Self is hidden by nescience, but the Self is always present, like the sun

---

[92] CW 7, § 405
[93] Jung, 1996, p. 74
[94] CW 7, p. 77, n. 15
[95] Coward, 1983

behind the clouds. When ignorance is gone, the Self is realized. An obvious question is how to bridge the apparent gap between the two orders of reality, between the phenomenal realm and the transcendent level of Consciousness. Advaita assumes that this radical discontinuity is only a problem for the human ego. Jung's approach to the numinous symbolic manifestations of the Self may act as such a bridge, although I believe the strict Advaitin might deny the possibility of any such possibility on the grounds that the Self itself has no quality of the kind found in a symbol, which is at best a pointer to the noumenal realm. However, my thesis is that numinous symbols are manifestations of Saguṇa Brahman,

The caveat here is that Jung warned against building "false and dangerous bridges over yawning gaps" between East and West.[96] He believed that Westerners should not simply imitate Eastern philosophy; he wanted the West to discover Eastern truths in the way of the West, which he believed would "produce its own yoga" in the course of time.[97] One of Jung's major concerns was the healing of the Western psyche, and he did not think that the adoption of Eastern religious practices would do so.

Two Levels of Consciousness

In the Advaitic system, from the ego's perspective, absolute Consciousness is differentiated from phenomenal or modified consciousness,[98] but this does not lead to an ultimate duality; Brahman, or absolute, Consciousness is the unifying ground of all phenomenal states of consciousness, and it persists throughout them. This means that the ground of our existence is also the source of our subjective experience. The ego distinguishes them, even though they are not truly different. The hierarchy only obtains from the lower point of view.

---

[96] CW 11, § 961
[97] Ibid.
[98] Indich, 1980

Jung distinguished between egoic consciousness and the unconscious, but Śaṅkara's distinction between two distinct levels of Consciousness corresponds to a more radical discontinuity between absolute reality and appearances.[99] For Śaṅkara, the Self is transcendent or absolute Consciousness, which is universal, undifferentiated, self-luminous, unchanging, and transcendent of all limitations, while a lower level of modified consciousness mediates apparent reality, including the empirical personality, the ego, or the personal self. Modified consciousness, or the constantly changing world of appearances, distorts reality by separating subject and object. This level appears to be individualized within separate beings; it is said by Advaita to be the result of the combination of absolute Consciousness with ignorance or illusion. According to Śaṅkara, because of a failure of discrimination, the limitations and manifestations of mind and body that do not belong to the Self are superimposed onto it, but Brahman remains unchanged. The Self illumines whatever condition the mind is in, and whatever state the mind is in obscures the Self or is superimposed on it. Only by stilling the mind is the Self revealed. Advaita teaches that the association of the Self with ignorance leads to an "internal organ" known as the antaḥkaraṇa, which is described in different ways, but typically consists of a combination of the discriminating intellect, the sense of "I-am," the perceiving mind, and memories that affect present activities.

The Advaitic distinction between two levels of consciousness is consistent with the notion of the ego-self axis. However, whereas Jung wants the ego level to pay attention to the manifestations of the Self within the psyche, for example in the form of dream imagery, Advaita wants all forms of personal experience to be seen through or eliminated, in order to reveal the underlying Ātman, as if the personal material were a cloud obscuring the sun. Since the absolute level of Consciousness is unchanging, development of the

---

[99] Vimuktananda, 2020

personality within the individuation process must occur by means of modified consciousness, even though the unchanging level remains a background presence. However, if these levels are truly radically distinguishable, as Advaita claims, the reconciliation of the development of modified consciousness with the presence of unchanging Consciousness is a confusing paradox. This may be why Sri Aurobindo speaks of two modes of Brahman, the Silent and the Active; in the active mode, Brahman transforms into the universe.[100]

Jung believes that there are levels of the psyche that are entirely autonomous; the overlap would be that for Advaita, absolute Consciousness is autonomous from the point of view of empirical consciousness. Although it is not clear whether the Advaitin's pure Consciousness is the same as Jung's collective unconscious, Occam's razor suggests that perhaps they are the same. Both point to a universal level of psychic reality that is not knowable within ordinary waking consciousness. As Whitfield suggests, Jung's model can be extended by considering Brahman as the invariant pure Consciousness or noumenal level of Jung's Self.[101]

What is Real?

According to Advaita, empirical existence seems to be real, but it is only relatively real or it is true for practical purposes; it is sublated or contradicted by knowledge of absolute reality, from which point of view phenomenal reality is an appearance. Following the Upaniṣads, Śaṅkara believes that only that which never changes and never ceases to exist is real. In this view, no thing and no knowledge are absolutely real if they only exist temporarily. "Absolute reality implies permanent existence."[102] In this account, whatever can be modified or contradicted (sublated) as a result of new experience is not real. (Here, "not real" does not mean nonexistent; an illusion

---

[100] Aurobindo, 1996
[101] Whitfield, 2009
[102] Prabhavananda & Isherwood, 1975, p. 7

exists even though it is not factual; it is not as real as it seems to be.) Only the Self cannot be negated; it is the constant feature of all experience, including deep sleep. The world is subject to change, so it only appears to be real, but no experience can cancel or contradict the immediacy of Awareness. In this tradition, only the "non-temporal, non-spatial, and non-causal absolute Brahman" is real.[103]

Jung insists that the psyche is real, and its images are real. However, dream images are not permanent, and so in the Advaitic view, they are only apparently real but cannot be ultimately real. Advaita sees the dream as a product of the jīva, the individual soul. Dream images are essentially dualistic, because they are specific and limited. However, if we see the totality of the psyche as synonymous with the totality of Consciousness, the contents of the psyche are its manifestations. The psyche can be thought of as the substrate of dream images, like a matrix or like the screen on which a movie appears. In this metaphor, the screen is not affected by the images projected onto it, but it is inseparable from them. Thus, the Consciousness out of which dream imagery arises is real, even if any particular imagery within it is transient. Intrapsychic images of the Self are like reflections in a mirror; they are not unreal, but they are only appearances. Jung intuited this when he said that "there is an original behind our images, but it is inaccessible. We could not even be aware of the original since its translation into psychic terms is necessary in order to make it perceptible at all."[104]

For Advaita Vedānta, māyā is the inexplicable power of the divine that produces relative or conditioned existence, which has a phenomenal reality, but it is illusory in the sense that it is not ultimately real. Its actual ground is the infinite Brahman. Śaṅkara's metaphor is that a rope may look like a snake until we realize its true nature; the erroneous perception is due to māyā. The illusion occurs because we have superimposed the memory of the snake onto the rope, but this

---

[103] Prajnananda, 1973, p. 44
[104] CW18, § 1589

mistake is corrected, or sublated, when we see the reality. Analogously, the knowledge of the phenomenal world is sublated by knowledge of Brahman, and this knowledge cannot be contradicted. The relationship between the nondual reality of Brahman and the apparent phenomenal world is attributed to māyā, and is an indescribable mystery. This difficulty only arises at the level of duality.[105]

The Approach to the Dream in Jung and Advaita

Not surprisingly, Jung's approach to dreams is much more central to his theory than is the Advaitic analysis of dreams to that tradition. Indich points out that there are at least six different analyses of the nature and origin of dreams in classical Indian thought.[106] An important difference between Jung and Advaita is that Jung values dreams very much, while Advaitic thinkers emphasize the superiority of the waking state over dreams, which they believe represent the experience of a vague consciousness in which the mind "functions in a disorderly manner with little thought and many conflicting, unstable, and unreliable images."[107] Advaitic thinkers prefer the logical thinking of the waking state. Advaita argues that the empirical personality during a dream remains "involved in the causal or karmic order as a result of his identification with" the dream content.[108] Thus, consciousness in dreams is as bound as it is in waking experience. The Advaitic approach to dreams therefore fails to realize their importance for communicating between the Self and empirical consciousness.

In Conclusion

Jung had the following experience of the Self as the totality after a heart attack in 1944. At the time, he was close to death in a

---

[105] Radhakrishnan, 1923/2008, vol. 1
[106] Indich, 1980
[107] Ibid., p. 64
[108] Ibid., p. 82

"state of unconsciousness."[109] He describes the experience of being high up in space, seeing the earth far below bathed in glorious blue light. Then:

> I had the feeling that everything was being sloughed away; everything I aimed at or wished for or thought, the whole phantasmagoria of earthly existence fell away or was stripped from me. ... Nevertheless something remained; it was as if I now carried along with me everything I had ever experienced or done, everything that had happened around me. I might also say: it was with me, and I was it. I consisted of all that, so to speak. ... there was no longer anything I wanted or desired. I existed in an objective form. ... I had everything that I was, and that was everything.

The hegemony of Jung's ordinary consciousness was paralyzed by his illness, which allowed him an experience from the timeless and unitary perspective of the Self, *sub specie aeternitatis*, from which Jung eventually returned to the limitations of the ego world. He then referred to mundane reality as the "box system" because it then seemed to him as if "each person sat by himself in a little box."[110] In spite of this experience, perhaps because of his reluctance to let go of a Western prejudice, Jung maintained his emphasis on the importance of the ego. For many of us interested in the interface between his work and the Upaniṣadic traditions, the ego can be relativized by seeing it as nothing more than the practical mind of everyday necessity. The Self is our ultimate nature.

---

[109] Jung, 1965, pp. 290-291
[110] Ibid., p. 292

References

Aurobindo, Sri. (1996). *The Synthesis of Yoga*. Twin Lakes, WI: Lotus Light Publications

Borelli, J. (1985). Jung's criticism of yoga spirituality. In H.G. Coward, *Jung and Eastern Thought*. pp. 79-92. Albany, NY: SUNY Press

Clarke, J.J. (1994). *Jung and Eastern Thought: A Dialogue with the Orient*. New York: Routledge

Corbett, L. (2006). Varieties of numinous experience. In A. Casement (Ed.), *The Idea of the Numinous*. New York: Brunner-Routledge

Corbett, L., & Whitney, L. (2016). Jung and non-duality: Some clinical and theoretical implications of the self as the totality of the psyche. *International Journal of Jungian Studies, 8*(1), pp. 15-27

Coward, H.G. (1983). Jung and Karma. *Journal of Analytical Psychology, 28*(4), 367-375

Coward, H. (1985). *Jung and Eastern Thought*. Albany, NY: SUNY Press

Indich, W.M. (1980). *Consciousness in Advaita Vedānta*. Motilal Banarsidass Publishers: Delhi, India

Forman, R.K.C. (1990). *The Problem of Pure Consciousness*. New York: Oxford University Press

Jung, C.G. (1939). *The Integration of the Personality*. S. Dell, Trans. New York: Farrar and Rinehart

_____. (1965). *Memories, Dreams, Reflections*. New York: Random House

_____. (1973). *Letters*, Vol. 1. G. Adler and A. Jaffe, Eds. R.F.C. Hull, Trans. Princeton, NJ: Princeton University Press

_____. (1975). *Letters*, Vol. 2. G. Adler and A. Jaffe, Eds. R.F.C. Hull, Trans. Princeton, NJ: Princeton University Press

_____. (1996). *The Psychology of Kundalini Yoga*. Princeton, NJ: Princeton University Press

Katsky, P. (2021). Enlightenment, individuation, and nonduality: Reflections on a dream. *Jung Journal: Culture and Psyche, 15*(1), 104-128

Prabhavananda, S. & Isherwood, C. Trans. (1975). *Śaṅkara's Crest-Jewel of Discrimination (Viveka-Chudamani)*. Hollywood, CA: Vedānta Press

Prajnananda, S. (1973). *Schools of Indian Philosophical Thought*. Calcutta, India: Firma K.L.Mukhopadhyay

Radhakrishnan, S. Ed. (1953). *The Principal Upanishads*. London: George Allen & Unwin

Radhakrishnan, S. (2008/1923). *Indian Philosophy: Volumes 1 and 2*. New Delhi, India: Oxford University Press

Sachdeva, I.P. (1978). *Yoga and Depth Psychology*. Delhi, India: Motilal Banarsidass

Schlamm, L. (2010). Revisiting Jung's dialogue with yoga: observations from transpersonal psychology. *International Journal of Jungian Studies, 2*(1), 32-44

Stein, M. (2019). Psychological individuation and spiritual enlightenment: Some comparisons and points of contact. *The Journal of Analytical Psychology, 64*(1), 6–22

Vimuktananda, S. (Trans. 2020). *Śri Śaṅkarācārya's Aparokṣanūbhuti or Self-realization*. Kolkata, India: Advaita Ashrama

Whitfield, C. (2009). *The Jungian Myth and Advaita Vedānta*. Chennai, India: Arsha Vidya Publications.

Whitney, L. (2017). Depth psychology through the lens of Classical Yoga: A reconsideration of Jung's ontic reality. *International Journal of Jungian Studies, 9*(1), 17-27

DAOISM
AND SUFISM

6

The "Secret" of the Golden Flower: The Individuation Process by Way of Daoist Practice

Ann Chia-Yi Li

Jung claimed the significance of the Daoist treatise, The Secret of the Golden Flower, for his research. This chapter explores the resonance between analytical psychology and Daoist alchemy, despite the abstruse Daoist terminology. After clarifying the difference in understanding of the term consciousness from the perspectives of Jung and this treatise, the Daoist alchemical opus is explored by way of circumambulating the concepts of primal spirit and conscious spirit. Next, Daoist practice is explained with reference to the alchemical opus formulated by Dorn and Paracelsus. Finally, the "omnipresent center" phenomenon is elaborated as a mandala, a formation process, and the essential nature of the great One, which resonates with the Self in terms of the Jungian individuation process.

The centre is omnipresent;
everything is contained in it;
it is connected with the release of the whole process of creation.[1]

---

[1] Wilhelm, 1975, p. 35-36

Prelude

The image of water, either a lake or an ocean, constantly came to mind during the days when I was pondering the theme "Eastern Practice and Individuation," to the extent that I eventually had to take a long walk through the woods where I finally arrived at Zurich Lake. Only when sitting by the lake, did I realize the tension hidden in this water image. Namely, the scene was peaceful, but I was not in peace. The medical mask in my hand was especially odd in this setting.

It was a beautiful autumn afternoon in 2020 amid the COVID-19 pandemic. Country borders were closed, cities were locked down, and people had to keep social distance and avoid even family gatherings. Although the internet helped maintain connections, somehow life became surreal. It was as if people were still together, but in fact, life fell apart; we were functioning instead of living. The many gaps in life naturally remind me of sections of a drought-affected rice field and, hence, the story of the rainmaker.

Jung was very fond of the rainmaker story told to him by sinologist Richard Wilhelm about a great drought he had experienced in China. According to Wilhelm, after many prayers and rituals had failed to stop the drought, the village people decided to fetch a rainmaker from another province — a "dried up old man."[2] The rainmaker asked for a small house, and he locked himself inside for three days. Then, on the fourth day, there came a great snowstorm, which was unexpected in that area at the time of the year. Jung further reported what Wilhelm experienced:

> The town was so full of rumours about the wonderful rain-maker that Wilhelm went to him to ask the man how he did it. In true European fashion he said: 'They call you the rain-maker, will you tell me how you made

---

[2] CW 14, § 604, n. 211

the snow?' And the little Chinese said: 'I did not make the snow, I am not responsible.' 'But what have you done these three days?' 'Oh, I can explain that. I come from another country where things are in order. Here they are out of order, they are not as they should be by the ordinance of heaven. Therefore the whole country is not in Tao, and I am also not in the natural order of things because I am in a disordered country. So I had to wait three days until I was back in Tao and then naturally the rain came.'[3]

This story beautifully reveals how the Daoist philosophy has been integrated and put into practice. It is the fundamental principle of the *I Ching* that motivates the whole process: the relatedness of the universe and humans, the macrocosm and the microcosm, within an organic wholeness. Hence, the rainmaker was not responsible for making the snow; what the rainmaker did was to be "back in Tao," and thus have the agency to mediate the reconnection of the disordered country with the "ordinance of heaven," the "natural order of things."

"Back in Tao"[4] is the core of Daoist philosophy and alchemy, it naturally includes the Daoist alchemy treatise *The Secret of the Golden Flower*. Daoist alchemy is like mysticism in that it shares a similar goal with Western alchemy; that is, to restore and redeem the celestial nature given to us in order to reunite with the ultimate One World. Daoist practice is, however, both metaphysical and physical because despite being so incomprehensible, everyone can experience it. The widespread practice of mindfulness and the "moving meditation" (動禪) seem to me to be modern and yet practical versions of Daoist inner alchemy practice, all aiming for resonation with the flow of nature. Being present in the "here and now," a subtle

---

[3] Ibid.

[4] Wilhelm chose the translation *Tao* instead of *Dao*, which keeps the Chinese pronunciation. In this chapter, *Tao* is kept when quoting Wilhelm.

communication and connection with the great One, marks Daoist alchemy as unique. This uniqueness especially attracted Jung, as he expressed in 1938 in his foreword in the second German edition of Wilhelm's translation of *The Secret of the Golden Flower*: "It was the text of the *Golden Flower* that first put me on the right track. For in medieval alchemy we have the long-sought connecting link between Gnosis and the process of the collective unconscious that can be observed in modern man."[5]

As indicated by this chapter's title, "The 'Secret' of the Golden Flower: Individuation Process by Way of Daoist Practice," I explore the essential practical and experiential nature of Daoist practice. By stressing the "secret," I mean to limit the discussion to focus only on the secrets: empty heart, the light, and the center, which are indicated in the original Daoist treatise, *The Secret of the Golden Flower*, with the hope of revealing the individuation process in terms of the Daoist alchemy opus.

Jung's Encounter with The Secret of the Golden Flower

In 1928, Wilhelm sent a copy of his translation of *The Secret of the Golden Flower* to Jung, enclosed with an invitation to Jung to write a commentary on this Daoist treatise. This commentary, together with Wilhelm's translation, was published in 1929 in German, and it took another two years to have the English version published.

Jung's commentary and elaboration on *The Secret of the Golden Flower*[6] are superb, in that he addressed the core directly. He declares, "I devoured the manuscript at once, for the text gave me an undreamt-of confirmation of my ideas about the mandala and the circumambulation of the centre."[7] Jung asserts that the text did not consist of "sentimental, overwrought mystical intuitions of pathological cranks and recluses";[8] instead, he understands the text

---

[5] CW 13, p. 4
[6] CW 13, Chap. 1
[7] Jung, 1963, p. 223
[8] CW 13, § 2

as grounding its teachings in practical insights, acknowledging the paradoxical nature of life.[9]

Jung's words mirror his intense emotions; however, at this point, it cannot be overlooked that before his encounter with *The Secret of the Golden Flower*, he had already traveled a very long and lonely way seeking an answer to unresolvable psychic phenomena. The initiation of this journey can be traced back to the two mystical accidents that Jung experienced in his early 20s at his home in the summer of 1898. Recalling them both, Jung asks, "Why and how had the table split and the knife shattered? … It seemed highly improbable to me that the Rhine would flow backwards just once, by mere chance — and all other possible explanations were automatically ruled out."[10] He was utterly at a loss for an explanation; moreover, he was annoyed at being so profoundly impressed by this impossible situation.

In 1900, after two years of experiments with a 15 ½-year-old medium, Jung concludes his observations in his doctoral dissertation, titled *On the Psychology and Pathology of So-Called Occult Phenomena*.[11] Even though it was another unfinished problem that Jung was unable to resolve, what was important to him was that he derived a psychological point of view and trusted that some objective facts exist in the human psyche. In other words, Jung seemed to have noticed that there might be an unknown force operating in our lives. Somehow, this unknown force is not strange to those who grow up within Chinese culture. For example, when the rainmaker explained to Wilhelm that he was not responsible for making the rain, he indirectly pointed out the existence of a greater force in life.

Jung furthered his research with his famous word association experiments conducted in collaboration with Franz Riklin in 1904 and discovered autonomous feeling-toned complexes in the psyche. Consequently, Jung considered the existence of an objective layer in the unconscious realm that is collective, instead of merely repressed

---

[9] Ibid., § 2-7
[10] Jung, 1963, p. 127
[11] CW 1, Chap. 1

and forgotten individual memories, as Freud claimed. In 1912, Jung published this discovery under the title *Transformations and Symbols of the Libido*,[12] which eventually caused his splitting with Freud.

Jung suffered torment from parting with Freud. As Jung puts it, "All my friends and acquaintances dropped away. My book was declared to be rubbish; I was a mystic, and that settled the matter."[13] Jung admits the inner uncertainty derived from this challenging situation, and a state of disorientation overtook him. He felt suspended in midair, as he says, "for I had not yet found my own footing."[14]

Subsequently, however, in November 1913, Jung started his many years of self-experimentation in encountering his unconscious world. These experiences and materials are the predecessors of Jung's well-known *Red Book*.[15] Moreover, Jung continued presenting papers that characterized the Zurich School of Analytical Psychology, despite the many critics from German-speaking regions. He published these papers in two books in 1916 and 1928, respectively, titled *Collected Papers on Analytical Psychology* and *Contributions to Analytical Psychology*. At this stage of his research, Jung had settled on his viewpoint that the unconscious consists of individual and collective levels; that the ego is the subject of consciousness; and that "the psyche itself, in relation to consciousness, is pre-existent and transcendent."[16]

The main occurrence that brought Jung out of his darkness after his split with Freud was his creation of a series of mandala drawings in 1918-19. In these mandalas, Jung could observe his psychic development, as he depicts it, quoting Goethe, "Formation, Transformation, Eternal Mind's eternal recreation."[17] Jung recalls:

---

[12] Later to be revised as *Symbols of Transformation*, CW 5.
[13] Jung, 1963, p. 191
[14] Ibid., p. 194
[15] Jung, 2009
[16] CW 17, § 169
[17] Jung 1963, p. 221

> Between 1918 and 1920, I began to under-
> stand that the goal of psychic development is
> the self. There is no linear evolution; there is
> only a circumambulation of the self. Uniform
> development exists, at most, only at the be-
> ginning; later, everything points towards the
> centre.[18]

Jung found the mandala to be a symbolic expression of Self. This
helps explain the crucial significance of his encounter with the
Daoist text *The Secret of the Golden Flower* in 1928. "That was the
first event which broke through my isolation," Jung claims.[19]

The Daoist Treatise: *The Secret of the Golden Flower*

In identifying the individuation process, Jung refers to the
psychic transformation that "follows the natural course of life — a
life in which the individual becomes what he always was."[20] He sees
the individuation process as a synthesis, integrating the unconscious
elements of one's personality through disintegration, letting go
of identification with the roles one plays. He finds an analogy in
alchemical distillation operations — burning away the rough *prima
materia* to obtain the purified undestroyable essential part, the *lapis*.
Jung explains this process with a metaphor: "Each step forward in
psychological development means tearing off a new veil; we are like
onions with many skins, and we have to peel ourselves again and
again to get to the real core."[21]

Whether to become what one always was or to obtain the
"real core," it extends the thought Jung claims earlier: The psyche
itself is "pre-existent and transcendent." *The Secret of the Golden
Flower* shares this same belief that life contains the celestial aspect

---

[18] Ibid., p. 222
[19] Ibid., p. 223
[20] CW 9i, § 84
[21] Jung, 1976, p. 334

with which each person is born. Despite different cultures and religions, people strive to find the origin of life. Some call it God or, as Western alchemists named it, the *unus mundus*, the One World. This ultimate reality is synonymous with what Jung referred to as the Self, an autonomous archetypal force that is the drive and goal of one's individuation process. *The Secret of the Golden Flower* depicts a similar formula in its opening paragraph:

> Master Lü-tsu said, That which exists through itself is called the Way (Tao). Tao has neither name nor shape. It is the one essence, the one primal spirit. Essence and life cannot be seen. They are contained in the light of Heaven. The light of heaven cannot be seen. It is contained in the two eyes.[22]

Dao is one of the synonyms for the preexistent and transcendent aspect of life; it is the "one essence" that enables one's life. Notably in the text, this one essence is divided into *hun* (魂) and *po* (魄) at the moment when the person was born into the physical world. *Hun* dwells in the person's heavenly heart, which lies between the two eyes, and is named "primal spirit"; *Po* binds itself to fleshly heart and is the "conscious spirit."[23] This one essence is invisible but could reveal itself in the form of the "light of Heaven."[24] However, the light of heaven is mostly invisible; hence, Daoists try to practice and regain inner tranquility and thereby to energize the primal spirit and distill the conscious spirit. The text provides a detailed explanation, as will be discussed. In general, when one closes one's eyes, one sees darkness; however, if the Daoist practice goes well and the primal spirit is strengthened, one might start to see a dim light emerging

---

[22] Wilhelm, 1975, p. 21

[23] Ibid., p. 28 In the text, Wilhelm translated *hun* and *po* as animus and anima.

[24] Ibid., p. 21

from the dark, though one's eyes are closed. This light's emergence characterizes the moment of one being "back in Tao."

Like most Daoist treatises, the central teaching of *The Secret of the Golden Flower* is in the first paragraph, and the elaborations follow thereafter with more significant details. What is unique in Wilhelm's version is that the text is accompanied by an added set of four images to help depict and elaborate on the Daoist practice process.[25] The editor of Jung's commentary on the text mistook these four images as those from the Daoist text, *Hui Ming Ching*;[26] in fact, they are the images in a well-presented Daoist treatise, *Juan Yin Zhenren Xingming Guizhi Quanshu*, published in 1622.[27] Nevertheless, this Daoist treatise grounds in the same Daoist tradition as *The Secret of the Golden Flower*; hence, from my point of view, the use of these four images to help illustrate the text's teaching for the Western readers is appropriate.[28]

The following exploration of the individuation process as experienced through Daoist practice is based on Wilhelm's translation of the Chinese edition published in 1921 by Daoist scholar Zhanran Huizhenzi (湛然慧貞子).[29] When Wilhelm was translating *The Secret of the Golden Flower*, the respected Chinese sage Lao Nai-hsuean, to whom Wilhelm referred as his honored teacher, passed away in 1921 after he completed the *I Ching* translation with Wilhelm.[30] Even so, there is no doubt that the experience of translating *I Ching* had granted Wilhelm a particular foundation for understanding Chinese culture and philosophy. In addition to this

---

[25] Ibid., pp. 27, 37, 47, 57

[26] Jung, CW13, p. 29, n. 1

[27] 《鎸尹真人性命圭旨全書》, 滌玄閣印本 (1622). See U.S. Library of Congress digital edition at https://www.loc.gov/item/2014514151/ (Last accessed 20.02.2022)

[28] Wilhelm took these four images to indicate different stages of meditation.

[29] In the preface of this edition, the publisher, Huizhenzi, explains the reason why he combines two treatises in one book and gave it a new title *Chang Sheng Shu Xu Ming Fang* 《長生術續命方》, wherein *Tai I Chin Hua Tsung Chih* 《太乙金華宗旨》, the original Chinese title of *The Secret of the Golden Flower*, appears as *Cheng Sheng Shu* 《長生術》

[30] School of Wisdom, n.d., paras. 8–10

advantage, Wilhelm was not alone. It is not difficult to imagine that the Chinese scholars who joined the Confucius Society founded by Wilhelm in Tsing Tao[31] still offered him great accompaniment in exploring and translating the Chinese religious and spiritual text. Although there might be unavoidable limitations to Wilhelm's translation work due to the language barrier, he faithfully translated and transmitted its messages. The translation is by no means a "corrupted version of *The Secret of the Golden Flower* rendered by Wilhelm," as claimed by Thomas Cleary,[32] a later translator of the text. In addition, Jeremy Zhu has pointed out that there is no reference to the sourcebook on which Cleary based his translation,[33] which makes comparison impossible.

Notably, Hedaozi (合道子), editor of the sourcebook published by Huizhenzi, explained in the epilogue[34] how others contributed to completing this edition with these seven rediscovered prefaces. However, according to these prefaces, even though the context of the treatise was revised a few times, the structure of the 13 chapters was maintained. Many Daoist alchemy treatises were initially transmitted orally, so that each edition is slightly different in wording. Nevertheless, the teachings keep the same track. Even though Wilhelm decided to translate only the first eight chapters, the original Chinese copy he read indeed consisted of 13 chapters. Compared to another version of *The Secret of the Golden Flower* previously published in 1831, for example, the version which Huizhenzi published and Wilhelm read keeps the same format. I therefore find no grounds for Cleary's critique that Wilhelm had "misconstructed the text on many points."[35]

---

[31] Ibid.

[32] Cleary, 1991, p. 136

[33] Zhu, 2009

[34] "Epilogue," *Chang Sheng Shu* (Huizhenzi, 1921, p. 43)

[35] Cleary, 1991, p. 134

Mandala, the Light Buried in the Water-Region

The following vital sentences in the first chapter of *The Secret of the Golden Flower* once more paraphrase the primary teaching of this treatise: "The Golden Flower is the light. What colour is the light? One uses the Golden Flower as a symbol. It is the true energy of the transcendent great One. The phrase 'The lead of the water-region has but one taste' refers to it."[36]

Daoist alchemy terminology can be abstruse. To account for this, the readers of Wilhelm's edition will notice paragraphs printed in a smaller font amid the text. This is the commentary especially added by the Daoist scholar and publisher Huizhenzi (慧貞子) in his 1921 edition to help readers who are either beginners or non-Daoist practitioners to understand the treatise at the critical historical moment of China's religious reawakening against the invasion from the Western World.[37] Now, these notes are a tremendous help, making it possible for readers to decode the Daoist perspective on the metaphysical concepts presented.

What is the "one taste" in the "water-region"? Huizhenzi explains, "Heaven created water through the One."[38] This instruction reveals that Daoist alchemy has its root in *I Ching* philosophy. Cary F. Baynes is the translator of the English edition of Wilhelm's *I Ching* and *The Secret of the Golden Flower*. She received permission from his son, Hellmut Wilhelm, to omit this statement because "in

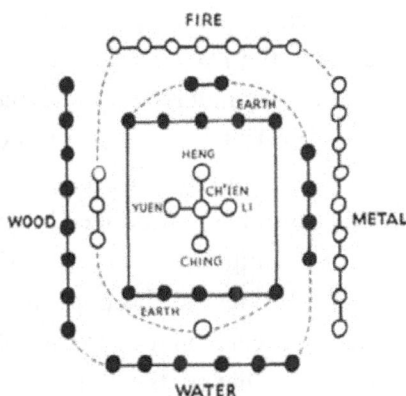

Figure 1: River Map

---

[36] Wilhelm, 1975, p. 21

[37] For more information on the background of this edition of *The Secret of the Golden Flower*, please see Wilhelm's discussion in "Origin and Contents of the *T'ai I Chin Hua Tsung Chih*" in *The Secret of the Golden Flower* (1975, pp. 3-10).

[38] Cited in Wilhelm, 1975, p. 21

the German text the *Book of Changes* is said to be the origin of this sentence. It does not occur there."[39] In fact, the related oral instruction of the *I Ching* principle can be found in Wilhelm's (1977) translation, "Book II," "*Ta Chuan*: The Great Treatise," in "Chapter IX: On the Oracle:" "Heaven is one, earth is two; heaven is three, earth four; heaven is five, earth six; heaven is seven. Earth eight; heaven is nine, earth ten."[40] These numbers map out the diagram known as *Ho T'u*, the "River Map," and often it is depicted together with *wu hsing*, the Five Elements System. For example, in "Concerning Mandala Symbolism," Jung presents the integrated diagram (Figure 1) as an example of a mandala.[41]

Jung describes the legend of the River Map (Figure 1) and in it "the laws of the world-order."[42] Jung also notices that the knotted cords signify numbers: "All uneven numbers are masculine, even numbers feminine." In *I Ching* terminology, the opposite masculine and feminine pair is termed Heaven and Earth, clarifying that in this very sentence, "Heaven created water through the One," these words — "Heaven ... water ... One,"[43] are not symbols but the signs and terms in the *Ho T'u* and *wu hsing* system.

To understand the dynamic of "the laws of the world-order" in Figure 1, it must be combined with the third *I Ching* instruction — the postnatal eight trigrams. In this postnatal eight trigram system, each trigram is symbolized by a specific natural element; for example, the Arousing is thunder, the Abysmal is water, and the Clinging is fire.[44] Besides, in the postnatal eight trigrams, the Abysmal (K'an) trigram locates in the direction North, where the number 1 of *Ho T'u* is located; hence, the "Heaven One" location is the Abysmal "water-region." Moreover, the term *Abysmal water* could also refer to the

---

[39] Ibid., 1962, p. 21, n. 2
[40] Wilhelm, 1977, p. 308
[41] CW 9i, p. 356f, fig. 2
[42] Ibid., § 642
[43] Wilhelm, 1977, p. 308
[44] Ibid., p. 226-227

midnight of the day, the winter of the year, the color black, the abyss of darkness, the uncertainty of psychic disturbance, and the chaos of *prima materia* in alchemy. All depict different facets of a decisive transitional moment.

Psychologically, this "Heaven One water-region" location could be the borderland, where conscious and unconscious both are present. It could also be the liminal space, possibly transitioning to another psychic state. This is the threshold of a life-or-death decisive moment, which, in *The Secret of the Golden Flower*, is particularly depicted with the time slot *Zhi Shi* (子時). In *I Ching* instruction, this is a unit of a time system, and it overlaps the location of the Abysmal (K'an) trigram when compared with the postnatal eight trigrams. In its current expression, *Zhi Shi* refers to the duration from 11:00 p.m., at midnight, to 1:00 a.m., the dim new dawn of the next day! Moreover, it is equivalent to the term *third watch* when counted in another Chinese ancient time system. It is the deepest night and can be compared to the alchemical stage of *nigredo*.

With the help of these Daoist terms, we may start to understand what is so crucial in this "Heaven One water-region." Huizhenzi (慧貞子) indicates that it holds "the true energy of the great One."[45] Daoist Master Lü-tsu, whose teachings are documented in *The Secret of the Golden Flower*, uses the undivided yang line, which is contained in the middle of the Abysmal (K'an) trigram, to depict the location and nature of the true energy of the great One: "The third watch is the Abysmal (K'an, water). The sun's disk is the one polar line in the trigram for water, which is about to turn into the Creative."[46]

As this may be arcane terminology, perhaps the text by Paracelsus, a 16th-century Swiss alchemist, helps to rephrase the same phenomena. He claims that the dim light that reveals itself in the critical situation of *nigredo* is the *lumen naturae*, that is, the light

---

[45] Cited in Wilhelm, 1975, p. 21
[46] Wilhelm, 1975, p. 58

of nature. It is "the divine spark buried in the darkness."[47] Moreover, it is not the light that shines from above or from outside; instead, "the *lumen naturae* is the light of the darkness itself, which illuminates its own darkness, and this light the darkness comprehends."[48] The Gnostic view adopted by Western alchemists also resonates, as they "took the *prima materia* to be part of the original chaos pregnant with spirit";[49] here, "spirit" refers to the divine *anima mundi,* which "remained in matter in a potential state."[50]

In discussing some specific problem of psychotherapy, Jung expresses another similar observation: "The unconscious is not just evil by nature, it is also the source of the highest good: not only dark but also light, not only bestial, semi-human, and demonic but superhuman, spiritual, and, in the classical sense of the word, 'divine.'"[51]

Neurosis often announces itself in the form of unbearable anxiety and endless entanglement with unresolvable problems. However, as Jung observes from his experience and his clinical practice, "mandalas ... usually appear in situations of psychic confusion and perplexity."[52] This indicates the existence of an invisible and latent operation in the larger scope of one's life that attempts to restore the balance. Therefore, as Jung points out, alchemy's aim is "to extract the original divine spirit out of the chaos."[53]

What about the metal lead in the water-region? In general, Daoist alchemists use the metal mercury as a metaphor for restless thoughts; and the metal lead is the metaphor for the primal spirit. It depicts the phenomenon that in the heating and fusion process, the metal lead is able to stabilize the everchanging mercury. It is also worth noticing that, when freshly cut, the metal lead reveals its

---

[47] CW 13, § 197
[48] Ibid.
[49] CW 11 § 160
[50] Ibid.
[51] CW 16, § 389
[52] CW 10, § 803
[53] CW 11, § 160

essential silvery whiteness. It is oxidization that turns its surface into dull gray. I argue that this phenomenon also depicts the divine nature being clouded, which responds to the teaching in *The Secret of the Golden Flower*, owing to the "deepest secret"[54] of Daoist practice: "This is the washing of the heart and the purification of the thoughts; this is the bath."[55] Naturally, both the rediscovered whiteness of the lead and "the sun's disk"[56] remind me of the *albedo*. Daoists view this light that is incubated in the water as one's true essence given by the great One. In other words, at birth, one brings with oneself part of the ancestral spirit as one's nature, thus everyone has the birthright to be at home and rooted in the original oneness; however, this true essence is deeply concealed in the dark physical world. It is therefore crucial to revive the preexistent and transcendent aspect of life, *the Creative*, a synonym for the primal essence. Huizhenzi's comment, "If man attains this One he becomes alive; if he loses it he dies,"[57] reflects the standpoint of Daoist practice, which resonates with Jung's thoughts: We are paradoxically searching for what we have already had.

"Consciousness" and the *Klesha*

Based on his central teaching, Master Lü-tsu elaborates in great detail on rediscovering the latent primal, essential nature by circulating the light. First, he depicts the different essential natures of the primal spirit and the conscious spirit: "When men are set free from the womb, the primal spirit dwells in the square inch (between the eyes), but the conscious spirit dwells below in the heart."[58] Understanding this sentence is especially crucial because it maps out Daoists' perspective on an individual's relationship with the universal great One. This statement provides a more precise impression that a

---

[54] Wilhelm, 1975, p. 59
[55] Ibid.
[56] Ibid, p. 58
[57] Cited in Wilhelm, 1975, p. 21
[58] Ibid., p. 25

transcendent eternal life preexists before one is born into a physical body, a notion that resonates with Jung's assumption in his doctoral dissertation mentioned above. There is a greater and collective subject prior to an individual's life.

As mentioned, the great One is the primal spirit dwelling in the Heavenly heart, and it is perceived by the individual's bodily heart as conscious spirit. In other words, when personal life takes form, it naturally falls into the duality of form and formless; thus, in some way, one is no longer home with the origin of life, the great One. Instead, one carries it within and sets out on a personal life journey in a dualistic mode. Consequently, in their practice, Daoists strive to face the necessary dualism in the individual's world and, at the same time, maintain within themselves the nondual, great-One homeland. Essentially, Daoists navigate balance and relatedness by "action through non-action."[59]

Before speculating on the relationship of this pair of opposites — the *primal spirit* and the *conscious spirit* — the nature of *consciousness* must be clarified in the context of *The Secret of the Golden Flower*. This might help explain some confusion when reading Jung's commentary on Wilhelm's translation because Jung and the Daoists use the same term to refer to different things. Jung identifies *individuation* as a process of becoming conscious; however, in terms of Daoism, Master Lü-tsu explains the conscious spirit, which "dwells in the heart," in this way: "This lower fleshly heart has the shape of a large peach; it is covered by the wings of the lungs, supported by the liver, and served by the bowels. This heart is dependent on the outside world."[60]

This "fleshly heart" where the conscious spirit dwells is not the same as the "heavenly heart," which is in the square inch between two eyes, where the primal spirit lives. The "fleshly heart" indicates the connection of conscious spirit with one's fleshly

---

[59] Ibid., p. 53
[60] Ibid., p. 25

physical sensations; in other words, the consciousness derived from the conscious spirit is very possibly the result of one's perceptions entangled with one's sensed desires. Consequently, if the conscious spirit "hears something terrifying, it feels extremely uncomfortable. If it hears something enraging it stops; if it is faced with death it becomes sad; if it sees something beautiful it is dazzled."[61] Moreover, "it is the conscious spirit which after death is nourished on blood, but which, during life, is in great distress. The dark returns to darkness and like things attract each other according to their kind."[62]

Daoists apparently use the term *consciousness* in a specific way. It seems that this kind of consciousness derived from the fleshly attached conscious spirit is susceptible to its surroundings and that within it, there is an autonomous dynamic that reminds me of the "feeling-toned complex," as described in Jungian psychology: "Every constellation of a complex postulates a disturbed state of consciousness. The unity of consciousness is disrupted and the intentions of the will are impeded or made impossible."[63] It might appear confusing when first reading the two streams of thought — Jungian and Daoism — using the same term in different ways, not to mention all the related synonyms. Radically speaking, in the context of *The Secret of the Golden Flower*, *consciousness* is more likely to refer to the psychic state in which, as Jung reminds us, "complexes can *have us*."[64] From the Jungian perspective, this state signals the outbreak of neurosis: "The complex establishes itself on the conscious surface; it can no longer be circumvented and proceeds to assimilate the ego-consciousness step by step."[65]

The viewpoint on consciousness presented in *The Secret of the Golden Flower* might be due to the impact of Buddhism, which Daoist alchemy integrates into its teaching. The dialogue between

---

[61] Ibid.
[62] Ibid., p. 28
[63] CW 8, § 200
[64] Ibid.
[65] Ibid., § 207

Jung and Zen master Shin'ichi Hisamatsu[66] is a possible reference point for this discussion. In 1958, Jung received this special guest at his house in Küsnacht and had the following conversation on the joys and sorrows that emerged in fairy tales:

> Jung: They are instinctive activities which
> can be observed in animals. Probably
> one can say that the issues surrounding
> the so-called Kleśa concern the
> various aspects and symptoms of the
> unconscious.
> Hisamatsu: From our point of view, the
> Kleśa belong, rather, to the sphere of
> consciousness.[67]

Regarding the *Klesha* (Kleśa), Jung understands them according to Sanskrit as the instinctual forces of the psyche, and "the yoking aims at controlling these forces that fetter human beings to the world."[68] The clear response from Hisamatsu is that from the perspective of Zen Buddhism, the chaotic instinctual forces instead belong to "the sphere of consciousness."[69] This example illustrates that Eastern practice and analytical psychology might share a similar process of becoming conscious, or individuation, but express the same phenomena with different terminology. In terms of consciousness, they even endow different definitions to the same word.

The Conscious Spirit

The kind of consciousness referred to in *The Secret of the Golden Flower* as involving the *Klesha* needs distillation and purification to avoid the consequent neurotic dissociation of the personality. The conscious spirit might play the key role in this

---

[66] Shin'ichi Hisamatsu (1889-1980), Japanese Zen scholar and philosopher.
[67] Jung & Hisamatsu, 1992, p. 105
[68] CW 11, § 912
[69] Jung & Hisamatsu, 1992, p. 105

distilling process. The text reads, "The primal spirit loves stillness, and the conscious spirit loves movement. In its movement it remains bound to feelings and desires. Day and night it wastes the primal seed till the energy of the primal spirit is entirely used up."[70]

The role of the conscious spirit, which dwells in the "lower fleshy heart," is as the agent for an individual's life in the physical world. In the context of *The Secret of the Golden Flower*, this conscious spirit, which "remains bound to feelings and desires,"[71] seems to be driven or impeded. Its situation reminds me of an ensnared ego that is not capable of integrating the unconscious materials and, instead, can only be taken away and alienated from Self. Master Lü-tsu thus wants his pupils to distill their consciousness, to bathe and "to wash the heart"[72] to purify their thoughts.

To help clarify the importance of this distillation process of "washing the heart," I borrow the formula expressed by the 16th-century alchemist Gerhard Dorn. From his point of view, alchemical distillation would help complete the union of the trinity — spirit, soul, and body — and thus achieve *unus mundus*. Basically, the "inextricable interweaving of the soul with the body"[73] would only occur in the state of *nigredo*, wherein the soul mingles with the body and what they produce is but "a dark unity."[74] The alchemists' task for this stage of work is *separatio*, which means setting the soul free from its fetters in bodily desires. Psychologically, *separatio* could also mean recognizing one's shadows and withdrawing one's projections, or as Master Lü-tsu says, distilling the thoughts and "melt[ing] out completely the slag of darkness."[75]

In regard to redeeming one's true divine quality, Dorn claimed that first, the purified soul would be set free from the body

---

[70] Wilhelm, 1975, p. 29
[71] Ibid., p. 29
[72] Ibid., p. 53
[73] CW 14, § 696
[74] Ibid.
[75] Wilhelm, 1975, p. 26

and reunited with the spirit. In this way, soul and spirit form the state of *unio mentalis*, "which is at the same time a substance-like 'truth' hidden in the body."[76] Then, to produce the quintessence in the individual, the last stage is the *unio mentalis* returning and reuniting with the body, thus achieving the phenomenon of *unus mundus*.

I assume that the Daoist term *conscious spirit* relates to two entities — the body and the soul. Compared with Dorn's formula, the *conscious spirit* is parallel to the soul, and the *fleshly heart* is similar to the body. Here, I am not equating the conscious spirit with the soul. By a parallel, I mean to address the importance of distilling the *Klesha* 'consciousness' away from the conscious spirit, so as to set the conscious spirit free from the fetters of bodily desires. This would be the beginning of resuming the dialogue with primal spirit.

Not to be overlooked is the Daoist message that "the deepest secret of the bath that is to be found in our teaching is … confined to the work of making the heart empty."[77] In this context, *heart* refers to the *fleshly heart*, the emptiness refers to *Klesha* "consciousness" being washed away. Nevertheless, Daoists also attempt to "yoke" the fleshly heart by guiding its chaotic movement into another form of movement: continuous rhythmic breathing. The movement is thus transformed, not changed. In my view, this approach also exemplifies the Daoist way, which makes progress by way of acceptance. The following quote from *The Secret of the Golden Flower* offers a clear example of how the Daoists put their metaphysical thoughts into practice:

> So, then, should a man have no imaginings in his mind? One cannot be without imaginings. Should one not breathe? One can not do without breathing. The best way is to make a medicine of the illness. Since heart and breath are mutually dependent, the circulation of

---

[76] CW 14, § 695
[77] Wilhelm, 1975, p. 59

the light must be united with the rhythm of
breathing.[78]

This passage reminds me of Dorn's formula in that the last
stage of the alchemical process of reviving the *unus mundus* is
reuniting spirit and soul with the body. In this way, paradoxically,
the body and the sensing fleshy heart are prepared as the furnace to
contain the spirit and soul for the alchemical process:

> For this, light of the ear is above all necessary.
> There is a light of the eyes and a light of the
> ear. The light of the eyes is the united light of
> the sun and moon outside. The light of the ear
> is the united seed of sun and moon within. The
> seed is thus the light in crystallized form.[79]

How, then, is the heart used during the practice? It follows
the principle of action through nonaction; hence, in meditation, "it
is a use without use,"[80] as described in reference to other sensing
organs: "In this sort of hearing, one hears only that there is no sound;
in this kind of seeing, one sees only that no shape is there. ... Only
when one looks and hearkens inward does the organ not go outward
nor sink inward."[81]

The fleshly heart is "washed" and tamed and is functioning.
Eventually, the conscious spirit becomes as free as a piece of mirror,
not being affected or dominated by what it encounters, meaning both
the bodily sensations and the greater archetypal forces. These might
occupy the mirror's surface but may not be capable of altering its
essential nature and clarity; hence, the refined conscious spirit will
not be captured by either a complex or inflation. As in actual practice,
"all entanglements must be put aside, one must be detached and

---

[78] Ibid., p. 40
[79] Ibid.
[80] Ibid., p. 43
[81] Ibid., p. 44

independent."[82] Notably, the original Chinese phrase for "detached and independent" is *XingXing Ziruo* (惺惺自若). The word *Xing*[83] consists of a heart and a star. It depicts the mind staying awake in the night, like the dim light of a star in the dark. The phrase *XingXing Ziruo* thus initially intimates that during the practice of meditation, one remains stable with awareness in the incomprehensible process, like the stars in the night. This is the ideal objective conscious spirit for which Daoist practitioners strive and which makes the witnessing and bridging of the inner process possible.

I assume that *conscious spirit* could be a synonym for *ego*, but maybe not in the way that Jung perceives and interprets it in his understanding of Eastern practice: "Such an ego-less mental condition can only be unconscious to us, for the simple reason that there would be nobody to witness it."[84] Instead, in Daoist terms, *ego-less* is more an attentive psychic mode and therefore a fully present ego in a way that the conscious spirit can simply *be* and not become entangled. Master Lü-tsu clearly explains, "To kill the heart does not mean to let it dry and wither away, but it means that it has become undivided and gathered into one";[85] therefore, "one hears only that there is no sound," and "one sees only that no shape is there."[86] In actual practice, this attentive psychic mode can be experienced as a kind of presence when one is simply perceiving and being, not moving one step further to name, to judge, and to analyze. The ego-less state of the conscious spirit could also be a type of subtle relatedness to surroundings rather than purposive attachment. In this mode, the universal great One lives through the individual; both exist to contain each other.

---

[82] Ibid., p. 46
[83] 《康熙字典》 See https://zd.hwxnet.com/search/hwxE6hwx83hwxBA.html (Last accessed 20.02.2022)
[84] CW 11, § 774
[85] Wilhelm, 1975, p. 42
[86] Ibid., p. 44

The Center, the Blooming Mandala

The center is the gate to reach the light; or paradoxically, the center is the light. I perceive three layers of meaning for *center* in the context of *The Secret of the Golden Flower* — its presence as a mandala, its formation as a process, and its essential nature as the great One. In general, Daoists depict the attentive state of the psyche in their meditation practice as the phenomena of "center." As Master Lü-tsu reveals, "the centre is omnipresent; everything is contained in it; it is connected with the release of the whole process of creation."[87]

This particular existential phenomenon of the center might relate to Jung's understanding of Self. In discussing the process of individuation, Marie-Louise von Franz posits that "the organizing centre from which the regulatory effect stems seems to be a sort of 'nuclear atom' in our psychic system. ... Jung called this centre the 'Self' and described it as the totality of the whole psyche."[88] Jung figuratively depicts the Self as "God within us"[89] and elaborates: "The beginnings of our whole psychic life seem to be inextricably rooted in this point, and all our highest and ultimate purpose seem to be striving towards it."[90] The center introduced in *The Secret of the Golden Flower* is also a paradox: It characterizes the start point, the process, and the totality of one's life.

Despite this ancient wisdom and Jung's theory, we might still be left with endless wonderings about where this center is located, how it presents itself in everyday life, and the ways in which we can be in touch with it and experience it. The text claims that "the centre is omnipresent."[91] In terms of psyche, Jung comments that "the East has produced nothing equivalent to what we call psychology, but rather philosophy or metaphysics."[92] Regarding where the center

---

[87] Ibid., p. 36
[88] von Franz, 1978, p. 161-162
[89] CW 7, § 399
[90] Ibid.
[91] Wilhelm, 1975, p. 35
[92] CW 11, § 759

is, this question resonates with Jung's observation that alchemy explains "the obscure by the more obscure, the unknown by the more unknown."[93]

Figure 2

Based on my study of the Daoist treatises, it seems informative to research the Chinese etymology of the word *center*. According to *Shuowen Jiezi,* the first Chinese dictionary, circa early second century, in the Han Dynasty, the Chinese word for *center* is *zhong*.[94] We learn from the commentary of this dictionary that this pictogram *zhong* (Figure 2) consists of an interior space and a channel that accommodates the free flow of the above and below.[95] *Zhong* can be traced further back to 1,600 B.C.E., in the oracle bone script of the Shang Dynasty. The square in the middle is a neutral interior shared by both the two antagonistic military troops or political forces (Figure 3).[96] The confrontation of the hostile opposites is depicted by the flags standing on either side of the neutral interior. In this depiction, the

Figure 3

neutral interior is a space capable of containing both hostile opposites, though not without tensions. Notably, if there is no confrontation of the opposite antagonistic forces, there will be no neutral space created in between. It could be said that the hostile opposing forces give birth to the center's neutral point despite the uncertainties. To associate this definition of center with reviving the buried divine one essence, this neutral space shared by the opposites could be a synonym for the dark realm represented by the Abysmal (K'an) trigram. As previously described, this is a

---

[93] CW 12, § 332

[94] 《説文解字》 See https://ctext.org/library.pl?if=gb&fi le=77389&page=28 (Last accessed 20.02.2022)

[95] Duan Yucai, (1815) *Shuowen Jiezi Zhu.* 段玉裁 (1974)《説文解字注》台北：蘭台書局。（原版1815）

[96] From *Jia Gu Wen Zi Dian: Vol. 1* (Shu Zhong Shu, Ed.), 1989, Sichuan Dictionary Publishing, p. 39. 《甲骨文字典》卷一. 徐中舒編, 成都：四川辭書出版社

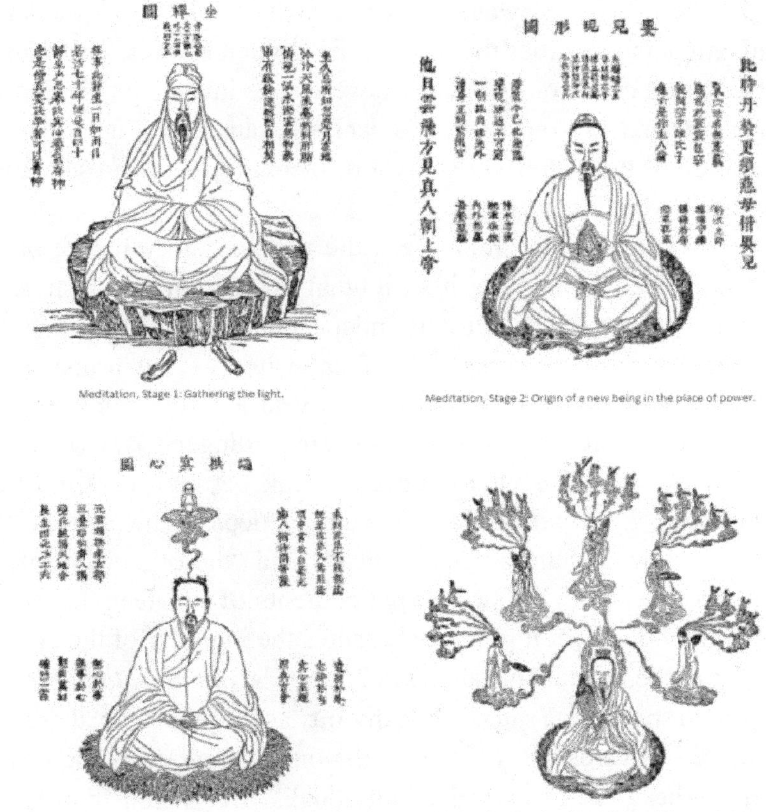

Meditation, Stage 1: Gathering the light.

Meditation, Stage 2: Origin of a new being in the place of power.

Meditation, Stage 3: Separation of the spirit-body for independent existence.

Meditation, Stage 4: The centre in the midst of the conditions.

Figure 4: The stages of meditation

borderland where night and day, unconscious and conscious meet. Their existence is equally granted, yet with tension.

Furthermore, it may be similarly fitting to zoom in and find that the center also indicates the exact point, the split second when the conscious spirit and the primal spirit restore the lost relatedness and connection. The Daoist text describes this dynamic in actual practice: "When a man can let his heart die, then the primal spirit wakes to life."[97] This is the meaningful transition taking place

---

[97] Wilhelm, 1975, p. 42

207

in *Zhi Shi* (子時). However dim the revived light is, it marks an awakening and signifies the birth of the Golden Flower, an initiation of becoming conscious of who we were. The images for meditation stages one and two represent this decisive transition (Figure 4). The revelation of the center's first layer of meaning — the presence of a mandala — begins.

Whereas Jung emphasizes the compensatory nature of the opposites, Daoists express it as mutual generation and restriction. Because the conscious spirit is independent and can perceive the presence of the other, this pair of opposites — the primal spirit and the conscious spirit — seem to reveal a further dimension, a phenomenon that resonates with Edward Edinger's description of the ego-self axis, the vital connecting link between ego and Self. In his book *Ego and Archetype*, Edinger depicts the Self as "the original mandala-state of personality"[98] and "the organic whole."[99] The encounter with the archetypal contents of life feels numinous to the individual, yet it possibly "ensures the integrity of the ego."[100]

In the formula presented in *The Secret of the Golden Flower*, the primal spirit is the same subtle divinity as the great One; therefore, the more it revives and circulates, the more it embodies the eternal truth of the great One in the individual's life. When the organic whole of life is bridged and operates in the individual's life, "just as when the master is quiet and calm, men-servants and maids obey his orders of their own accord, and each does it work."[101] Meanwhile, the refined, mirrorlike conscious spirit is competitive enough to hold the dialogue with the primal spirit. The continuous mutual generation and restriction form the back-and-forth communication of the primal spirit and the conscious spirit. With this continual rotation and circulation moving along, the great One submits to further embodiment in the individual with the help of the purified

---

[98] Edinger, 1972, p. 4
[99] Ibid., p. 100
[100] Ibid., p. 6
[101] Wilhelm, 1975, p. 22

conscious spirit that can perceive its energy and message. In this process, "related things attract each other. ... It is not only the light in the abyss, but it is creative light which meets creative light."[102] Reviving the primal spirit is a "moment of true creative union,"[103] and as the text expresses, "the Way of the Golden Flower depends wholly on the backward-flowing method."[104] (I would add, however, that one might risk misinterpretation if one takes this term literally and practices with energy "flowing backward.")

The "backward-flowing method" refers to meditation, the practical way and process of redeeming and circulating the light, which the Golden Flower symbolizes. This method, or process, is depicted as *Yuan Zhong* (緣中). Wilhelm translates this term as "the centre in the midst of conditions,"[105] whereas Cleary translates it as "focus on the centre."[106] Both translations depict one facet of this phenomenon. Because Chinese words are organic and living images, there is another aspect: The Chinese word *Yuan* means "hem," the margin or edge of clothing. When used as a verb, *Yuan* represents the way and process of "moving along" something; hence, it also signifies the intimate relatedness of the relationship with the other. When moving along, like the hem fitting to whatever shapes the piece of cloth takes, one relates to *Zhong*, the center, the eternal existence with eternal change due to the contentious dialogue between the primal spirit and the conscious spirit. One's subtle relatedness with the organic center is *Yuan Zhong*.

The text expounds on the process of *Yuan Zhong* with reference to Buddhist practice of "fixating contemplation" (or *Zhi Gwan*, 止觀), as translated by Wilhelm: "When the flight of

---

[102] Ibid., p. 55
[103] Ibid.
[104] Ibid., p. 31
[105] Ibid., p. 35
[106] Cleary, 1991, p. 20

the thoughts keeps extending further, one should stop and begin contemplating. Let one contemplate and then start fixating again."[107]

At this point, it is clear that, within the realm of the center, there is this circular process moving along with the dialogue of the primal spirit and conscious spirit, that is, tranquil infinity and restless thoughts. In the meditative process, one observes and perceives where the thoughts emerge and originate and where they head. One is reminded that something better or more will never come forth if one tries to push the reflection or trace the thoughts further. Doing so might lead one to risk giving power to external circumstances and falling into one-sidedness, whereby the practitioner becomes alienated from the root of life.

On the other hand, one is also reminded that it is not wise to hold on to the tranquility of contemplation, which is but another type of one-sidedness that leads the practitioner to dissociate from the physical world. Both *Yuan Zhing* and "fixating contemplation"[108] indicate the importance of navigating the subtle relatedness to let the great One become embodied in one's life; thence, one is based in a dual physical world but is capable of freeing oneself from the opposites and reconnecting the nondual part of life, the one essence. Put another way, practicing fixation and contemplation will naturally form a spiral process, like *Yuan Zhong*, or the alchemical distillation *opus*, or what Jung comprehends as "circumambulation of the centre."[109] Reporting this revelation with a phrase borrowed from Goethe, Jung writes, "Only gradually did I discover what the mandala really is: 'Formation, Transformation, Eternal Mind's eternal recreation.'"[110]

This image in figure 4, titled "The centre in the midst of the conditions," might exemplify this mandala formation as a blooming golden flower. We can see that this image depicts the practice of

---

[107] Wilhelm, 1975, p. 36
[108] Ibid., p. 35
[109] Jung, 1963, p. 223
[110] Ibid., p. 221

Yuan Zhong, which emphasizes the state of the individual when encountering the divine great One. However sublime the archetypal energy is, the individual remains attentive and competent to perceive and embody the divine energy, like a firm furnace that can hold the continuous transforming process. In this state, one might feel "a sense of great joy as if intoxicated or freshly bathed" and that "the earth is a world of light and brightness."[111] As the text states, "the fragile body of the flesh is sheer gold and diamonds. That is a sign that the Golden Flower is crystallized."[112]

The ultimate result of the practice is restoration of the divine nature given to us, being "back in Tao." Nevertheless, at this point, one has not yet reached the final destination. Paradoxically, it is equally dangerous to encounter the numinous crystallizing Golden Flower because the gravity of tranquility seduces one to overidentify with it. In that case, the practitioner will only fall into the other pole of one-sidedness. The practice revealed in *The Secret of the Golden Flower* encourages pupils to maintain the rotation of the primal spirit and the conscious spirit. This is the way. The goal of alchemy is the operation, the work, the *opus*; therefore, after the sage (Figure 4) forms the diamond body, the *opus* is not ended but instead takes place at a further-advanced level, resembling *the process of formation, transformation, and the Eternal Mind's eternal recreation.*

I am aware that this viewpoint is different from Jung's commentary on this Daoist treatise. He associates the fourth-stage meditation image with the understanding that the unconscious has "a decidedly disintegrating effect on consciousness."[113] Accordingly, he sees the head of the sage as surrounded by "tongues of fire, out of which five human figures emerge," and "these five again split up into twenty-five smaller figures," and Jung worries that this "would be a schizophrenic process if it were to become a permanent state."[114]

---

[111] Wilhelm, 1975, p. 49
[112] Ibid.
[113] CW 13, § 46
[114] Ibid.

I would reserve the possibility of not taking these small figures for "bizarre spirit-beings" and "fragmentary psychic systems," as John James Clarke expounds.[115] Instead, I argue that the fourth-stage meditation image in figure 4 depicts a state of *unus mundus*, a reunion with the divine great One. Hence, the individual is simultaneously present and beyond, as we can see that all these figures look the same as the practitioner. Moreover, it would be advisable to pay attention to the particular order defined by the repeated layers, whereby one spirit-being gives birth to five spirit-beings. The number five depicted in this image also reminds me of the *center*. According to Daoist alchemy and its use of *I Ching* terminology, the number five is located in the middle position of *Ho T'u*, the "River Map" (Figure 1). It is the pivot that bridges the pairs of Heaven and Earth numbers on each side; hence, the number five resembles the center in symbolizing the harmonious balance created by the antagonistic opposites. This is the moment the golden flower is blooming, the wholeness embodied after all the circumambulating process, hence the center is omnipresent.

Postlude

My impression is that the rainmaker, the "dried up old man," according to Wilhelm,[116] exemplifies the Daoist *Yuan Zhong* lifestyle encouraged in the alchemical treatise *The Secret of the Golden Flower*. *Yuan Zhong* synthesizes life as it was, situating one in the here and now. With this clarity in body, mind, and spirit, one is grounded and yet intimate with the metaphysical universe. Life might be simple, but it is contained. Acceptance of uncertainty and openness to the profound mystery become the basis of daily life.

This principle reminds me of one of my earliest memories — the days when I was wandering near my grandparents on our rice farm. "The rain might be coming! We shall be ready to go home,"

---

[115] Clarke, 1994, p. 86
[116] CW 14, p. 419, n. 211

said my grandpa, with his hands speeding up to finish the work. My grandma looked at the cloud and seemed to confirm his assessment by packing the tools and dragging me to wash my feet in the tiny ditch. I was fond of that rhythm of quietness and relatedness. It seemed to me that the sky always told my grandpa something. That's why he knew.

References

Clarke, J. J. (1994). *Jung and Eastern thought: A Dialogue with the Orient.* London: Routledge

Cleary, T. (1991). Translator's afterword: Modern applications of the golden flower method. In T. Cleary, *The Secret of the Golden Flower.* pp. 131–153. New York: Harper San Francisco

Edinger, E. F. (1972). *Ego and Archetype.* Boston: Shambhala

Jung, C. G. (1916). *Collected Papers on Analytical Psychology* (2nd ed)., C. Long, Ed.; M. D. Eder, A. A. Brill, E. Eder, C. E. Long, & D. Hecht, Trans. London: Baillière, Tindall and Cox

_____. (1928). *Contributions to Analytical Psychology.* H. G. Baynes & C. F. Baynes, Trans. London: Harcourt, Brace & Co.

_____. (1963). *Memories, Dreams, Reflections.* A. Jaffé, Ed., R. Winston & C. Winston, Trans. London: Fontana Press

_____. (1976). *The Visions Seminars: Notes of the seminar given in 1930-1934.* Vol. 2. C. Douglas, Ed. Zurich: Spring Publications

_____. (2009). *The Red Book: Liber Novus.* S. Shamdasani, Ed. S. Shamdasani, M. Kyburz, & J. Peck, Trans. London: Norton

_____. (1992). Self and liberation: A dialogue between Carl G. Jung and Shin'ichi Hisamatsu. In D. J. Meckel & R. L. Moore, Eds. *Self and Liberation: The Jung-Buddhism Dialogue.* pp. 103–113. New York: Paulist Press

School of Wisdom. (n.d.). Richard Wilhelm: One of the School of Wisdom's Most Notable Teachers. https://schoolofwisdom.com/about/richard-wilhelm-one-of-the-school-of-wisdoms-most-notableteachers (Last accessed 20.02.2022)

von Franz, M.-L. (1978). The process of individuation. In C. G. Jung & M.-L. von Franz Eds. *Man and His Symbols.* pp. 157–254. London: Picador

Wilhelm, R. Trans. (1975). *The Secret of the Golden Flower.* C. F. Baynes, Trans. London: Routledge & Kegan Paul

Wilhelm, R. Trans. (1977). *The I Ching or Book of Changes.* C. F. Baynes, Trans. Princeton: Princeton University Press

Zhu, J. C. (2009). Analytical psychology and Daoist inner alchemy: A response to C.G. Jung's 'Commentary on the secret of the golden flower.' *Journal of Analytical Psychology, 54*(4), 493–511

List of Figures

7

Rest in Peace: *Entering the Paradise of Consciousness Itself: Self-realization and Individuation*

Karin Jironet

> *"Consciousness can only exist through continual recognition of the unconscious, just as everything that lives must pass through many deaths."*[1]

Introduction

Carl Gustav Jung took an approach to research so bold that most scholars today would never dare: using himself, his subjective experiences, and a meticulous analysis of these as *prima materia* for the objectified theory that became known as analytical psychology. A primary goal of analytical psychology is individuation, or the achievement of self-realization through a process of integrating the conscious and the unconscious.[2] As Jung frames it:

---

[1] CW 9i, § 178-179

[2] http://journalpsyche.org/jung-and-his-individuation-process (Last accessed 02-02-2022). *Principium individuationis* is a concept borrowed from Arthur Schopenhauer (1819) in *The World as Will and Representation,* who in turn borrowed it from Scholasticism.

> Individuation means becoming an 'in-dividu-
> al,' and, in so far as 'individuality' embraces
> our innermost, last, and incomparable unique-
> ness, it also implies becoming one's own self.
> We could therefore translate individuation as
> 'coming to selfhood.'[3]

While individuation has become the property of the world of psychology, Jung intends it to be much more than that. To him, it encompassed the philosophical, mystical, and spiritual realms of the human experience: "The aim of individuation is nothing less than to divest the self of the false wrappings of the persona on the one hand and the suggestive power of primordial images on the other."[4]

To form a deeper understanding of individuation, it is helpful to juxtapose it with an Eastern practice with comparable aims, such as Sufism. I hold a deep personal affinity with Sufism, as an academic and a writer, and since 1993, as a practicing Sufi. The form of Sufism into which I have been initiated was instigated by mystic and musician Hazrat Inayat Khan (1882-1927) in the early 20th century. He first visited the West in 1910 and went on to be a visionary leader of the Sufi Movement in the West.

As a mystic and as a human, Inayat Khan's central inspiration was music. Music, in essence, is vibration: The vibrations that manifested the entire world from a vacuum are the same vibrations an individual creates when doing Sufi breath practices. To Inayat Khan, music was the profound and singular essence of creation (love), the ultimate form of divine realization (harmony), and the supreme expression of devotion to and communication with the divine (beauty).[5]

In this essay, we will place this form of mysticism alongside individuation. We will observe how core Sufi teachings and practices

---

[3] CW 7
[4] Ibid., § 269
[5] Khan, H.I., 1989, e.g., Vol II

aim to reach the same goal as individuation, a state known in Sufism as self-realization, a process of differentiation and unification of body, mind/heart and soul, that "is recognized by some religious-minded people as God consciousness, and by philosophical minds as cosmic consciousness."[6] In doing so, the aim is not to rank one against the other, but to provide a new angle from which to appreciate the nature and context of individuation and self-realization and create a fuller understanding of both.

We will first deepen our acquaintance with Hazrat Inayat Khan, his teachings as presented in *The Sufi Message* and supplementary papers,[7] and the role of music, mysticism, and psychology in the Sufi mureed (disciple) and Murshid (guide) relationship. We will become acquainted with stages of consciousness development as well as breath practices that may be given to disciples according to each individual's stage of consciousness development as determined by the guide. We will explore the underpinnings of the process of self-realization from Inayat Khan's Sufi perspective and of individuation from a Jungian perspective. Finally, we will witness an imagined conversation between Inayat Khan and Jung, which ties the foregoing together.

Combining Real with Imitation

Inayat Khan's mystical and musical training began at home.[8] He was born in Baroda, a modern Indian state influenced by European ideas and norms, with a multidimensional social and religious context. Inayat Khan was born and lived until 1901 in the mansion

---

[6] Ibid., Vol. V: Metaphysics, *The Experience of the Soul Through the Different Planes of Existence*

[7] Nekbakht Furnée, a Dutch mureed who assembled papers and documents for the Biographical Department, collected the supplementary papers. She created a Dutch foundation for this purpose, the Nekbakht Foundation, still today a most valuable resource.

[8] In his paternal line, it was expected that there be at least one full mystic in each generation. From their earlier Central Asian Bakhshe tradition, Inayat's 'Tayaji' (elder uncle) Mashaik Jafar Khan was the fifteenth such mystic.

of his maternal grandfather, Maula Bakhsh (1833-96),[9] together with 30 to 40 relatives, children, spouses, grandchildren, and servants.[10] Bakhsh was one of the most famous musicians of his time in India, with his skill in both northern and southern Indian styles setting him apart. At the same time, on his paternal side, Inayat Khan was part of a long line of Sufi mystics, and he attained *Samadhi*,[11] a state of God consciousness, as a young man. Though a Muslim by birth, he attended a Mahrathi, a Hindu school.[12] His Murshid, Abu Hashim Madani, was an independent representative of the Chishti Order,[13] and it was into this order that Inayat Khan was initiated first and foremost.[14]

Inayat Khan's early life was imbued with and defined by mysticism and music. When his second wife died in 1902, he left on a musical tour of the south of India, to Madras and Mysore, and later traveled throughout India.[15] At the same time, he was deeply ensconced in his spiritual training: Well before leaving India, he received his *ijazat*, an authorization to teach and practice the master's doctrines awarded upon completion of physical, intellectual, mental, moral, and spiritual[16] education, and rigorous training.

---

[9] Maula Bakhsh contributed in two different ways to Indian music: he wrote many published compositions and he developed an innovative system of notation that unified various traditions. It was the first system that could be read across social classes throughout India. Maula Bakhsh made classical music accessible outside the closed court circles and the ambit of southern Brahmins. See Khan, H.I., 1979. pp. 19-29; Jironet, K., 2002, p. 17; Khan, Z., 2001, pp. 17-19

[10] Khan, M., 1982, p. 17

[11] Khan, H.I., 1979, p. 111. See also fn. 9

[12] Hazrat Inayat Khan's skill in language and music were not recognized in the Hindu school the family had decided to send him to because it taught in the language of the dynasty and Mahrathi ruling minority: Ibid., p .45. He was described as a dreamer who could not concentrate on subjects such as maths, so he was often punished: Keesing, 1981, p. 7. His father also forbade Inayat Khan from writing poetry: Khan, M., 1982, p. 107

[13] Khan, H.I., 1979, p. 76; 1989, Vol. XII, p. 149

[14] He was also initiated into the Suhrawardiyya, Qadiriyya and Naqshbandiyah Sufi Orders of Sunni Islam.

[15] For a detailed presentation of Inayat Khan's travels in India, see Mahmood Khan's thorough Biochronological Survey in Khan, Z., 2001, pp. 81-95

[16] Khan, H.I., 1989. Vol. XII, p. 149

Inayat Khan was the first Eastern Murshid to travel to the West,[17] arriving in New York from Bombay by boat in 1910:

> When our ship arrived in the harbor of New York, the first land of my destination, I saw before me the welcoming figure of the statue of Liberty, an idol of rock, which I felt was awaiting the hour to turn into an ideal, awaiting the moment to rise from material liberty to spiritual liberty.[18]

During his travels in the United States, Inayat Khan saw a pressing need in the West for practices that would give rise to the experience of the unity of existence, *wahdat al-wujud*. Indeed, Inayat Khan identified a longing for the very gifts and initiations with which he had been bestowed: music and mysticism. However, he found connecting with people in the West by way of his music rather difficult. There was little appreciation for Indian music in the United States at that time, which forced him to adapt his music and, in doing so, sacrifice an essential aspect of what he wanted to convey.

> We had an interesting tour together throughout the States, and yet for the public, which was there for amusement, our music became merely entertainment. This was amusement for them, and therefore painful for us. Also it was not satisfactory to combine real with imitation. However, it helped to keep the wolf away from our door.[19]

Note the contrast of "real" and "imitation" here. In Inayat Khan's experience and training, the real was the *sama*; that is, the practice of listening to music and allowing it to carry one into

---

[17] See e.g. Rawlinson, 1997, p. 42. He traveled to the U.S. with his younger brother Maheboob Khan and cousin Mohammed Ali Khan.

[18] Khand, H.I,, 1979, p. 123

[19] Ibid., p. 124

the presence of the divine, into unity of existence.[20] The pain of having to decorate the real with the false in order to make his music palatable to the public prompted Inayat Khan to search deeper for a means of allowing Westerners to discover and experience true *sama* uncompromised.

This search would ultimately render his teachings as collected in *The Sufi Message*, formed from transcripts of lectures and speeches he gave in the West between 1910 and 1927. These teachings comprise an important cornerstone of the approach taken by Western Sufis, especially since its publication in consolidated form in the 1960s.[21] Inayat Khan himself did not view these talks as "his" nor as "teachings" but simply as God's message, the same eternal wisdom given to mankind in different forms at different times by different messengers.[22]

From 1910 to 1915, Inayat Khan traveled and performed his music in New York, London, Paris, Moscow, back to Paris, and back to London. It was there that what would become the International Sufi Movement was founded. Today, many different international organizations gather around the teachings and practices established by Inayat Khan, and his teachings are shared by Western teachers in mainstream Western society.[23]

Eastern mysticism, Western mind

> Not being aware of one's own neglect and fault, not being aware of the real self – this is the main reason for illness. Consciousness of

---

[20] For the relation between the lover (individual) and the beloved (God) as experienced through *Sama*, ecstasy, see Lawrence, 1983.

[21] Previously, Inayat Khan's teachings had only been available in separate books and papers. *The Sufi Message* consists of 13 volumes published in 1960-67. Titles include for example *The Way of Illumination, The Mysticism of Sound and Music, Mental Purification, The Alchemy of Happiness,* and *Sufi Mysticism.*

[22] See e.g., Khan, H.I., 1989, Vol. I, pp. 15, 33, 118; Vol. VI, p. 137; Vol. VIII, p. 38; Vol. IX, p. 125

[23] For more on contemporary Western teachers practicing within Eastern esoteric traditions, see Rawlinson, 1997.

the real self before God Almighty, means first
of all consciousness of others, consciousness
of everything surrounding you. For the self
does not exist alone.[24]

Spiritual development of the individual, the group, and
the world: This was the objective of Inayat Khan's teachings. The
spiritual development he propounded was a very different process
from that contemplated in the West at the time. Unlike the Western
perception of development as being learning through accumulation
of knowledge,[25] Inayat Khan stressed that the aim of his teachings
was "unlearning."[26] His teachings were originally silent: nonverbal,
or through music. No explanations. Discussion, in his view, was a
delay tactic: a mere postponement of application. Later, however,
realizing that this was *the* modus operandi for Western education, he
accommodated his students' need for verbal teachings.

He encountered another conflict regarding the nature of
the process of spiritual liberation. Inayat Khan saw growth toward
spiritual liberty as ongoing, not something that could be achieved
once and for all, then crossed off the to-do list. His Western mureeds,
however, were overwhelmed by the compulsion to determine their
goal in advance and a need to *know* that they were striving toward
it. One of the more challenging elements of following Inayat Khan's
teachings for Western mureeds was to make the shift from seeking
security through accumulating knowledge, practices, and tasks
within the organizational context to seeking the unspoken, innermost
experience — and to simply leave it there. Easier said than done, as
it were.[27]

To further complicate matters, Inayat Khan believed
spiritual development hinged on the individual having an attitude

---

[24] Pir-o-Murshid Ali Khan in *Zahur,* Unpublished paper in my private possession.
[25] See Jironet, 2002, pp. 189-191
[26] See Ibid., pp. 129, 190
[27] Jironet, 2009

of acceptance and that they surrender to life *as it is*. In the words of Mohammed Ali Khan, who was the Pir-o-Murshid (leader) of the Sufi Movement until his death in 1948, "Self-realization means to become aware of the world and of personal neglect and faults."[28] Self-realization involves overcoming the duality of good and bad and the inclination to see yourself as one or the other: "Goodness and badness exist together in man: if the one appears the other is hidden, as a lining in the coat."[29] This in turn entails integration of elements belonging to the unknown, to the rejected and repressed parts of the individual's psychological makeup and that of the organization. Another somewhat revolutionary aspect of Inayat Khan's approach was his emphasis on the unity of religious ideals,[30] which gives *The Sufi Message* a universal character. By emphasizing this as a central mystical tenet, rather than a natural outcome of individual spiritual illumination, Inayat Khan went beyond common manifestations of classical Sufism and the popular forms of Muslim and Hindu traditions in which he had been educated and trained.

Early mureeds of the International Sufi Movement found themselves at a crossroads. They had contributed to the development of a multireligious Western society and formed part of a Western tradition but simultaneously witnessed a deep inner isolation among groups and individuals within this society. One can imagine how, especially as the horrors of the First World War unfolded, new Western mureeds experienced the relief of homecoming that the organization offered. They found a meaningful spiritual life, but also community.

Becoming a Sufi in the West entails forming a new identity, partly rooted in dissatisfaction with the dominant religion (Christianity) in tandem with attraction to the Eastern (mysticism). The new identity is created through a kind of push-pull: rejection of

---

[28] See above, n. 24
[29] Khan, H.I., 2007
[30] This also forms the title of Volume 9

the dominant paradigm,[31] while at the same time adopting Eastern customs, such as a dress code or a Sufi name, alien to the dominant Western culture — especially, one can imagine, in Europe during the 1910s.[32]

Unorthodox, yet effective

During the first years in London, Inayat Khan offered his teachings through music, attunement, and stilling the mind in *sama* silence. One of the early disciples, Raden Jodjana, explains his method:

> Inayat Khan stayed true to his own vow — by singing in his unique sweet way, opening, for those who could listen, the path into the inner world to meet the Divine Presence within, and so to learn to serve the Presence silently in full acceptance of one's destiny, meeting all beings as expressions of the same Presence.

---

[31] By rejecting the prevailing cultural context and adopting foreign customs, the individual stands out. Ego-identity is developed and potentially inflated. Any sense of being "special," belonging to an exclusive esoteric movement, and progressing in an internal group-specific spiritual hierarchy is detrimental to self-realization — and individuation. Inner expectations as well as external ones may inspire self-consciousness, mannerisms, and "all-Sufi" like behaviors that strengthen the persona rather than the true Self. As a senior-most Murshid once told me, "The worst thing you can do to somebody is to give them a yellow robe," a yellow robe being a form of distinction of a certain rank within the Sufi Movement. I have kept that advice in mind.
[32] Theories abound within cultural studies regarding "hybrid" versus "perennial" orientations within Western Sufism. Marcia Hermansen (see: Hybrid Identity Formations in Muslim America: The Case of American Sufi Movements, 2000), pursues this garden metaphor, contending that hybrid movements tend to adapt to the American cultural context while perennial movements stress the unity of all religions. With their strong emphasis on the unity of being and of religious ideas, as well as their orientation towards adaptation and integration into daily life of Western cultural context, the teachings and movements formed around Inayat Khan are both perennial and hybrid. Pir Zia Inayat Khan, who leads the Inayatiyya Order, a development out of the Sufi Order, comments on the Inayatiyya Order's hybrid character: "The salient distinction … is not between hybridity and contrasting norm of 'purity,' but rather between the unconscious, organic hybridization that is intrinsic to the historical evolution of language, and the conscious, intentional hybridization that constitutes a distinct aesthetic strategy." Khan, Z., 2006, p. 3

In meditation I learned to enter within inner space, into inner silence, and began to become aware of the inner interrogative state. I started to know how to serve, what to do, and how to obey without the mind interfering, questioning or discussing. Just the clear inner awareness of what to do in the moment.

It was not easy, as I had never learnt before to accept with the whole body, mind and soul, this inner guidance. Never before had I known that the body can and should become wholly receptive. Therefore I had to teach the body to open to all sides its nervous system, the brain included, and to relax the whole muscular structure. The mind then stays receptive. The centers of attention absorb impressions and let them descend to the source of life.

Inayat Khan did not tell and explain all this to me, and no questions were allowed. But the questions were there, and the mind had to be silenced. Downwards the questions went, and created by and by, the inner interrogative state. Taking the habit of listening within, at last one discovers that the inner questions receive their true answer, awakening awareness of what to do or not to do, of what to say or not to say, in the moment.

From the center of gravity, from the center of balance and being, inspirations and ideas, inner awareness and intuition will be born and create intentions to act and to speak, or not to move and keep silent. In this way Inayat Khan was directing me to the deepest consciousness of life.[33]

---

[33] From R.A. Jodjana, *Autobiography*, in Khan, Z., 2001, pp. 387-388

The same disciple speaks as well to the typical way of training more advanced mureeds, a method one could think of as "deconstruction," or the "rock-the-boat" principle. When all seems stable, challenging but — with focus and dedicated effort — doable, BOOM! Something totally disturbing and unexpected comes, undermining all equilibrium. Jodjana, who had been invited to make a debut together with Inayat Khan and his ensemble at the well-reputed concert hall, Leighton House in London, gives the following example:

> The day before the performance I went to Ladbroke Road for the last rehearsal. I did not know that Inayat had told the boys [brothers] to play the accompaniment out of tune, and to upset the rhythmic structure of the songs. I made tremendous efforts and spent hours trying to adjust myself to accept the strain. Going home I became very distressed, not knowing how they would play in the performance. ... Another time, Inayat Khan was presenting me at the Queen's Hall... He was singing duets with me. Suddenly, during the performance, he began to sing my small solo part. My knees started to tremble. ... In moments of utter distraction, Inayat Khan, seeing my efforts to master the situation, laughed heartily, as if he enjoyed exposing me to public shame. In a quite incomprehensible way, I always felt an astounding inner help in these vexing moments. And these experiences formed the basis of a rare joy.[34]

---

[34] Ibid., p. 392. It is worth noting that Inayat Khan begged Jodjana never to join the Sufi Order. He wanted to teach her in the Eastern style, in which he himself was trained. It brings to mind an observation Jung is supposed to have made: "Thank God I'm Jung and not a Jungian."

Western Sufism and Consciousness

According to Inayat Khan, the basis of Sufi training is that the purpose of living is to experience the consciousness of God and that every individual can reach this goal through introspection. Man may identify with the divine aspect within, the true Self, and become conscious of God. Sufi mysticism consists of training in how to seek knowledge about the true Self and *to live it*. Inayat Khan's training silences the mind and thus enables the disciple's access to the inner reality for the unconscious to speak and inform consciousness. The path is not an accrual of knowledge, but an unlearning, freeing oneself from the false ego with which one identifies: that is, mental purification. Eventually, the mureed fully abandons rigid ideas about the world and the Self so that the mind can become open and reflect divine light. This freeing effect is why the Sufi Message is one of spiritual liberty.

This process involves reconciling opposites such as right versus wrong, good versus bad, pleasure versus pain, as these opposites block the mind from the unified Self, which otherwise remains largely unconscious. Turning consciousness inward, away from its observations of the external world, reveals consciousness to itself, allows consciousness to see itself and realize its true nature, and the Self in its original condition, the soul. As Inayat Khan puts it:

> Sufism, therefore, is the analyzing of the self, the self which has for the moment become a mixture of three things, of body, mind, and soul. By separating the outer garments of the soul the Sufi discovers the real nature and character of the soul, and in this discovery lies the secret of the whole life.[35]

---

[35] Khan, 1989, Vol. I p. 161

Today, *The Sufi Message* thrives in part due to its highly international reach. Adaption to online formats had already been made well in advance of 2020. Currently, online teachings[36] fulfill the role of teachings and practices in lieu of face-to-face and group settings. In my experience as a participant in and a leader of online Sufi gatherings, I find this medium not only effective but also deeply impactful. The reason is somewhat paradoxical: intimacy. With one person on the screen at the time, I can assimilate the teachings of Pir Zia, for example, without disturbance or distraction by a physical audience moving about, rustling papers, or sipping water. Similarly, when teaching an individual, there is both a "one-on-one moment" with our focus on each other on the screen, while reaping the benefit of the palpable presence of a larger group who do not interfere, but rather support through the art of listening with intention.

Stages of Consciousness in Sufism

> **Consciousness** is the wakeful state of the knowing faculty;
> **knowledge** is that of which the consciousness is conscious;
> **conscience** is a sense which is born when consciousness holds before itself a scale, on the one side an action and on the other side an ideal; and **intelligence** is the grasping faculty of consciousness, which by every means recognizes, distinguishes, perceives, and conceives all that is around it.[37]

There are five different, successive stages of Sufi consciousness: *Nasut, Malakut, Jabarut, Lahut* and *Hahut*.[38] Let us briefly contemplate each.

---

[36] See generally Rozehnal, 2019, and Piraino, http://scp.sagepub.com/content/63/1/93, (last accessed 02-02-2022)

[37] Khan, H.I., 1989, Vol. 1, p. 39

[38] Abridged from Ibid., Vol. V, pp. 24-30, Vol. VIII, pp. 196-198

Nasut is the consciousness that depends upon our senses. Whatever we see, hear, touch, smell, or taste, all that is experienced by means of material body, proves to us that this is a particular plane of consciousness, or a particular kind of experience of the consciousness.

Malakut is a further stage of consciousness working through our mental plane. This plane allows us to experience thought and imagination — beyond our senses. For example, a person passes you by and, immersed deep in thought upon some subject, does not notice you. You may speak, but the person will not listen, so deeply is that person absorbed. Though the ears are open the person cannot hear; though eyes are open the person cannot see. What does this mean? At that moment, the person' consciousness is experiencing life on a different plane. Though the person is before you with open eyes and ears, consciousness is on another plane, working through a different body.

The next stage is *Jabarut*, the plane of consciousness where the experience is like that of a person in deep, dreamless sleep who may be said to be sound asleep. The blessing here is greater still. In this higher experience, there is God's own Being through which we experience the life, peace, and purity that are within us. Moreover, while anyone may experience this blessing during sleep, the person who follows the path of spiritual development will also experience this joy of life, peace, and purity that the mystic experiences with wide-open eyes while awake.

A still further experience of consciousness is *Lahut*. This raises a person from the material to the immaterial plane. In this plane, the state of deep sleep is not necessary. There is greater peace and joy, and nearness to the essence, which is called divine.

Hahut, the final step to which is known as *Samadhi* may be described as merging in God. In this stage, we dive into our deepest selfhood; God is in our deepest Self. In this state, we are able to dive so far as to touch our deepest being, the home of all intelligence, life, peace, and joy, and where worry, fear, disease or death do not enter.

The Way There: Breath and Related Practices

> The true delight of the soul lies in love,
> harmony and beauty, the outcome of
> which is wisdom, calm and peace; the
> more constant they are, the greater is the
> satisfaction of the soul.[39]

According to Inayat Khan, breath is the channel through which all the expression of the innermost life can be given. Breath creates attunement between body and soul. In essence vibration, breath, forms the bridge between his affinity with music and mysticism — it is, to Inayat Khan, the alpha and the omega: Mysticism has been founded on the science of breath. "There is no mystic, whether Buddhist, Vedantic, or Sufi, who makes use of another process than that of breath. Breath is the first lesson and it is also the last."[40]

Breath also attunes different faculties, such as thought, speech, and action. Breath is the root of a silent mind, which is peaceful, peace being the secret of mysticism.

> It is the peaceful one who is observant; it is
> peace that gives him the power to observe
> keenly. It is the peaceful one, therefore,
> who can conceive, for peace helps him
> to conceive. It is the peaceful who can
> contemplate; one who has no peace cannot
> contemplate properly. Therefore all things
> pertaining to spiritual progress in life
> depend upon peace.[41]

To give some context, and before we draw in Jungian consciousness, let me share examples of several of the key breath practices.

---

[39] Ibid., Vol. II, p. 25
[40] Ibid., Vol. XIII, p. 138
[41] Ibid., Vol. I, p. 211

The first (and last) practice one must master is the purification breath. This practice is performed in the morning, setting the tone for the day, preferably outdoors or at an open window. I tend to sit on my terrace or balcony, so I may also drink in the first rays of the sun. It encompasses balance, grounding, and attunement with the elements. You breathe in for four counts, and out for four counts, with a short pause in between as the flow shifts as follows:

(1) Earth Breath: In through the nose, out through the nose, visualizing the color gold (five times).

(2) Water Breath: In through the nose, out through the mouth, visualizing the color green (five times).

(3) Fire Breath: In through the mouth, out through the nose, visualizing the color red (five times).

(4) Air Breath: In through the mouth, out through the mouth, visualizing the color blue (five times).

(5) Ether Breath: In through the nose, out through the nose, very refined, visualizing silvery transparency (five times).

After this purification breath, I turn to a short healing prayer called *Nayaz*, which goes like this:

> Beloved Lord, Almighty God,
> Through the rays of the sun, through the
> waves of the air, through the All-pervading
> Life in space,
> Purify and revivify me, and, I pray, heal
> my body, heart, and soul.

The *Wazifa* practice utilizes the breath to ennoble your soul with divine qualities. A *Wazifa* is the name of one of the attributes of God. By invoking this name, you draw closer to its essence. Your Murshid will give specific instructions, which might be to invoke a certain *Wazifa* a certain number of times at a certain time of the day.

By way of example, you may be instructed to use one of the 99 names or attributes of God, such as *al-Hayy*, meaning "the living." Inhale fully. Exhale as you recite *ya Hayy*. The number of breaths doesn't matter as much as intention. Then, on the last breath of the cycle, fully inhale and conclude with one extended, fully intentional *ya Hayy* on a slow out breath. Experience your living body.

This can also be done as a walking *Wazifa*. So, *ya Hayy* may be silently recited on the right foot striking the ground. Then, inhale *ya Hayy* as the left foot does the same.

The *Fikr* is a practice in which a sacred word swings out on the exhale then swings back into you, rhythmically according to your own breath, and can similarly be used as a walking *Fikr*. *Fikr* offers a natural a manner of awareness and concentration on the rhythm of breath in silence.

Finally, *Zikr*, which means remembrance of God or reminding oneself of God, is an essential practice on the Sufi path. Through different stages of repetition of the Arabic phrase meaning "there is no god but God," the disciple gradually attunes to the being of God. The practice encompasses posture, breath, sound, movement, focus of the mind, and quality of the heart.

Ideally, one sits cross-legged with the right foot's toes touching the inside of the bent left leg, which promotes opening of the heart and emptying of the mind. With an empty mind, one proceeds to turn and churn the upper body over the pelvis in a perpendicular rightward, circular movement, while intoning a: *la ilaha illa'llahu* 101 times.[42] After a short pause of observing the presence of God in silence, one proceeds with the second *Zikr* following the same movement and concentration, now invoking: *illa'llahu*. The third

---

[42] For an illustration, please see Shaik al-Mashaik Mahmood Khan in the first *zikr*. https://www.youtube.com/watch?v=K4qVZW8vgXA (Last accessed 02-02-2022).

Zikr follows in the same manner with *Allahu*. In the fourth and final *Zikr*, only *Hu* is repeated.

The aftermath of *Zikr*, silence, is an exquisite sense of being alive in all dimensions — body, mind, heart, and soul at once and to be present to that liveliness as vibration, as bliss.

Consciousness and Individuation

> The figures of the unconscious are as uninformed, and need man, or contact with consciousness, in order to attain knowledge.[43]

The Self is the whole of the psyche, including all its potential. Self has a teleological function: It is forward-looking, seeking fulfilment. The goal of the Self is wholeness, or, in Jungian terms, individuation, and the path to individuation is laid by bringing consciousness to the unconscious.

Consciousness is a cornerstone of our understanding of what it means to be human and has become an active field of scientific research, albeit with rather starkly conflicting theories. Some researchers contend that consciousness is a property of matter so fundamental that even an electron is conscious to a certain extent, a position known as panpsychism.[44] Integrated information theory (IIT) identifies consciousness as emergent: that is, consciousness emerging out of the complex behavior of the brain. It attempts to identify the essential properties of consciousness and account for them in the underlying system's complexity. Christof Koch, president and chief scientist of the Allen Institute for Brain Science in Seattle, states:

> Consciousness is a property intrinsic to organized matter. It's a property like charge and spin. We find ourselves in a universe that has space and time, and mass and energy,

---

[43] Jung, 2009, p. 357, n. 148

[44] https://aeon.co/ideas/panpsychism-is-crazy-but-its-also-most-probably-true; https://plato.stanford.edu/entries/panpsychism/ (Last accessed 02-02-2022).

> but we also find ourselves in a universe
> where organized systems that have [a value
> of] phi different from zero have experiences.[45]

IIT is a deep and complex theory, with mathematical foundations that predict new phenomena and recent anesthesia research findings, which may prove illuminating in allowing us to quantify consciousness.[46]

In Jung's view, individuation is an active, ongoing process of circumambulation of the Self and not a static state: "Consciousness should defend its reason and protect itself, and the chaotic life of the unconscious should be given the chance of having its way too — as much of it as we can stand. This means open conflict and open collaboration at once."[47] This correlates with Inayat Khan's view of self-realization as an ongoing process and not a single event, as we saw earlier. Further, individuation has a heroic aspect to it:

> Individuation is an heroic and often tragic task,
> the most difficult of all, it involves suffering,
> a passion of the ego: the ordinary empirical
> man we once were is burdened with the fate
> of losing himself in a greater dimension
> and being robbed of his fancied freedom of
> will. He suffers, so to speak, from the violence
> done to him by the self.[48]

Like many of life's most defining events, Jung's heroic journey into the depths was by no means premeditated.[49] On the first page of *The Red Book*, in an inscription dated 1957, Jung writes:

---

[45] Koch, *The Integrated Information Theory of Consciousness*, presented on 23 September, 2014. https://www.organism.earth/library/document/integrated-information-theory-of-consciousness (Last accessed 02-02-2022)

[46] See Koch's research with Tononi for example as set out in Koch, 2018.

[47] CW 9.1, § 522

[48] CW 11, § 223

[49] On the contrary, as we know, in 1913, aged 38, Jung had had a falling out with Freud, which resulted in a personal crisis.

The years, of which I have spoken to you, when I pursued the inner images, were the most important time of my life. Everything else is to be derived from this. It began at that time, and the later details hardly matter anymore. My entire life consisted in elaborating what had burst forth from the unconscious and flooded me like an enigmatic stream and threatened to break me. That was the stuff and material for more than only one life. Everything later was merely the outer classification, the scientific elaboration, and the integration into life. But the numinous beginning, which contained everything, was then.[50]

As for Jung's own individuation process, in Sonu Shamdasani's words, in his introduction to *The Red Book*:

The overall theme of the book is how Jung regains his soul and overcomes the contemporary malaise of spiritual alienation. This is ultimately achieved through enabling the rebirth of a new image of God in his soul and developing a new worldview in the form of a psychological and theological cosmology. Liber Novus presents the prototype of Jung's conception of the individuation process, which he held to be the universal form of individual psychological development. Liber Novus itself can be understood on one hand as depicting Jung's individuation process, and on the other hand as his elaboration of this concept as a general psychological schema.[51]

---

[50] Jung, 2009, p. vii
[51] Ibid., p. 207

Jung thus arrives at his theory of individuation through a *full* immersion method, *sine qua non*, documented in *The Red Book*. In this, his greatest experiment and the numinous beginning of a lifelong quest, he delved deep into his (and the collective) unconscious, faced it, endured demons' and angels' dwelling places. He meticulously noted his experiences in his journals, his daily mandala paintings, as well as sought numerous artistic forms of expression for what he had witnessed and experienced "down there." Gradually, he discovered a practice he was to call active imagination, an inner dialogue with his fantasies and with figures who emerged and engaged in his dialogue. Philemon, one of Jung's foremost inner guides, bestowed new insights, for "... he said things which I had not consciously thought. For I observed clearly that it was he who spoken not I."[52]

Conflict and differentiation are important components in this process of the individual coming to terms with multiple parts of the personality. It requires renouncing overidentification with one single identity imposed by external demands or inner fantasies, which in turn empowers a true identity to emerge, separate from the pool of all that is. In the last part of *The Red Book*,[53] Jung describes an encounter with Philemon, who earlier had explained that nothingness is the same as fullness and that in infinity full is as good as empty, and that this nothingness or fullness is called the *Pleroma*;[54] he continues:

> You ask: 'what harm is there in not differen-
> tiating oneself?' If we do not differentiate, we
> move beyond our essence, beyond creation,
> and we fall into nondifferentiation, which is the
> other quality of the Pleroma. We fall into the
> Pleroma itself and cease to be created beings.
> We lapse into dissolution in the nothingness.
> This is the death of the creature. Therefore we
> die to the same extent that we do not differ-

---

[52] Jung, 1989, p. 183
[53] Ibid., Scrutinies, a.k.a, The Seven Sermons to the Dead.
[54] Ibid., p. 347

> entiate. Hence the creature's essence strives toward differentiation and struggles against primeval, perilous sameness. This is called the *principium individuationis*. This principle is the essence of the creature. From this you can see why nondifferentiation and nondistinction pose a great danger to the creature.[55]

According to Jung, the assimilation of unconscious contents leads to a condition in which conscious intention is replaced by a (synthetic) process of development that may seem irrational. This process at the same time signifies individuation, and its product is individuality, both particular and universal.[56]

The unconscious — individual and collective — is (in) the Pleroma. And reaching in is a process characterized by the irrational, symbolic, archetypal, alchemical — what is up is down — chaotic, paradoxical, metaphysical. ... It *is* surrendering to no control; not conceptually but for real. Yet at the same time, the various elements of the process are intimately intertwined: Only in conjunction can differentiation and integration bring about the desired self-realization that forms the hallmark of individuation. This resonates with an important component of the Sufi notion of self-realization which, as we have seen, involves overcoming the duality of good and bad and the inclination to see yourself as one or the other. Again, "Goodness and badness exist together in man: If the one appears the other is hidden, as a lining in the coat."[57]

The Journey Is the Goal

We might say that Jung uses the concept of Self to describe the potential of who we are, and the concept of individuation as the

---

[55] Ibid.
[56] CW 7, § 505
[57] Khan, H.I., 2007

process by which we can fulfill that potential.[58] In a similar framing, for Sufis, the concept of Soul is reached through the process of self-realization. Both individuation and self-realization are ongoing processes that gradually reveal themselves: In essence, the journey is the goal. Both use assimilation of dimensions of consciousness; both yield a form of wisdom that is at once universal and satisfying to the individual. And, in both, there is an emphasis on stilling the mind and facing reality as it is. Jung reports a significant moment during his own experimentation with the process of individuation:

> It was during Advent of the year 1913 —
> December 12, to be exact — I resolved upon
> the decisive step. I was sitting at my desk
> once more, thinking over my fears. Then I let
> myself drop. Suddenly it was as though the
> ground literally gave way beneath my feet,
> and I plunged into the dark depths.[59]

Just as one does not rush into stilling the mind, one does not gulp in renunciation. These are tacit movements of the heart that manifest from the depth when the moment is mature. It is well understood among Sufis and practitioners of analytical psychology that these moments cannot be forced. Rather, when the mind is sufficiently still, the Self/Soul invites the stilled mind to delve in. Ease and peace are intuitive states that escape rational estimation, as they are products of irrational processes. Above Jung's front door at his home in Küsnacht is inscribed: Vocaus atque non vocatus deuas aderti: "Called or not called, God will be there." The critical point is, are you still enough to receive?

Imagination is a widely acknowledged tool within Sufism for manifesting the Soul's relations with dimensions beyond cognition. In Sufi terms, the primary principle for this transmission

---

[58] https://www.thesap.org.uk/resources/articles-on-jungian-psychology-2/about-analysis-and-therapy/individuation/ (Last accessed 02-02-2022)
[59] Jung, 1989, p. 179

is called creative imagination. As a practice, creative imagination has quite some overlaps with Jung's active imagination. Let us take a few moments to explore each of these.

Creative imagination occurs when the contemplator becomes the contemplated; for example, if one is contemplating God, creative imagination arises during union between Soul and God.[60] Indeed, Corbin suggests that by utilizing creative imagination, symbols and archetypes can fall away, leading to unity with reality as it truly is.[61] As he describes:

> The hermeneutic ability of the creative imagination to transmute all things into symbols destroys the distinction between psychology and cosmology and unites them in a psychocosmology in which Creator and the creature participate not as opposing terms with an unbridgeable gulf separating them, but as complementary poles of a divine drama.[62]

Within analytical psychology, the purpose of *active imagination* is to create a living bridge between the personal unconscious and personal consciousness, between images emerging from the unconscious, whether subjective or objective, as when interacting with archetypes pertaining to the collective unconscious. It has dreamlike qualities, but because it is conducted as a practice with conscious awareness, it is a realm in which the autonomous unconscious can be actively witnessed and interacted with by waking consciousness.

There are many ways to approach active imagination. At first, the unconscious takes the lead, while the conscious ego serves as a kind of attentive inner witness and perhaps scribe or

---

[60] For further detail, see Corbin, 1969
[61] See generally Corbin, 1994
[62] Ibid.

recorder. Second, as inner imagery, symbols, figures, dialogues form in consciousness over time, one may start to notice how these play out in daily life. Active imagination takes place in a process composed of different stages. Jung speaks of two parts: First, letting the unconscious come up; and second, coming to terms with the unconscious.[63] [64] It is in the second part of active imagination that consciousness takes the lead. For Jung, this second stage is the most important part because it involves questions of meaning and moral demands. In German, this is the *Auseinandersetzung*, which denotes a disambiguating or differentiating process, a real dialectic. In Jung's writings, *Auseinandersetzung* is usually translated as "coming to terms" with the unconscious: All the parts of an issue are laid out so that differences can be observed and resolved.

One major difference between creative imagination and active imagination lies in the position of the subject. Active imagination involves a dialogic modus in which the image and the subject are treated as separate and different, while creative imagination strives to achieve full unity between the two. Although neither practice involves the image stemming from deliberate action on the part of the subjective, the function of creative imagination is to typify and transform everything into symbolic images through perception of the correspondence between the visible and the hidden.[65] The idea is *not* to transmute a dream image into reality, but rather to look at it the other way around: How can this reality be considered as a spiritual occurrence? As Corbin points out, it is the dream image that carries

---

[63] Marie-Louise von Franz, 1997, a close adept and colleague of Jung's, proposed five stages: (1) Empty the 'mad mind' of the ego; (2) Let an unconscious fantasy image arise; (3) Give it some form of expression; and (4) Ethical confrontation. Later, she added: (5) Apply it to ordinary life.

[64] In Murray Stein's words, firstly, clear the mind and prepare to receive. Whatever comes; receive it. Secondly, once something comes from the unconscious into conscious mind, receive it freely. If it moves, follow it; if it speaks, listen. Thirdly, engage in a dialogue with the autonomous – oftentimes surprising (because they are not formed out of ego consciousness) – elements and figures of the unconscious. https://www.youtube.com/watch?v=Qx_xuwNKkS0 (Last accessed 02-02-2022).

[65] Corbin, 1998, p. 244

itself back up to its underlying truth in a process of dematerialization. Dream interpretation is key here, especially when the dream has a character of divine inspiration. According to Corbin, when the Prophet received divine inspiration, "Everything he apprehended was apprehended in the Imaginative Presence, and that precisely is why it all called for interpretation. ... If it had not been a dream in the true sense, there would have been nothing to interpret, that is, to see beyond it, for this 'beyond' is precisely the privilege of the Imaginative Presence as *coincidentia oppositorum.*"[66] This unity of opposites, or *coincidentia oppositorum*,[67] is a major theme in Jung's research and work. Just as consciousness and the unconscious may merge at critical points in life, so will the Soul with the body in the process of achieving *coniunctio*, as elaborated in alchemy. Similarly, Sufis recognize a realm where direct communion and revelation from God to prophets and messengers take place. Known as *Alam al-mithal*, the world of images, or *mundus imaginalis* in Latin,[68] it exists as a universe intermediate between God and manifestation, as real as the manifest world. It is a mind-world inhabited by subtle bodies, jinns, and angels as well as some minds of the dead.

In a comment on creative imagination that also extrapolates to active imagination, Inayat Khan notes:

> The mind is a magic shell, a shell in which a design is made by the imagination, and the same imagination is materialized on the surface. The question "then why does not all we think come true, why is all we wish not always realized," may be answered, that by our limitedness, we, so to speak, bury the divine creative power in our mind.[69]

---

[66] Ibid., pp. 241-242

[67] *Coincidence of opposites* is a neoplatonic definition attributed to 15 century German Nicolas of Cusa.

[68] See generally Corbin, 1977

[69] Khan, H.I. Vol.1, p. 157

Peace, Unity and Wholeness

> Only by living life you can free yourself from
> it. So live it to such a degree that it benefits
> you.[70]

Rest in peace, *requiescat in pace*, colloquially denotes the mainly Christian notion of a person passing peacefully and resting eternally united in Christ. The meaning in this essay, however, is another kind of dying: the death of the false ego, which preempts the resurrection of the true Self: self-realization. Nevertheless, as we may deduce from Jung's own experience described in *The Red Book*, this psycho-spiritual passing resembles *actual* death quite graphically:

> If you comprehend the darkness, it seizes
> you. It comes over you like the night with
> black shadows and countless shimmering
> stars. Silence and peace come over you if
> you begin to comprehend the darkness. Only
> he who does not comprehend the darkness
> fears the night. Through comprehending the
> dark, the nocturnal, the abyssal in you, you
> become utterly simple. And you prepare to
> sleep through the millennia like everyone
> else, and you sleep down into the womb of the
> millennia, and your walls resound with ancient
> temple chants. Since the simple is what always
> was. Peace and blue night spread over you
> while you dream in the grave of the millennia.
> ... I awaken, the day reddens the East. A night,
> a wonderful night in the distant depths of time
> lies behind me. In what far-away space was I?
> What did I dream?[71]

---

[70] Jung, 2009, p. 371
[71] Ibid., p. 270

In Sufi terms, dying before death, comprehending the dark, is known as *Fana*. It consists of annihilation, an experience that precedes awakening, merger with God, and true self-realization.

> It is the annihilation of the false self, which gives rise to the true self; once this is done, from that moment man approaches closer and closer to God, and stands face to face with his Divine Ideal, with whom he can communicate at every moment of his life.[72]

Fana is equivalent to "losing the false self" (*Nafs*), which again culminates in *Baqa* (resurrection); that is, to survive the annihilation, but transformed. The experience of losing oneself progresses through different stages. One such stage,[73] familiar to most of us, is when we are so absorbed in a thought or an activity that consciousness of the body, environment, and self dissolves in a dim background. Unconsciousness of the false self gradually becomes the true Self-consciousness, or, consciousness of consciousness itself.

Duality and unity form a pair of opposites that is fundamental to the philosophy and psychology within both analytical psychology and Sufism. Duality, in turn, is composed of pairs of opposites, a model countlessly utilized by Jung and Inayat Khan, which through a dynamic process, demonstrates the Hegelian dialectical model. Jung refers to Hegel,[74] whom he says hypostatizes the idea in a tripartite system of the concept, the reality of the concept, and the union of both. Inayat Khan also refers to Hegel,[75] whom he quotes saying, "If you believe in one God, you are right; if you believe in two Gods, that is true; but if you believe in three Gods, that is right also; for the nature of unity is realized by variety."[76] Inayat Khan concludes that

---

[72] Khan, H. I, 1989, Vol. IX, p. 266
[73] See e.g., Csikszentmihalyi, 1990
[74] CW 6, § 735
[75] Khan, H,I, 1989, Vol. V, p. 13
[76] Ibid.

the idea of opposites keeps us trapped in an illusion. He goes on to argue that, although distinguishing between two opposites (analysis) is necessary, the important step lies in realizing the idea of unity, which comes through the synthesis of life, by seeing the One in all things and in all beings. Realizing unity is, beyond "seeing," an act and product of love, ultimately:

> When *Ahad*, the only Being, became conscious of his *Wahdat* only existence, through His own consciousness, then His predisposition of love made Him project Himself to establish His dual aspect, that He might be able to love someone. This made God the lover, and manifestation the beloved; the next inversion makes manifestation the lover, and God the Beloved.[77]

In Jung's view, the divine manifests its wholeness in the form of spontaneous or autonomous symbols, above all in the mandala. The squaring of the circle, he says, could be seen as the archetype of wholeness:

> ... I gradually come to what the mandala really is: 'Formation, transformation, the eternal mind's eternal recreation.' And that is the Self, the wholeness of the personality, which, when everything is well, is harmonious, but which can bear no self-deception.[78]

The mandala according to Jung thus signifies the wholeness of the Self: "This circular image represents the wholeness of the psychic ground or, to put it in mythic terms, the divinity incarnate in man."[79]

---

[77] Ibid., Vol. V, p. 17
[78] CW 9ii, §§ 59-60
[79] Jung, 1989, pp. 334-335

Dropping the false self, self-deception, however familiar and safe it may appear, is an act of personal courage coinciding with the grace of God. It sets off self-realization in an entirely new dimension:

> Whether the conditions become better or worse, the first thing is to seek the kingdom of God within ourselves, in which there is our peace. As soon as we have found that, we have found our support, we have found our self. And in spite of all the activity and movement on the surface we shall be able to keep that peace undisturbed if only we hold it fast by becoming conscious of it.[80]

While we have explored some of the overlap between the enormously influential thinking and work of Carl Gustav Jung and Hazrat Inayat Khan, I suspect further investigation will reveal even more of these commonalities and similarities in formulation of experience.[81] What follows is a harmonious conversation, as my fantasy envisions it, between Inayat Khan and Carl Jung. The dialogue, while moving through motifs of shared interests, gives words to the sentiment of common understanding that unites mystics through direct experience over time and space — eternally and in the present now. May I invite you to join me in my vision of their encounter.

An Envisioned Dialogue

Once upon a time, in New Delhi, it's a late afternoon in early spring. Carl Gustav Jung and Hazrat Inayat Khan sit facing one another; black tea with ample sugar is sipped. Cicadas play their music in the background. By the end of the conversation, we find them sitting

---

[80] Khan, H.I., 1989, Vol I p. 212

[81] For example, the notion of "attitude" which Jung and Inayat Khan each apply in various contexts including the affirmation of a religious attitude free and independent of religious creed.

*on the same rotan bench, looking out across the patio to see a bird
landing in the lush greenery. They share the sunset in sacred silence.*

Carl Gustav Jung: So, here we are. I'm only seven years your senior.

Hazrat Inayat Khan: Close in age but culturally afar.

Jung: I think culture, aside from politics, is formed largely by
the collective unconscious, and the stuff of which it is made —
archetypes, images that go back as far as the beginning of time. And
these are shared images. I've visited India before, for a conference,
but I made my own plans and traveled to the South by train and cars.
It was strenuous and fascinating. I found that, there, the architecture
mirrors the mind of the people. Dreamlike, feminine, musical, even.
As different as the entire scenery seemed from Küsnacht, I could still
relate to it, something in my unconscious somehow recognized its
meaning. I witnessed my dreams immersing into its mood; the scent
of India reached into my dreams.

Inayat Khan: To me architecture is music, gardening is music,
farming is music, painting is music, poetry is music. Everywhere
that beauty has been the inspiration, where the divine wine has been
poured out, there is music. And, you know, the art of music has been
especially considered divine, because it is the exact miniature of the
law working through the whole universe. For instance, if we study
ourselves, we shall find that the beats of the pulse and of the heart,
the inhaling and exhaling of the breath, are all the work of rhythm.
Jung: Yes, yes, the breath. ... I found it fascinating. During my
encounters with tantric yoga, it was precisely the breath, and the
bodily movements it brings forth, that establishes that link between
the unconscious and the conscious ego, which has a most luminous
quality; the light of *the man of light*. The breath is not yet part of
Western psychoanalytical treatment. But it will surely become.
Inayat Khan: The breath makes a circuit through the body, and the
channel through which it makes the circuit is the spine. Imagine it

247

as a serpent holding its tail in its mouth. As you know better than most, in almost all symbols, the serpent represents the channel of the breath. When the method of breath clears this channel, this is not only a help to the physical health but it also opens up the faculties of intuition but also the inner doors that lead to real happiness. To clear away blocks in this channel, one must, of course, follow the rules of mystical ablutions and rhythmic breathing. Not occasionally or intensely or in strained bouts. No, gently, steadily, every day. In my view, the soul in its manifestation on Earth is not at all disconnected from the higher spheres. It lives in all spheres, though it is generally conscious on only one plane. And thus it becomes deprived of the heavenly bliss, and conscious of the troubles and limitations of life on the Earth.

Jung: Analysis — and kundalini yoga, or any form of yoga or meditation or active imagination — these are different means to the same goal. So that's where culture shows up again. I had a period of intense encounters with figures of my phantasy; as a matter of fact, they seemed more real than my neighbors. It brought home to me that entities, spirits, deep down in the collective unconscious have the same traits as the living. Good and evil coexist in equal measure, and the one doesn't cancel out the other. But what was more: It was overwhelming. There were times when I thought these encounters would get the better of me. I did yoga to calm my system, but only in order to continue my work on the unconscious, just as the alchemists. Making gold was their form of Western yoga, as they went about the frightening mission of uniting heaven and Earth in the vas. But I don't feel too sorry for myself, because it was precisely the troubles and limitations that demons brought on that showed me the world of psyche's objective reality.

Inayat Khan: You know, when I think about what you just said about your dream about knowing India's spirit, as foreign as it is to your conscious mind, it reminded me of the five different phases of consciousness that we Sufis recognize. It is a mistake to think of this evolution as a woken, rational process. Rather it dwells in the mystery of sleep, and even more so in dreams. During sleeping and

248

dreaming everyone experience all phases, if one is only aware of it. The end phase is most difficult to retain, and if one does, it generally only lasts for a heartbeat. Still, it makes an impression. It is the soul who knows and experiences, the soul is awake in your dream, experiencing directly those elements of Indian nature. Consciousness observes its own knowing. Such knowing is different from reading a guidebook or going on a tour. That glimpse is more.

I didn't go into psychoanalysis, but the deep spiritual connection between my Murshid and I had profound transformational proportions in the same vein, like a dream if you will. In a subtle, nonverbal way, it opened me up to the reality of truth, through the heart, to that which can never be gained through discussion or argument, reading, writing, or any mystical exercises.

Yet, at the same time, naturally I studied as much as possible, the Quran, Hadith, and Persian mysticism and more. You know, my prayers and practices gave rise to clairvoyance, clairaudience, intuition, inspiration, impressions, dreams, and visions: These formed my teachings. I also, like you, communicated with both the living and the dead. I delved into the occult and psychic sides of mysticism, as well as realizing the power of devotion to the God-ideal, which can help keep one sane. Slowly I deepened into knowing my inner nature and with that, well, the outer world.

Jung: Self-realization! This, this is what I wanted to talk about with you. Acquiring self-knowledge demands perseverance because the unconscious ego strives to trick you. Just think of the story of Siddhartha, seated under the Bodhi tree, waiting for enlightenment to come, tricked and tested and threatened by Mara and consort, demons of the senses and illusion. Mara flung all sorts of terrifying projections from the unconscious upon him, but Siddhartha prevailed and defied Mara, interestingly with the help of touching the ground with his fingertips. Then one day, the throne was empty. And the Buddha was simply not there! … I see you understand what I mean.

I had a patient and what she did during her analysis: persisting in prayers. She approached archetypal figures as creative fantasy equivalent to *samskara*. She used this to get to know herself and her own myth. The unconscious is the medium through which religious experiences flow. Individuation follows a similar process that begins with the Self removing itself from the ego, passions, and entanglements. This leads to the experience of the numinous, call it God or not, which needs no rational verification. The soul then expresses itself as it is. It is this freeing that leads to wholeness.

Inayat Khan: Ah, what you are saying now is very interesting, because it resembles the purification process through the different *Nafs*, egos or concepts of self, described in the Quran and in Sufi philosophy and psychology. The first is called *Nafs al-Ammara*. It is those self-centered passions that determine a person's course of action unconcerned with the needs of others. Then, we have the *Nafs al-Lawwama*, the self-blaming mind. With the view that approval and admiration of others is detrimental to spiritual development, at this stage, the person moves toward indifference to others' opinions, good or bad: irrelevant. The third stage, *Nafs al-Mutmainna*, is a stage of peace, ease, and contentment. Mental purification and the practice of *Zikr*, remembrance of God, is such a most important practice at this stage.

Jung: Hmmm ... Recognition of the shadow, including what you allude to, matters such as reckless greed or the vanity of false humility, may lead to true modesty and surrender to imperfection. In the face of God, we are, every day, every minute, infinitely imperfect. And this conscious recognition of bottomless fallibility is what we need because it informs conscience and the ethical imperative of human relationships, which are based on what is weak and helpless and in need of support. Relationships that understand and acknowledge how interdependent we all are. What would a "perfect" person need or depend upon from someone else? That brings us back to the notion of culture and individuation. Naturally, differentiation is essential, but it does not make us basically different. When you allow the love of your fellow man to be a felt reality, this becomes completely clear. Then, that inner light you speak of as a third *Nafs, Nafs al-Mutmainna,* can manifest in the form of social cohesion. Because the conscious man sees through the power hunger, terror, discrimination, and violence carried out by fellow man due to their absence of love. One could then say individuation is a form of intercultural psychology.

Inayat Khan: I think of spirituality as the water hidden in the depth of the Earth: buried in the heart of man and that this water must be, so to speak, dug out. This digging occurs when one takes pains in awakening one's sympathy for one's own helplessness and weakness, and that of others. In harmonizing with others and in understanding that we have very much in common on a very deep level. The knowledge of plurality begins life; but in the consciousness of unity is life's culmination.

May I tell you something? There are further stages in development of the *Nafs*. The furthest being the *Nafs al-Salima*, in which man's consciousness is removed to an abstract plane. In the heart of a person at this point of evolution, love is raised from admiration to worship; love is his being. Such a person lives on a higher plane of life, judging by different standards, though his inspiration springs from the ordinary. Whatever you do, whether you're a thinker, visionary, or laborer, you become absorbed in the contemplation of the essence of things. This means you become incapable of regarding anything as common or unclean. Eventually, in your contemplation of the mystery of life, your devotion to the pursuit of truth, and self-sacrifice to the cause of humanity, may gradually etherealize you above every material object.

Jung: May I ask, do you believe your Sufi teachings and practices amplify the progress of individuation and self-realization as I have described these processes?

Inayat Khan: I know. I don't need to believe it.

References

Corbin, H. (1969). *Creative Imagination in the Sufism of Ibn `Arabi*, R. Manheim, Trans. Princeton, NJ: Princeton University Press

_____. (1977). *Spiritual Body and Celestial Earth*. Princeton, NJ: Princeton University Press

_____. (1994). *The Man of Light in Iranian Sufism*. Amherst, MA: Omega Publications

_____. (1998). *Alone with the Alone: Creative Imagination in the Sufism of Ibn 'Arabi*. Princeton, NJ: Princeton University Press

Csikszentmihalyi, M. (1990). *Flow: The Psychology of Optimal Experience*. New York City: Harper & Row

Hermansen, M. (2000). *Hybrid Identity Formations in Muslim America: The Case of American Sufi Movements*. Boston: Harvard Canvas

Jironet, K. (2002). *The Image of Spiritual Liberty*. Leuven: Peeters Publishers

_____. (2009). *Sufi Mysticism into the West: Life and Leadership of Hazrat Inayat Khan's Brothers 1927-1967*. (New Religious Identities in the Western World). Leuven, Belgium: Peeters Publishers

Jung, C.G. (1989). *Memories, Dreams, Reflections*. A. Jaffe, Ed., R. & C. Winston, Trans. New York: Vantage Books

_____. (2009). *The Red Book: Liber Novus*. S. Shamdasani, Ed. S. Shamdasani, M. Kyburz, & J. Peck, Trans. New York: W. W. Norton

Khan, Hazrat Inayat. (1989). *The Sufi Message*. Vol. I. The Way of Illumination. New Delhi: Motilal Banarsidass

_____. (1989). *The Sufi Message.* Vol. II. The Mysticism of Music, Sound and Word. New Delhi: Motilal Banarsidass

_____. (1989). *The Sufi Message.* Vol. III. The Art of Personality. New Delhi: Motilal Banarsidass

_____. (1989). *The Sufi Message.* Vol. IV. Mental Purification and Healing New Delhi: Motilal Banarsidass

_____. (1989). *The Sufi Message.* Vol. V. Spiritual Liberty. New Delhi: Motilal Banarsidass

_____. (1989). *The Sufi Message.* Vol. VI. The Alchemy of Happiness. New Delhi: Motilal Banarsidass

_____. (1989). *The Sufi Message.* Vol. VIII. Sufi Teachings. New Delhi: Motilal Banarsidass

_____. (1989). *The Sufi Message.* Vol. IX. The Unity of Religious Ideals. New Delhi: Motilal Banarsidass

_____. (1989). *The Sufi Message.* Vol. XI. Philosophy, Psychology, Mysticism. New Delhi: Motilal Banarsidass

_____. (1989). *The Sufi Message.* Vol. XII. The Divinity of the Human Soul. New Delhi: Motilal Banarsidass

_____. (1996). *Diwan of Inayat Khan.* Westbrook, J. D. Trans. New Delhi: Motilal Banarsidass

_____. (1997). *Biography of Pir-O-Murshid Inayat Khan.* Guillaume-Scamhart, E. & van Voorst van Beest, M.. Eds. London: East-West Publications

_____. (2007). *The Dance of the Soul: Gayan Vadan Nirtan: Sufi Sayings.* New Delhi: Motilal Banarsidass

Khan, M. (1982). *Pages in the Life of a Sufi.* The Netherlands: Mirananda

Khan, Zia Inayat. (2001). ed. *A Pearl in Wine: Essays in the Life, Music and Sufism of Hazrat Inayat Khan.* New Lebanon, NY: Omega Publications

_____. (2006). *A Hybrid Sufi Order at the Crossroads of Modernity: the Sufi Order and Sufi Movement of Pir-o-Murshid Inayat Khan.* Department of Religion in Graduate School of Duke University, Durham, NC

Lawrence, B. (1983). *The Early Chishti Approach to Sama.* New Delhi: Manohar

Rawlinson, A. (1997). *Book of Enlightened Masters: Western Teachers in Eastern Traditions.* Chicago: Open Court

Schopenhauer, A. (2010). *The World as Will and Representation.* Vol. 1. Norman, J.; Welchman, A.; Janaway, C., Eds. Cambridge: Cambridge University Press (1819)

Piraino, F. (2016). Between real and virtual communities: Sufism in Western societies and the Naqshbandi Haqqani case. *Social Compass,63*(1), 93-108

Rozehnal, R. (2019). *Cyber Sufis: Virtual Expressions of the American Muslim Experience (Islam in the Twenty-First Century).* London: Oneworld Academic

Stein, M. (2020). *The Collected Writings of Murray Stein: Volume 1: Individuation.* Asheville, NC: Chiron Publications

Von Franz, M-L. (1997). *Alchemical Active Imagination: Revised Edition (C. G. Jung Foundation Books Series).* Boston: Shambhala

THE BUDDHIST
NO-SELF

8

The Cuckoo's Call of Instant Presence: Self and Nonself in Jung, Bion, Buddhism and Dzogchen

Judith Pickering

This chapter examines the interface between Jung's concept of Self and Buddhist teachings on śūnyatā and anātman, or emptiness and nonself. A clinical case of "Ester" shows the importance of having a healthy sense of self before undergoing intensive Buddhist practices involving teachings on śūnyatā and anātman and certain contraindications for patients suffering a disorder of self. Jungian analysis may here help develop a sense of continuity, ongoing being, individuation and self-hood, all of which are necessary psychological developments before challenging the sense of self and ego-centricity. A second case, that of "James" shows how when a person already has a healthy sense of self, Buddhist meditation practices and analysis may be mutually beneficial.

Ester

Ester has a haunted, hollowed-out look. She feels no more than an amoebalike semblance of prelife, an alien, alienated and amorphous, with no sense of ongoing being. She is skinless and porous — the emotional states of others pass through her like the tides of an ocean. Ester feels she is falling forever into an abyss of no-thing-ness. No one is there for her. She is alone. She doesn't exist. Picking up a self-help book on mindfulness in her local bookshop, she feels drawn to its descriptions of Buddhist teachings on nonself and emptiness. She then attends a retreat run by Western neo-Buddhists in northern Queensland, Australia, near the sea. The daily routine consists of teachings followed by 12 hours of alternating single-pointed mindfulness and walking meditations. The retreat is conducted in strict silence, all interaction with other participants forbidden, including eye contact. There is no opportunity to discuss disturbing experiences and perceptual distortions arising during meditation. After a teaching on emptiness, Ester feels literally mortified, suspended in thin air, but there was no one to be suspended because she doesn't exist and there was no air to suspend her as there is no air either. In fact, it felt as if there was no one, no-where, no-thing but pure no-thing-ness, and this nothingness was "evil."

Ester is found by a passerby wading naked into dangerous surf on a beach near the retreat. She tells me how she was supposed to owe her life to that person, for the area was known for its dangerous rips and there had been previous drownings. But, she comments, 'What life is there to save for someone who doesn't exist in the first place?'

The retreat director had, it seems, presented the Buddhist view of *śūnyatā,* or emptiness, in a way that for Ester implied annihilation, nonexistence, a void of nothingness. Ester also did not receive the benefits of a committed one-to-one student-teacher relationship with a realized master, nor was there any supportive psychological care, care that she now entered sought to find in therapy with me.

James

James is a seasoned Buddhist meditator. He enters Jungian analysis seeking help, both to integrate his spiritual experiences with the goal of individuation, and to work on psychological obstacles to the path of enlightenment. In his first session, he relates the following dream:

> I dream that I am at a Buddhist retreat. My teacher looks directly into my eyes, and I feel I am seen utterly to my core. There is no intermediary, just his looking directly into my mind, and I look into his, and his wisdom-mind is what is transmitted. It is so personal, yet a wisdom that pervades all, beyond all concept, yet it is full of boundless love and compassion for all. I feel like all last traces of old complexes, defensive tendencies and impure vision fall away. I feel I could melt into rainbow light, and I have no fear of dying, my entire body is filled with peace beyond understanding. At the same time, I feel at one with the world and full of compassion for all the needless suffering based on ignorance of our true nature that leads to aggression, possessiveness, concepts of me and mine, you and yours, hope and fear, conflict, war, all the troubles of the world. I find myself crying uncontrollably, and I want to do all I can to help others.
>
> Afterward, I walk outside, and the grass is vibrating with light of the early sun shimmering on the dewfall. Each blade of grass is refracting dancing rainbows of light. The world has never seemed so radiant, so alive, so real before, as if I had lived all my life with cataracts and only now can I see clearly. I was half asleep, and only now awakened to true reality.
>
> I hope that nothing can take away this realization, but how will I keep this inner vision clear and untarnished, how will I abide by and in it without grasping it or turning away? That is the question I bring to you as my therapist.

259

I don't quite know how to answer such a vitally important question. I tentatively reply, "Perhaps it's about not grasping after this experience but integrating it, keeping it alive, freshly knowing it and discovering it again and again."

Ester and James both attended Buddhist retreats but what they experienced could not be more divergent. For Ester, it led to an experience of annihilation, for James, one of beatitude. What was the reason for such difference, given they were both doing similar practices? In essence, Ester did not have a healthy sense of self to begin with, and teachings on *anatman,* or nonself, and emptiness, or *śūnyatā,* given in a context without psychological support served to aggravate her disorder of self, leading to fragmentation. James had a well-developed healthy sense of self; he was resilient, flexible, grounded, and so meditation led to realization.

Introduction

This paper presents a quaternity of interrelated matters concerning self and nonself in Jungian Analysis and Buddhism, illustrated with two clinical vignettes. We will compare convergences and divergences in Jung's Self and Buddhist nonself, the path of individuation and the path of enlightenment. The two clinical vignettes show how a healthy sense of self is necessary before one begins to challenge or deconstruct it. Ester suffered a disorder of self and profound experiences of derealization and depersonalization. Buddhist teachings on emptiness and nonself unfortunately exacerbated her existential anxieties to the point of attempted suicide. Jungian analysis served to shore up a healthy sense of self, enabling her to later approach Buddhist practices in a more grounded, gentle way. James had a healthy sense of self to begin with and found a sense of joy, peace, infinity, timelessness, and fulfilment through Buddhist practice. He also found Jungian analysis helped him work through psychological obstacles to his spiritual path.

Patients such as James also raise questions concerning the compatibility of a Buddhist path toward enlightenment and the Jungian path of individuation. The Buddhist path toward enlightenment involves realization of nonself. The Jungian path of individuation involves realization of the true Self. How might a Buddhist concept of nonself be reconciled with Jung's Self as being the center and circumference, and its realization through the process of individuation as the ultimate goal of life?

There are other vital questions for psychoanalysis. Is the Self something that we are born with or that is there in *potentia*? Is individuation about *creating* a sense of the true Self, or is it about *discovering* what was there all along? Is psychotherapy a developmental progression or one of uncovering what is already there through removing all that is false, all that obscures our true nature?

The mystic path toward ultimate reality is often described as one of ever-closer union. Yet for apophatic mystics, the ultimate level at-one-ment is not actually becoming one with absolute reality because we were never separate to begin with. We do not attain anything because there is nothing to attain. It is what the ancient Greeks called *alétheia*, unconcealment. We break through myriad layers of psychological, intellectual, emotional, and spiritual obscuration preventing this realization.

As Thomas Merton put it, the true self is like an apple ripening in the sun: All one can do is bask in the sunlight. Mystical experience for Meister Eckhart (1260-1328) is one of discovery, realizing what was always there, homecoming, the recovery of a lost identity or memory in the uncreated ground of being, a return to our Origin in God:[1] "Truly you are the hidden God in the ground of the soul, where God's ground and the soul's ground are one ground. The more one seeks you, the less one finds you. You should so seek God that you find God nowhere. If you do not seek God, then you will find God."[2]

---

[1] Turner, 1995, p. 177
[2] Eckhart, 1981, p. 192

Jung writes of how: "… even the enlightened person remains what he is, and is never more than his own limited ego before the One who dwells within him, whose form has no knowable boundaries, who encompasses him on all sides, fathomless as the abysms of the earth and as vast as the sky."[3]

Self in the Jungian Context

Jung's concept of Self is enormously complex, Self being "an extremely composite thing" a "conglomerate soul,"[4] "paradoxical, animoninal," male and female, "old man," child, …. a true complexion oppositorum.[5] One classic definition of the Self is as follows: "The self is not only the centre, but also the whole circumference which embraces consciousness and unconscious, it is the centre of this totality, just as the ego is the centre of consciousness."[6]

Jung's concept of Self is much more than having a sense of self. For Jung, this personal self is not merely the ego or personal identity. Self for Jung is "the potential for integration of the total personality, including all psychological and mental processes, physiology and biology, all positive and negative, realised or unrealised potential, and the spiritual dimension."[7] It includes both consciousness and unconsciousness. Jung used Self to denote the most central archetype, the archetype of order. The Self is psychic totality, and the psychic function is to "balance and pattern *all* of a person's life in terms of purposes as yet unconsidered and unlived…. The self functioning as a synthesiser and mediator of opposites within the psyche … [and] prime agent in the production of deep, awesome, 'numinous' symbols of a self-regulatory and healing nature." [8]

---

[3] CW 11, § 758
[4] CW 9i, § 634
[5] CW 9ii, § 355
[6] CW 12, § 444
[7] Samuels, 1985, p. 72
[8] Ibid., p. 92

The Self as representing the totality of the person, the center and circumference, enables one to discover the meaning of one's life. Jung drew on Meister Eckhart, who, in Sermons 1-4, put forward a mysticism based on the ground of being (*grunt*). Within the ground there is the eternal birth of the Word in the soul, one's ground is God's ground, and the soul is empty, naked and pure.[9] Jung speaks of the Pleroma, an "uncreated potentiality beyond time and space from which all being emerges. It is a given state of oneness or unity in which all potential opposites commingle in their uncreated state"[10] and which is related to "primordial unconsciousness, undifferentiated nothingness and fullness," a "mysterious Nothingness,"[11] which is boundless, continuous, and eternal.[12] Jung links the *unus mundus* with the psychoid, in which matter and psyche are two aspects of one substance.

Self and Nonself in Buddhism: Śūnyatā and Anātman

How might Jung's Self relate to teachings on nonself (*Anātman*) in Buddhism? Jung discussed this very issue with a Zen master.

On May 16, 1958, a meeting took place between Jung and the Zen master Hisamatsu Shin'ichi (1889-1980). At this meeting, Hisamatsu asked Jung whether the true self was the conscious or unconscious. Jung replied: "The consciousness calls itself 'I' while the 'self' is not 'I' at all. The self is the whole, because the personality — you as the whole — consists of the 'conscious' and the 'unconscious.' That is the whole, or the 'self.' But 'I' knows only the consciousness. The 'unconscious' remains to me unknown."[13]

Another question concerning Jungian and Buddhist views of the self is its origin. Is there a primary self there from the beginning,

---

[9] Walsh, 2008
[10] Madden, 2008, p. 79
[11] Ibid., p. 83
[12] Ibid., p. 84
[13] Jung & Hisamatsu, 1968, p. 27

or does it come into being over the course of our life? Michael Fordham's concept of 'the primary self' is a model of the Self as a preexisting totality,[14] a separate, unique individual from the dawn of life, relating to "cosmic experiences extending to the limits of space and time."[15]

As Colman observes, this is reminiscent of the Zen Buddhist question, "What is the face of the Buddha before you were born? The primary self is the original Buddha face. Once again we find that we are brought up against the limits of what is thinkable."[16] Young-Eisendrath seeks to avoid essentialism and reification of the Jungian Self, instead taking a constructivist position.[17] Colman describes the Self as both totality and process, emerging out of a primary wholeness, yet also a being of interconnection and oneness with the entire universe.[18]

Teachings on *anātman* point to the absence of a permanent, autonomous, persisting, unchanging, independent, eternal ego. Self in the Buddhist context is not a permanent, unchanging, static entity cut off from the world, but is constantly in flux, changing, interdependent, intersubjective, interconnected: devoid of inherent, independent existence, yet it appears. Although it appears, it is empty; although it is empty, it appears. If we really examine our mind, there is not one aspect that is not always changing: Our thoughts are changing, our emotions are changing. They arise, and they disperse. Thoughts are fleeting, coming and going like waves on the surface of the ocean. We are not who we were yesterday. At a cellular level, our entire body is replaced every seven years. If we really examine our body, we soon see it is not permanent, singular, independent but breaks into constantly changing, interacting impermanent cells and molecules.

---

[14] Colman, 2000, p. 12
[15] Fordham & Zinkin, 1987, p. 143
[16] Colman, 2000, p. 16
[17] Young-Eisendrath, 1997
[18] Colman, 2000

The Buddhist view of nonself (*anātman*) does not mean that we have no self and do not exist. Śūnyatā is often translated in the general Mahāyāna context as emptiness, referring to the absence of inherent existence. The view of śūnyatā does not mean simply emptiness in a nihilistic sense, that all is nothing or nonexistent. *Śūnyatā* is a difficult term to translate, usually rendered as "emptiness" or "void-ness." It refers to the negation of all possible conceptualizations of "reality" and a transcendence of both eternalism and nihilism.

Yongey Mingur Rinpoche laments the fact that śūnyatā is "one of the most misunderstood words in Buddhist philosophy." It is not a void but more a sense of great openness and peace. In Tibetan, śūnyatā is *stong pa nyid, tongpa* meaning "empty," in the sense of beyond conceptualization. He suggests that a better translation might be "inconceivable" or "unnameable." The word *nyid* when added to another word gives the sense of "possibility," a "sense that anything can arise, anything can happen," so śūnyatā is closer to meaning "an unlimited potential for anything to appear, change, or disappear."[19]

Buddhism emphasizes self as being fluid and multiple, a moving continuum. Just as Heraclitus (533–473 B.C.E.) also observed, we might step into a river, but the river is not the same river. So too, we are and we are not, just as the river does not contain the same water. William James grappled with the problem of how to reconcile identity and continuity of self with the flux of consciousness as process. The stream of consciousness or mind, although ever changing, continues like a river. The same metaphor of a stream is used in Buddhism to explain the paradox of how the self seems to be eternal and unchanging when it is dynamic and impermanent. When we look at a particular river, it *appears* to be the same water, although the water we look at is never the same water, and what we looked at a moment ago has flowed onward. We create a construct of something that seems to stay the same and bestow upon our vision of the moving droplets of water the name "river." This "name-

---

[19] Yongey Mingur, 2007, pp. 59-60

making" practice, imputing identity, continuity, cohesion, sameness, permanence, and autonomy, is, according to Buddhism, the very basis of the unknowing (*avidyā*), which is seen as the root cause of all suffering and delusion. James avoids this philosophical error by emphasizing self-as-consciousness-as-process, as a function, not an entity in itself. Self is an awareness of the movements of an inner life. The "self" carries feelings of basic unity and continuity, and a recognition of change, contingency, as well as agency, the sense of freedom of choice. The "self" is not a static structure but a process.

Unfortunately in the West, Buddhist teachings on emptiness and nonself have often been misunderstood as implying a void of nonexistence and that "I do not exist." Many Westerners suffering disorders of self, such as Ester, have found these teachings amplifying their sense of unreality and nonexistence.

An important aspect of feeling real and alive is having a sense of continuity, of going on, being, that we are integrated, coherent, continuous, even if we are also deintegrated, incoherent and discontinuous. Winnicott's "going on being" depicts a sense of continuity of a sense of being real, creatively alive, through the vicissitudes of life. "Going on being" is also relational: the sense that another continuously holds us in mind gives rise to a sense of continuity of being.

In Buddhism, the word "tantra" also means continuity, without interruption. Guenther compares tantra to a loom, and figuratively "a weaving of one's life."[20] He relates tantra to interdependence and interrelationship. Such "continuity of being ... arises out of the question of how we are going to *be*. Tantra also sees the question of how we are going to be in terms of relationship, realising that [one] is always related to something or someone."[21] Chögyam Trungpa uses the analogy of that which threads things together: "In Tibetan tantra is called *rgyud*, which is like the thread that runs through beads."[22]

---

[20] Guenther, 1996, p. ix
[21] Guenther, 1975, p. 2
[22] Trungpa, 1975, p. 8

Misunderstandings of what nonself means in Buddhism can cause difficulties for Westerners who encounter Buddhist teachings. My patient James had a good sense of self to begin with, so it was not a problem for him to meditate on selflessness, nor through analysis to further a path of individuation that also involves surrendering the omnipotence of ego in the service of Self. But others who suffer depersonalization and derealization sometimes find that misunderstandings of teaching on *anatman* exacerbate pathologies of self, as it was for Ester.

Ester and the thread of nonbeing

When Ester arrives for her next session, I open the door to a white, frozen mask. Ester has disappeared into a void of nothingness. Lying on the couch, she turns away from me, staring in stony silence at the blank wall as if staring into vacant space. She is totally isolated in a realm of nonexistence. I feel myself fading into nothingness, absence, unmitigated bleakness, and blankness. An abyss opens up between us. On her side, she is sucked into the evil eternity of a psychic black hole, evil because the isolation is for her absolute. On my side, I feel helpless: How can I cross the abyss of agonized alienation?

Ester turns to me, breaking the silence says: "I am not in the hell realms. I am the hell realms. I am nothingness incarnate."

We sit for what feels like an agonizing eternity, listening to the deafening silence of the void.

Ester both feared that she did not exist as well as doubted the existence of the outer world. In place of a healthy sense of self and ongoing being, she had but an empty core inside. She also suffered what was termed "nameless dread" by Bion[23] or "primitive agony" by Winnicott[24] (1974) or a black hole in the psyche.[25] Not only did Ester

---

[23] Bion, 1962
[24] Winnicott, 1974
[25] Bion, 1962; Winnicott, 1974; Grotstein 1990

fear that "I do not exist," but there was also a fear that "others do not exist for me." In addition, others, in their otherness, are experienced as threatening, if not annihilating.

Ester found herself drawn to philosophies that seemed to make sense of the experience of derealization. She constructed a heady combination of Western existential, postmodern and neo-Nietzschean readings with those of Buddhist teachings on *nirvāṇa*, *anātman* and *śūnyatā*, which Ester interpreted as meaning, in turn, total extinction, nonexistence and "the void."

Ester's existential predicament exemplifies a more general area of concern found in situations involving Western practitioners of Buddhism, whether in traditional settings in Asia or Western settings ostensibly adapted to the Western mind. Have there been problems of translation in regard to Buddhist teachings on *anātman* (nonself) as implying the self is completely nonexistent, and interpretations of *śūnyatā* (emptiness) as meaning all reality is nonexistent, or void?

Such nihilistic readings may have adverse psychological consequences when they are used for defensive reasons to make sense of, yet thereby exacerbate certain forms of psychopathology. In such situations, psychotherapy may be a useful adjunct to meditation practice, helping a meditator identify, resolve, dissolve, and ultimately heal psychological wounds that obstruct realization.

This relates to another issue concerning situations where Westerners attend large Buddhist retreats in which personalized psycho-spiritual care may be lacking. Traditionally, a Buddhist master would know the student well and carefully select appropriate teachings and practices according to a disciple's psychological, physical, and spiritual predispositions, proficiency, and maturity. For example, teaching emptiness, or *śūnyatā*, to someone who is not ready can be extremely harmful. Skilfull means and discernment are required in knowing how best to help a given person on the path to enlightenment. In the traditional context, it was an established ethical principle that one should not teach *śūnyatā* or *anātman* to those who are not ready. One can see here the difference between a patient such as James who did have a healthy sense of self and for whom Buddhist meditation on *śūnyatā* was experienced as one of beatitude, entering a realm of infinity, whereas for Ester it was one of abject terror.

A metaphor given in many Buddhist teachings is that the Buddha is like a doctor, the teachings like medicine, and the student like a patient who is ill. It is said that Buddha observed that there were over 84,000 forms of emotional and psychological disease; consequently, he taught over 84,000 forms of meditation as psychological medicine to be applied judiciously according to need. So too, the Buddhist teacher needs to diagnose the particular psychological, physical, and spiritual conditions pertaining to a given student. The teacher can then prescribe the right teachings and meditative practices for that student. What is medicine for one student might be poison for another. A student suffering fear of ego loss can have adverse reactions when introduced to teachings on *śūnyatā*. Even highly experienced meditators tend to find *śūnyatā* confronting. It is said that Bodhisattvas on the Path of Accumulation, when beginning to truly realize *śūnyatā*, may be terrified that they are being extinguished and becoming nonexistent.

Therapy for Ester gradually afforded her first a sense of ongoing being, of continuity, of cohesion, such that she gradually developed a healthier sense of self, Jung's ego, as well as agency and a sense of aliveness. I steered her away from doing meditations on nonself or even mindfulness, toward meditations on loving kindness, firstly directed at herself (self-compassion). A Buddhist mantra she found useful was "May I be well, may I be happy," then "May all be well, may all be happy." She began to feel a sense of peace, part of her natural surroundings, experiencing moments of joy witnessing the play of sunlight on a wall, a sense of belonging, of the vastness of space as a realm of interconnection rather than alienation.

Ester's initial experiences of nameless dread also raise two further considerations. First, there is the question of what *śūnyatā* and *anātman* might inconceivably mean in the original Buddhist context (remembering that there are different points of view in different schools). Second, there is the traditional teacher-student relationship and the specific circumstances in which a teacher would ordinarily give teachings on *śūnyatā* and *anātman*. Both *śūnyatā* and *anātman* are apophatic terms designed to transcend what are seen as the two extreme views: those of eternalism (Skt. *nitya dṛṣṭi*) and nihilism (*uccheda dṛṣṭi*). Eternalism refers to the belief in oneself being concrete, independent, eternal, and singular. Nihilism is the belief that nothing exists, there is no ultimate reality. Unfortunately, due to misinterpretations of both terms, Ester initially fell into nihilism.

So, we can see that a major difficulty is that Buddhist teachings on emptiness and nonself are all too readily misread. While the essence of mind is described as empty, it is not nonexistent or nonsentient like a stone. We are aware, and this awareness is what is known as cognizant nature, or clarity. We perceive, understand, know, and are aware. This clarity aspect is sometimes known as "luminosity" or "Clear Light." In the Prajnaparamita Sutra, it is said:

> The mind is devoid of mind
> For the nature of mind is clear light.

We are not our projections, stories, traumas, habitual tendencies, emotions: All these are like weather patterns on Mount Zion. There is, however, a ground of awareness, of clarity: From waking to sleeping, and even through sleep, there is a clear, knowing consciousness or awareness, of whatever we are experiencing. Awareness is our mind-stream; it is also pure heart. We are aware of being happy, sad, joy, loneliness. This fundamental pure awareness is the cognizant aspect of mind and is the innermost, essential nature of mind.

The basis of both *saṃsāra* and *nirvāṇa* is the same ground that is primordially pure and self-perfected. The person who has realized enlightenment realizes phenomena are merely projections of the deluded mind, lacking inherent existence, "like a rainbow in the sky or like the water in a mirage."[26] A metaphor for the difference between *nirvāṇa* and *saṃsāra* is of water and ice:

---

[26] Khyentse, in Berzin, 1993, p. 606

> Just as water, which exists in a naturally free-
> flowing state, becomes frozen into ice under
> the influence of a cold wind, so the ground
> of being exists in a naturally free state, yet
> the entire spectrum of cyclic existence is
> established solely due to the underlying
> conception of an individual self and a self-
> nature of phenomena.[27]

Such an image is evocative of when patients find themselves caught up in a traumatic memory system that activates primitive defenses, they respond to the world of others in a repetitive, concrete, and hardened way. When they are freed from such traumatic complexes, they respond more freely, with flow, spontaneity, and softness.

What are other possible implications of teachings on *anātman* for psychotherapy? In psychotherapy, the aim is to find the Self. In Buddhism, the aim is to un-find the self. Yet these aims are not as divergent as they might seem. What is being refuted in Buddhist teachings on *anātman* is not the self *per se*, but an abiding, eternal, inherent, and independent ego. For the Buddhists, such self-grasping is a root cause of mental illness, and hence realization of nonself is vital to psychological well-being. Such Buddhist teachings on *anātman* may help overcome ego-centricity and narcissistic defenses of the false self in patients who cling to a rigidly reified view of their existence.

Dzogchen

Dzogchen is an ancient spiritual tradition. Although associated with Tibetan Buddhism, Dzogchen is beyond a school or religion. The word *Dzogchen* is an abbreviation of *Dzogpachenpo* (*rdzogs pa chen po*; in Sanskrit *Mahāsandhi* or *Atiyoga*) often translated as the "Great Perfection" or "Great Completeness." Dzogchen is called the

---

[27] Dudjom Lingpa, in Barron, 1994, p. 157

"Great Perfection" because "it is complete and perfect (rdzogs-pa) in itself, with nothing lacking, and because there exists nothing higher or greater (chen-po) than it."[28]

From the perspective of Buddhist Dzogchen, our true nature is there all along, but it is covered over in illusions, delusions, projections, the mire of emotional baggage we carry around us. The task of spiritual practice is to remove all that is occluding realization of our real nature. Our fundamental ground of being is not created but uncovered, recognized, and realized. The fundamental nature of the mind is the *tathāgatagarbha*, "or essence of enlightenment in all beings," which is "present from the beginning."[29] Applied to psychotherapy, the implication is that therapy is about removal of complexes, defense systems, and distorted views, so that one's true nature can manifest and shine forth.

Dzogchen is useful in the context of Ester because Dzogchen emphasizes that *śūnyatā* is not the end of the story: Although things are empty, they also appear; there is spontaneous presence. *Rigpa* refers to a nondual realization of pristine awareness and transcendence, an awakening to infinity, a direct revelation of ultimate reality, the discovery of the primordial ground of all beings, that, underneath all that occludes it, is like the adamantine purity of a diamond. Such a ground is ever present, like the sun behind the clouds. The path to realization is based on pure awareness unconditioned by thought, emotionality, or conceptualization. From the perspective of Dzogchen, everything is pure, perfect, undefiled, merely covered over with cognitive and emotional obscuration.

Real nature

What is our real nature from the perspective of Dzogchen? One metaphor often used is that our true nature is like the sky, and the psychological confusion that obscures it is like the clouds. Behind

---

[28] Reynolds, 1996, p. 21
[29] Guarisco, 2015, p. 36

the clouds is an infinite expanse of clear blue space. Another is that of a mirror. The mirror's nature is to reflect whatever is placed in front of it, but the mirror in itself is not that which it reflects. The mirror is pure, limpid, clear. Reflections never stain the mirror; they just appear in it.

The ground of our nature is said to have an essence that is empty, a nature that is cognizant, and a compassionate energy that is all pervasive.

> Imagine a sky, empty, spacious, and pure from the beginning; its essence is like this. Imagine a sun, luminous, clear, unobstructed, and spontaneously present; its nature is like this. Imagine that sun shining out impartially on us and all things, penetrating all directions; its energy, which is the manifestation of compassion, is like this: Nothing can obstruct it and it pervades everywhere.[30]

By empty essence, it is meant that mind is devoid of permanence, independence. It is "pure from the beginning (ka dag) ... because, like space, it is free of all impediments" and is the basis for all manifestation.[31] "This consciousness is the innermost subtle mind. We call it the buddha nature, the real source of all consciousness. The continuum of this mind lasts even through Buddhahood."[32]

It is the "fundamental innate mind of clear light." It is "self-perfected (lhun grub) ... because it exists spontaneously from the beginning, like the sun which shines in space. Clarity is the pure quality of all thought and of all perceived phenomena, uncontaminated by mental judgement."[33] An example is that of the difference between apprehension and perception. We see a flower,

---

[30] Sogyal Rinpoche, 2002, p. 153
[31] Chögyal Namkhai Norbu, 1996, p. 53
[32] HH Dalai Lama, 1988, p. 45
[33] Chögyal Namkhai Norbu, 1996, p. 53

and at first, there is no mental judgment; it is simply a flower. Then we begin the process of judgment, categorizing our perception as "nice" or "ugly," then "I like" or "I do not like." Clarity is when there is simple perception.

It is also sometimes referred to as "ordinary mind" or "ordinary wisdom" or "the wisdom of ordinariness."[34] It is ordinary because it is natural, primordial, pure, pristine, clear, limpid, awareness that is cognizant, radiant and awake: "It is simply your flawless, present awareness, cognizant and empty, naked and awake."[35]

Path

Although there is no difference at the ultimate level between the Buddha and ordinary beings, at the relative level there is: Buddha Shakyamuni realized his nature, we have not. This is known as "one ground, two paths." We took the path of delusion and ignorance, and we live in a mire of psychological confusion and obscuration. The dualistic state of mind filled with concepts such as me and mine, subject and object, good and bad is the fundamental error. An example is a beautiful statue. We see the statue and judge it as beautiful. Then we say to ourselves, "I want it." We grasp at it. This desire and attachment bring suffering. Or we see something ugly. We feel aversion to it. We divide the world of others into like and dislike, want and don't want, attachment, and aversion. It is not the awareness that causes problems but the grasping of ego: involving a subject and object and an emotional reaction to the object of grasping or aversion. Pure awareness has no duality of subject and object, no grasping or aversion.

Primordial Ground

Bion talks of ultimate Truth, Absolute Reality, O, as

---

[34] Chögyam Trungpa Rinpoche, 1975
[35] Sogyal Rinpoche, 2002, p. 50

denoting "ultimate reality, absolute truth, the godhead, the infinite, the thing-in-itself," the "unknown," "the void and formless infinite."[36] Apophatic Christian mystics talk of inherent godliness, Advaita Vedanta of the nonduality of **Ātman** and *Brahman*. Dzogchen describes the primordial condition of each individual as being pure and empty, with infinite potential. Ultimate Reality in Dzogchen is described as the ground (*gzhi*), which is unchanging, indestructible, perfect, incorruptible, unborn, nondual, all-pervasive, spontaneous, luminous, and unobstructed. The Tibetan *gzhi* has also been translated as Ground, Base, Foundation, Primordial Basis, and Being. In its most general sense, *gzhi* refers to an "eternal, pure, and luminous reality that is the source of all phenomenal appearance."[37] "Self-arising wisdom" in its original condition is "intrinsically pure," free of dualistic thought, ineffable, inconceivable, the "base of all primordial purity." This is the "natural condition of primordial enlightenment."[38]

This is the numinous ground of being that James experienced in his practice of meditation. It was not one of nihilistic psychological annihilation, as it was for Ester.

A major principle of Dzogchen is the recognition that our pure nature is the fundamental reality underlying all appearance to the contrary, underneath all the pervasive ignorance that obscures this. There is nothing to achieve, nothing to strive for, "for one has already acquired it all … every wish has already been fulfilled," and one is "intrinsically endowed with all." So instead of striving, one effortlessly "rests with spontaneity," as there is nothing that needs to be done. One is "always in being," "never lacking anything" and so "nothing more is needed."[39] One leaves oneself undisturbed in the state of such-ness.[40]

---

[36] Bion, 1965, p. 171
[37] Studstill, 2005, p. 148
[38] Ibid., p. 130
[39] Karmay, 2007, p. 49
[40] Ibid., p. 54

> Those who search for an enlightenment
> outside their actual condition are moving
> further and further away from it. Reality is
> the emptiness, the primordial purity, that is
> the basis from which all phenomena arise,
> and these phenomena have no essence....
> Luminous awareness of one's self, beyond
> subject and object, expands without the need
> for an intentional meditation ... one finds that
> all things are perfect.[41]

From Mind to the Nature of Mind

Because the nature of mind is primordially pure with radiant spontaneous presence, nothing can ultimately pollute its fundamental purity. Thoughts and emotional defilements are merely adventitious stains that can be removed. Adventitious stains (*glo bur gyi dri ma*) refer to obscuration that is not intrinsically part of our primordially pure buddha nature but are layered upon its inherent luminosity. It is possible to remove them, like stains on a mirror. There are four categories of obscuration: karmic, emotional, cognitive, and habitual. This has implications for the ways in which psychological defense systems operate to alienate us from the world of others, where we construct what feels from within a wall of protection from potential hurt but is experienced from the outside as a wall of fortification fending others off. Dissolving defenses opens us to others and affirms a common humanity and continuity of being, the basis of compassion. This is why mystics observe that union with God or the Absolute automatically opens the heart.

The Ground is described as indescribable, unnameable, and ineffable. In the Commentary to the *Tun-huang* Manuscript IOL 647, it is said that language is a "deviation from the principle" and nothing can be predicated of pure Being. "The Absolute (*dharmatā*) has, from

---

[41] Guarisco, et al, 2013, p. 24

the very beginning, never been pronounced."[42] Although Absolute
Reality cannot be described in words, there is a state of contemplation
in which it can be realized, a formless and nonconceptual system
of contemplation, a "direct experience of the true nature of reality,
which is immediately present"[43] and which goes beyond any form of
prayer, spiritual practice or transformational method of meditation.
One abides in "ever-present, nondual and conceptual awareness and
spontaneous presence (*lhun gyis grub pa*), indicating immediate and
unfabricated presence."[44]

Self-liberation or individuation?

A patient may hope to find ways to overcome habitual
destructive emotions and impulses such as anger, depression,
anxiety, fear, and addiction. How might Buddhist teachings help such
a patient? The Hīnayāna path of renunciation would use methods
based on calming the mind, the Mahāyāna path of bodhicitta would
apply methods based on compassion, the Vajrayāna is a path of
transformation, and Dzogchen is said to be a path of self-liberation
(*rang grol*).

If one was afflicted by one of the "five poisons" (desire,
anger, delusion, pride, and jealousy) in the Hīnayāna path, one would
seek to overcome destructive emotions through practices based on
renunciation. For example, if the afflictive emotion besetting a person
was excessive sexual desire, one might meditate on the desired object
as a corpse or take a vow of celibacy. Mahāyāna methods are based
on compassion and bodhicitta. If one feels strong antipathy toward
a colleague, one might apply an equalizing meditation in which one
visualizes the disliked person as well as a person one likes and a
person to whom one feels neutral. One meditates on how all three
are equal in desiring happiness and wanting to be free of suffering,

---

[42] In Karmay, 1988, pp. 54-55
[43] Van Schaik, 2004, pp. 4-5
[44] Tiso, 2016, p. 210

and gradually one extends the same feelings of loving kindness felt toward the person who is close to the disliked person. Another practice known as *gtong len,* or giving and receiving, involves imagining one takes in all the suffering of the person in question and sends loving kindness to them.

In the Vajrayāna path of transformation, through symbolically rich deity meditations involving combinations of visualizations, mudras, and mantra, one engages directly with destructive emotions transforming them into their enlightened beneficent counterparts. Yet from the Dzogchen view, this still involves dualistic thinking, regarding one form of emotion as negative and needing to be transformed and one as good.

In the Dzogchen approach, being in the state of instant presence, whatever emerges is simply liberated like writing on water.[45] For example, in the very moment of becoming angry, one neither represses nor transform the anger but simply observes it without judgment. If there is no aversion or grasping, just simple awareness, the "anger will dissolve by itself, as if it had been left in its natural condition, allowing it to liberate of itself."[46] An example given is a snake-knot naturally unraveling, where, without fabrication, manipulation, or applying an antidote, there is an intrinsic freedom. The practice of letting be means that if one simply allows whatever thought or emotion to arise and disperse of its own accord, neither accepting nor rejecting, all such mental constructions are "self-liberated": "all thoughts vanish into emptiness like the imprint of a bird in the sky, or like writing on water."[47]

The implications for how one lives ordinary life, how one might even approach the practice of psychotherapy, is one in which, at the level of pure Being, one realizes that whatever arises in one's mind is the "play (*rol pa*) of the ultimate nature."[48]

[45] Namkhai Norbu, 1996, p. 59
[46] Ibid.
[47] Trungpa, 2004, xxiv
[48] Tulku Thondup, 1989a, p. 86

Ester tells me that she has to keep herself frantically busy because if she stops and does nothing, she feels assailed by what she describes as a hurricane of conflicting, confusing, disordered thoughts. In the Dzogchen practice of liberation through bare attention, having gained confidence in the state of contemplation, when thoughts arise, one does not allow them to proliferate, nor do we allow ourselves to "become entangled in a net of memories created by the mind." Instead, we "allow thoughts to dissolve in the sky of the mind without leaving a trace behind." "When thoughts arise, we turn our attention to them, recognize them for what they are, and without following them, allow them to remain in their own native condition ... and dissolve of their own accord."[49]

Such practices may be helpful for psychotherapy in regard to contemplation, reverie, and Freud's free-floating attention in the analytic setting. Practices of "letting be" enable the mind to find a natural presence and clarity, just as water that is not stirred naturally becomes clear. In the state of analytic reverie, one observes all one's thoughts and emotions like fish in a pool of water, potential sources of information about what is occurring in the here and now, dynamics of the analytic encounter. Yet one is not caught up in them, and neither does one reject or grasp after them, but without memory, desire, or understanding, one merely takes note of them, sees them, watches how they emerge and how they dissolve again. "A mind that has developed some familiarity with the state of immediate presence ... remains undistracted."[50] Longchenpa advises that "remaining with that state of contemplation, the thoughts release themselves right away like a drawing on water."[51]

---

[49] Reynolds, 1996, p. 111
[50] Studstill, 2005, p. 168
[51] Longchenpa, in Lipman & Peterson, 1987, p. 37

Ground, path, and fruit

Ultimate Reality in Dzogchen is described as the ground (*gzhi*), which is unchanging, indestructible, perfect, incorruptible, unborn, nondual, all-pervasive, spontaneous, luminous, and unobstructed. The mystical path involves returning to this fundamental ground of our true nature.

From the Dzogchen perspective, we are already self-perfected, the ground of all is inherent purity, and we are already Being, so to realize enlightenment is "nothing other than being naturally and spontaneously present in a state of immediate awareness."[52] Dzogchen practice involves letting be, relaxing into the natural state, "doing nothing" (*bya bral*). One's true nature is already perfect, so "there is nothing to correct, or alter, or modify."[53] Structured contemplative practices are replaced with the immediacy of awareness beyond all mental constructs. Yet such seemingly simple practices of just being are not so easy for the complicated mind!

> The practice of 'doing nothing' as a resting in the immediacy of the moment is diametrically opposed to the mind's habitual tendencies of grasping and distraction. It requires constant, non-wavering mindfulness, and therefore involves a very *active* and *effortful* 'holding' to the immediacy of present awareness. 'Doing nothing' turns out to be an extremely difficult psychological feat.[54]

Consequently, there are also a wealth of preliminary practices that, while not the state of contemplation itself, prepare one to enter the state of contemplation. The distinction is that in meditation there is something to be done; in the state of contemplation, there is not.[55]

---

[52] Studstill, 2005, p. 160
[53] Namkhai Norbu, 1989, p. x
[54] Studstill, 2005, p. 162
[55] Namkhai Norbu, 1986, p. 77

In Dzogchen, realization is not something to be constructed or achieved. Realization and self-liberation merely deepen until one simply remains continuously in the primordial state. There is no need to renounce the world, since "whatever arises has arisen as the play (*rol pa*) of the ultimate nature," so one can "simply enjoy all phenomena."[56] There is no need to change any outward forms, clothes, or habits. Maintaining a vibrant awareness and presence, all that arises spontaneously liberates, without effort. All "one's habitual vision, the limited cage, the trap of ego" simply collapses, opening "out into the spacious vision of what is. The bird is free, and can finally fly without hindrance. One can enter and enjoy the dance and play of energies, without limit."[57]

Primordial purity and Bion's O

Both Christian and Dzogchen mysticism describe an ultimate, absolute Reality that is the ground of one's being. This ultimate Reality is seen as ineffable and beyond the constructions of the ordinary mind. In both traditions, the most fundamental problems of existence derive from the alienation arising from an erroneous view of individual selfhood and the experience of separation consequent upon dualistic divisions of self and other, self and godhead or ultimate reality. Both traditions observe that "letting be" (Dzogchen) and abandonment (Christian apophaticism) is predicated on the knowledge that the goal is realization of our primordial nature, awakening to what we already are. Eckhart asks, "Why do you not stay in yourself and hold on to your own good? After all, you are carrying all truth in you in an essential manner."[58]

Both Christian apophatic mysticism and Dzogchen speak of absolute reality that is the ground of being and of the Absolute as ineffable, beyond ordinary ways of knowing. The meaning of

---

[56] Tulku Thondup, 1989, p. 86
[57] Namkhai Norbu, 1986, p. 118
[58] Eckhart, 1981, p. 184

life is to be found as a return to the primordial ground of being. In Dzogchen, we are that reality. For the apophatic mystics, we ultimately become one with the godhead, which is also our true nature. In both traditions, intellectual knowledge falls short of this aim in favor of direct, unmediated, mystical experience of Reality. This also entails transcending the strictures of egotism and awakening into a state of universal love and compassion for others. Both traditions teach contemplative methods for achieving their goals, the formless practices transcending concepts common to both. Yet in both traditions ultimately one leaves behind any techniques. In both, the goal of life may be to realize absolute truth, but ultimately goals are also abandoned. One abides in the bare immediacy of pure awareness, an aliveness and vibrancy without clinging to past or future, and without attempts to reify or conceptualize Being. Such Being Bion calls O.

Bion uses the sign "O" to "denote that which is ultimate reality, absolute truth, the godhead, the infinite, the thing-in-itself.[59] O does not fall in the domain of knowledge or learning save incidentally; it can be 'become,' but it cannot be 'known.'"[60]

Bion sought to find language capable of gesturing toward the indescribable nature of absolute truth, language that undid itself, opening one out to a domain beyond words. Bion uses "O" as a symbol unsaturated with preconceptions, ideas, or theories that obscure rather than reveal Ultimate Reality.

"O" denotes absolute truth, a numinous domain of reality that is beyond all concepts and that passes beyond all understanding. It refers to the core truth of an analytic situation, of an object, of each other. O can only be realized through processes of transformation in O, that is, becoming O. O cannot be known; it can only be becomed, yet we so often put up resistances to realization of O.

---

[59] Bion, 1965
[60] Bion, 1970, p. 26

Transformations from knowing to being

James describes how on a retreat he had a profound experience of primordial awakening. He was in the desert, doing a solitary retreat in a tent. He describes to me how one night he woke to feel the tent bathed in the silvery light of the moon. He clambered out to find himself illuminated by this light. He describes to me how:

> It was eerie, the desert was so quiet, a kind of hush, as if the world stood still. I looked out at the desert stretching into the horizon but the horizon seemed to dissolve into the inky blackness of the sky illuminated by the moon and stars, which shone with a light I had never seen before. They too stretched into the vastness of space. It seemed so totally still, yet there was a wind blowing the sand into furrows, blowing the sand into the sky where the light of the moon illuminated each grain of sand, so they too took on the appearance of stars, the sand becoming one with the Milky Way. I saw how small and insignificant I am, a grain of sand among countless grains of sand, yet also like a star. So I had this inexplicable sense of wonder and joy. Something indescribable but utterly precious entered my soul.
> I long to regain this intimation of eternity I had that night, but the more I grasp after it, the more it seems to elude me. I'm really worried I'll just go back to living life in the shadows, you know, just going through the motions. How can I keep the flames of inspiration that I had that night in the desert burning within me?

A patient might have a profound insight but resist the implications such insight brings: to become rather than know. Intellectual knowledge of one's faults is very different from a relationally embodied realization leading to change. Bion asks, "Is it possible through psychoanalytic interpretation to effect a transition from knowing the phenomena of the real self to being the real self?"[61]

This relates to the distinction between insight and structural change in analysis. It is much easier to have insight into our complexes than to do what it takes to liberate ourselves from their grip. Change requires consistent and incremental and sometimes humbling practice. We bump up against our habitual tendencies over and over. We often substitute intellectual knowledge for realization that brings change. For Bion, resistance is related to the fear of moving from knowing to becoming:

> The gap between reality and the personality, or, as I prefer to call it, the inaccessibility of O, is an aspect of life with which analysts are familiar under the guise of resistance. Resistance is only manifest when the threat is contact with what is believed to be real. ... Resistance operates because it is feared that the reality of the object is imminent.[62]

There is a difference between knowing and being. Interpretations are part of the K link. Bion notates three emotional intersubjective links between human beings as Love (L), Hate (H), and Knowledge (K).[63] What Bion calls the K link refers to the emotional experience present when two persons are related to each other, or two parts of a person: It is both intra- and inter-relational. The K link is a dynamic interrelational link that holds the tension between seeking to know while tolerating the frustration of not knowing. We inhibit the K link if we are saturated with prejudgments, stale memories, and old insights.

As Bion explains, often patients experience anxiety that transformation in K (an intellectual insight, for example) might lead to actual transformations in O, and this is responsible for the form of

---

[61] Bion, 1965, p. 148
[62] Ibid., p. 147
[63] Bion, 1962, p. 43

resistance in which interpretations appear to be accepted but, in fact, the acceptance is with the intention of "knowing about" O rather than becoming O.[64] Transformations in K may be described loosely as akin to "knowing about" something, whereas transformations in O are related to becoming or being O or to being "become" by O.[65] "Acceptance in O means that acceptance of an interpretation enabling the patient to 'know' that part of himself to which attention has been drawn is felt to involve 'being' or 'becoming' that person."[66]

There is often, Bion warns, "intolerance and fear of the 'unknowable' and hence of the unconscious in the sense of the undiscovered or the unevolved."[67] Patients may seem to agree with an interpretation, but their hidden intention is to "know about" rather than undergo the transformation required by truly accepting an interpretation. Furthermore, the patient may well attempt to "inveigle the analyst" by seeming to agree with the interpretation "into a collusive relationship to preserve K," that is intellectual knowledge about, rather than become O.[68] Both patient and analyst need to face the fear of the transformation from knowing oneself to becoming oneself. For Bion, interpretations "should be such that the transition from *knowing about* reality to *becoming real* is furthered."[69]

> If I am right in suggesting that phenomena are known but reality is "become" the interpretation must do more than increase knowledge. It can be argued that this is not a matter for the analyst and that he can only increase knowledge; that the further steps required to bridge the gap must come from the analysand; or from a particular part of the analysand, namely his 'godhead', which must

---

[64] Bion, 1965, pp. 159-160
[65] Ibid., p. 163
[66] Ibid., p. 164
[67] Ibid., p. 171
[68] Ibid., p. 162
[69] Ibid., p. 153

consent to incarnation in the person of the analysand.[70]

James described how, at first, he had tended on the side of reading about Buddhism, and it had taken him a long time to actually practice it. He initially read a mass of Buddhist self-help books and was very inspired by them but always stopped short of actually going near a monastery. Yet, he eventually came to realize that he needed to take seriously the voice that kept coming to him in quiet moments, that he should actually go and do a retreat at a Buddhist retreat center with a recognized and qualified teacher rather than think about it. In the end, it was abject despair and a sense of meaninglessness and emptiness that propelled him to visit a Buddhist monastery, and there, on retreat, he felt a subtle yet radical shift from "knowing about" the contemplative path to "experiencing it." On retreat, James "consented" to letting something indefinably mysterious into his heart. He said he felt more alive than he had ever been. Before, it was as if he had lived in the shadows, merely going through the motions of life, only half alive. The emptiness he felt before now felt like the emptiness of a cave that could be filled, the cave of the heart. He knew on retreat that something utterly precious had entered his heart, that the despair and sense of meaninglessness were necessary prerequisites. James then feared what would occur when he left the monastery after the short retreat. He feared he would harden his heart and cover over this deep sense of peace.

Returning from retreat, he discussed his dilemma with me, the fear he would return to the state of knowing about rather than being at one with his experience of contemplation. How might I be able to help him continue to heed this inner voice without trying to

---

[70] Ibid., p. 148

influence, persuade, or have desires for his spiritual well-being? It had to be up to James to heed this call, in his own way and time.

Taking one's life "watered down" and "diluted" was the dilemma James described in therapy on his return. How could he keep the flame burning within? How to avoid indefinitely postponing "the state of 'being' O"?[71]

Not only the analysand but also the analyst needs to confront fear of becoming in O. The "psycho-analyst can know what the patient says, does, and appears to be, but cannot know the O of which the patient is an evolution: he can only 'be' it. He knows phenomena by virtue of his senses but, since his concern is with O, events must be regarded as possessing either the defects of irrelevancies obstructing, or the merits of pointers initiating, the process of 'becoming' O. Yet interpretations depend on 'becoming' (since he cannot know O). The interpretation is an actual event in an evolution of O that is common to analyst and analysand."[72]

The implication here is that the analyst as well as patient becomes in O. Even when sitting with patients who are anti-religious, atheistic, disinterested in spiritual questions, our own capacity for at-one-ment, for negative capability, for reverie and contemplation as well as compassion and care remain vital healing elements of our work.

Conclusion

In this chapter, I have presented two clinical cases relevant to the interface between Buddhism and Jungian Analysis, and a common situation involving patients who practice Buddhism as well as seek analysis. One case, that of Ester, was used to illustrate situations when those suffering disorders of self and depersonalization find that Buddhist teachings on *śūnyatā* and *anātman* amplify and worsen their disorders of self. Here, Jungian analysis may help develop a sense

---

[71] Ibid., p. 149
[72] Bion, 1970, p. 27

of continuity, ongoing being, cohesion, agency, individuation, and self-hood, all of which are necessary psychological developments before challenging the sense of self and ego-centricity. The second case, that of James, shows how when a person already has a healthy sense of self, Buddhist teachings may be of great benefit. James also sought Jungian analysis to enable him to work through psychological complexes that he found obstructed his meditation practice. Here analysis and meditation were mutually beneficial.

Both cases show how spiritual and psychological development may be greatly enhanced by the long-term commitment of therapy involving a deeply personal relationship whereby the analyst can help with the specificity of the patient's psycho-spiritual complexes and challenges.

The chapter also compares the path of individuation and path of enlightenment, showing ways in which they may converge or diverge, how they both might in fact enhance the other. I also argue that Jung's Self and Buddhist nonself may not be as diametrically opposed as one might think, and in addition, Western misunderstanding of Buddhist nonself has at times led to nihilistic interpretations. Dzogchen teachings on primordial purity and the nature of mind point to a numinous and apophatic realm beyond concept that cannot be known, only become, just as Jung saw the Self as numinous and full of mystery and just as Bion sees O as a mystical realm of unknowable ultimate reality that is the ground of being and the goal of analysis.

References

Barron, R., Trans. (1994). *Buddhahood without Meditation: A Visionary Account Known as Refining Apparent Phenomen (nang-jang)*, by Dudjom Lingpa [*Bdud-'joms gling-pa*, b.1835]. Junction City, CA: Padma Publications

Berzin, A., Trans. & Ed. (1993). *The Four-Themed Precious Garland: An Introduction to Dzog-ch'en, the Great Completeness*, by Longchenpa with explanation and oral commentary by Dudjom Rinpoche & Beru Khyentze Rinpoche, Sherpa Tulku, M. Kapstein (Trans. & Ed.). Dharamsala, India: Library of Tibetan Works and Archives

Bion, W. (1962). *Learning from Experience*. Northvale, NJ: Jason Aronson

_____. (1965). *Transformations*. London: Karnac

_____. (1970). *Attention and Interpretation*. London: Tavistock

Colman, W. (2000). Models of the Self. In *Jungian Thought in the Modern World*. E. Christopher & H. Solomon, Eds. London: Free Association Books

Eckhart, M. (1981). *The Essential Sermons, Commentaries, Treatises, and Defense*. E. Colledge & B. McGinn, Trans. The Classics of Western Spirituality Series. New York: Paulist Press

Fordham, M. & Zinkin, L. (1987). Correspondence between Louis Zinkin and Michael Fordham. In H. Zinkin, R. Gordon & J. Haynes, Eds. *The Place of Dialogue in the Analytic Setting: The Selected Papers of Louis Zinkin* (1998) (pp. 133-148). London & Philadelphia: Jessica Kingsley

Guarisco, E., Clemente, A. & Valby, J., Trans. (2013). *The Marvelous Primordial State: The Mejung Tantra*. Arcidosso, Italy: Shang Shung Publications

_____. (2015). *Secret Map of the Body: Visions of the Human Energy Structure*. Arcidosso, Italy: Shang Shung Publications

Guenther, H. (1975). Tantra: Its origin and presentation. In H. Guenther & C. Trungpa, Eds., *The Dawn of Tantra*. pp. 6-12. Berkeley, CA: Shambhala

_____. (1996). *The Teachings of Padmasambhava*. New York: Brill Leiden

Karmay, Samten Gyaltsen (1988). *The Great Perfection (rDzogs-chen): A Philosophical and Meditative Teaching in Tibetan Buddhism*, 2nd ed. Leiden, Netherlands: E.J. Brill

Madden, K. (2008). *Dark Light of the Soul*. Great Barrington, MA: Lindisfarne Books

Namkhai Norbu (1996). *Dzogchen: The Self-Perfected State*. Ithaca, NY: Snow Lion Publications

Reynolds, J., Trans. (1996). *The Golden Letters: The Three Statements of Garab Dorje, the First Teacher of Dzogchen, attributed to Garab Dorje [dGa'-rab rdo-rje]*, with commentary by Dza Patrul Rinpoche, entitled *The Special Teaching of the Wise and Glorious King*. Ithaca, NY: Snow Lion Publications

Samuels, A. (2003). *Jung and the Post-Jungians*. London: Routledge

Sogyal Rinpoche (2002). *The Tibetan Book of Living and Dying*. New York: Harper Collins

Studstill, R. (2005). *The Unity of Mystical Traditions: The Transformation of Consciousness in Tibetan and German Mysticism*. Leiden, Netherlands: E.J. Brill

Tiso, F. (2016). *Rainbow Body and Resurrection*. Berkeley, CA: North Atlantic Books

Trungpa, C. (1975). Laying the foundation. In H. Guenther & C. Trungpa, Eds. *The Dawn of Tantra*. pp. 6-12. Berkeley, CA: Shambhala

Tulku Thondup, Trans. (1989). *Buddha Mind: An Anthology of Longchen Rabjam's Writings on Dzogpa Chenpo* [translated selections from the works of Longchenpa (kLong-chen rab-'byams-pa), b.1308], Buddhayana Series. Ithaca, NY: Snow Lion Publications

Turner, D. (1995). *Darkness of God: Negativity in Christian Mysticism*. Cambridge, England: Cambridge University Press

Van Schaik, S. (2004). *Approaching the Great Perfection*. Boston: Wisdom Publications

Vermote, R. (2011). Bion's critical approach to psychoanalysis. *Bion Today*, C. Mawson, Ed. pp. 349-366. London: Routledge

Winnicott, D. (1974). Fear of breakdown. *International Review of Psycho-Analysis*, Vol. 1, pp. 103-107

Yongey Mingyur Rinpoche & Swanson, E. (2007). *The Joy of Living: Unlocking the Secret Science of Happiness*. New York: Three Rivers Press

9

On a Possible Bridge between Individuation Theory and Dzogchen Psychology: Challenges, Pitfalls, Opportunities for a Transcendent "Third": A Dialogue between Murray Stein and Jim Manganiello

Murray Stein
Jim Manganiello

In this chapter, the authors attempt to forge a dialogue between the Jungian theory of progressive individuation, based on stages of work in Jungian analysis and Jungian depth therapy, and the Dzogchen psychology theory of immediate individuation based on nontemporal direct experience of the mind's Natural State. The goal is to discover a "transcendent third" position that would harmonize the two positions and create a new model of theory and practice. In one aspect, this is an attempt to harmonize West and East; in another, it is to dispense with the duality in favor of a trans-binary position. The authors remain cautious and aware of cultural differences while at the same time searching for commonalities. It remains a work in progress.

After many conversations and various attempts to write this article, the authors have chosen to present their views in three parts:

first, an extended statement by Jim Manganiello about Dzogchen psychology because it will be less familiar to this readership than Jung's theory of individuation; second, a brief statement on the individuation process by Murray Stein; third, a conversational dialogue between the two authors.

Jim Manganiello

I sought Murray out for collaboration on this chapter because of his celebrated work on individuation. Murray's book, *The Principle of Individuation: Toward the Development of Human Consciousness*, moved me to reflect on the psychology and spirituality duality. And on how Jungian depth psychology and Dzogchen psychology address what each other is missing.

A focus on individuation provides an opportunity for Jungian depth psychology and Dzogchen psychology to meet, greet, and engage in meaningful conversation. A challenge for sure, but one worthy of the effort. Jungian psychology's view of individuation and Dzogchen psychology's view of individuation — i.e., becoming who we truly are — seem diametrically opposed. But disagreement could be good news. Because the conflict between them may generate the heat and light needed to give rise to something new, necessary, and real. I hope that a dialogue between the Dzogchen psychology and Jungian depth psychology holds some promise for a new day based on a true and deep understanding of what a sound mind and heart look like. And how to cultivate and protect them both.

Before we consider what Dzogchen is, let me note a few things about myself. I'm a clinical psychologist working in the depth psychology and depth therapy tradition. I have an academic rank of associate professor. I've done many years of Jungian analysis with several analysts. After more than 35 years in both the depth psychology and Dzogchen domains, the line separating them is often hard to find. Interesting forces in me still seem to be pushing them toward each other. Thus, this chapter.

On a Possible Bridge between Individuation Theory and Dzogchen
Psychology: Challenges, Pitfalls, Opportunities for a Transcendent
"Third": A Dialogue between Murray Stein and Jim Manganiello

When I asked Lopon Tenzin Namdak Rinpoche why
Dzogchen is considered to be the highest spiritual teaching, he said:
"Because there's nothing beyond it." I probably would not have
believed him, if not for the fact we were in a three-week teaching
and practice retreat. And he was explaining a complex Dzogchen
teaching very clearly and carefully. What he was explaining abruptly
opened up to me like a developing photograph emerging from
darkness. I suddenly saw what he was teaching me. And as I did, I
burst into tears, uncontrollably.

Don't misunderstand, please. I am not in any projection-
based swoon over Dzogchen teachers and teachings. I just directly
experienced and realized what Dzogchen is. And my soul experienced
it as remembrance of something buried deep in my heart. I've been
in considerable conflict with younger Tibetan Dzogchen lamas over
the way they teach in the West and how they behave. I also have
great regard and affection for Jungian depth psychology. I consider
it the only deep end of the Western psychology pool. I am not trying
to present Dzogchen as something better or more important. I just
know that in some way, somehow, a connection between Jungian
depth psychology and Dzogchen psychology will be good for each,
and very possibly, for the world.

Dzogchen calls us to awaken completely from the waking
dream state we are in much of the time. A dream state in which we
identify with a fictive conditioned identity, as "I" or "me," "in here,"
and we project a world, as an external reality, "out there." When, in
fact, neither actually exists. They both appear, on close inspection,
as absence. The experiential awareness that is the direct experience
of this truth — is Dzogchen revelation. Dzogchen revelation unveils
who we truly are in our innermost nature. This is an experience of
Gnosis as divine knowledge and wisdom, outside the box of any
tradition. Dzogchen is the experience of sacred knowledge that is
the a priori revelation to any form of spiritual or religious tradition.

Dzogchen revelation is Gnosis experienced on its own, in
the nontemporal state. As the unspeakable, indescribable Timeless
Awareness that is the mind's essence, the Nature of Mind. Holy of

Holies. But no fireworks or trumpets are necessary here. It's the silent timeless awareness of who and what we are, complete, in our innermost nature.

We come to discover and know who we truly are in the experience of Being who we truly are. In the experience of Rigpa, the timeless nondual awareness of the mind's innermost core recognizes itself as nonidentity. Pure, awareness-based nonidentity dwelling in the experience of vast, indescribable Mystery. Any idea of an "I" or "me" in this experience is an absurd and hilarious tautology. From the Dzogchen View, nonidentity is ultimate individuation.

Dzogchen is not a view of what is, it *is* what is. A "viewless view" we could say. The Dzogchen View tells us that as depth psychologists, we should know that ultimate identity is nonidentity. And that the only thing to hold onto is the knowledge that there is nothing to hold onto.

Dzogchen revelation doesn't have to be a strike-up-the-band affair. It can be a quiet, unshakably certain realization, in the Timeless Moment, of who and what we are. It's the unveiling of our true condition. In our waking dream, we sometimes can feel that we belong somewhere else, somewhere where our true home is, where our real friends and family can be found. For me, and perhaps for you, the mind's innermost nature is home for the finding and recognizing.

When we talk about timeless awareness of ultimate identity and so on, it can sound a bit trippy — unless we have the ears to hear it at the right pitch, even faintly. We don't have to negate, dismiss, or undervalue embodied life in time. Temporal individuation and nontemporal individuation must be reciprocal. Or else we will have a separated psychology and spirituality, and both are now already tired words. It seems that alone and separate, neither will do any longer. Throwing them in a box together willy-nilly won't do either.

Once we realize our timeless experience of nonidentity, we can't package it and carry it back into time, as if it's a one-and-done affair. It's not. There's nothing more egoic than claiming to have lost your ego. We need to humbly work to learn how to integrate our Knowledge into our psychology and our own life circumstances —

On a Possible Bridge between Individuation Theory and Dzogchen
Psychology: Challenges, Pitfalls, Opportunities for a Transcendent
"Third": A Dialogue between Murray Stein and Jim Manganiello

in time. We need to refresh our experience often and learn how to deepen and extend it, or we will forget, and then forget that we have forgotten.

This is where we as depth psychologists face an adventure exploring Dzogchen psychology experiential methods. And our individuating conscious ego can and must be an ally on our adventure. Dzogchen is not about Tibet. It's the discovery of our true condition and it must be understood from our own sensibilities, not from those from another time and place. No need to go to Tibet or become like Tibetans. No need to alter our external lives in any direction, Dzogchen is an internal matter. We just need to know what Dzogchen is through direct experience. Dzogchen is a discovery of who we truly are already, as we are, complete in our innermost essence. No transcendence necessary.

There's individuation in time and individuation beyond time. This needs to be worked out as a meta depth psychology. The depth psychology alchemical opus can be both temporal and nontemporal. Time and Timelessness can lean into each other with mutual recognition. Timelessness is the unmanifest source of Time, and Time is the manifestation of Timelessness.

The depth psychology idea that we can individuate beyond our conditioning in a gradual process that will lead us into the Rubedo and the Self is a thing of striking beauty. But it must be reconsidered in a new light and in relationship to individuation beyond time. Beyond time individuation unveils a bold truth: we are in the Rubedo NOW, always. NOW is all there is. The future never arrives because when it does, it's now. And the past always shows up as now, as well. NOW is the only real thing going on, ever.

From the Dzogchen perspective, the Rubedo is the nontemporal first and last step because it's the only step. Whether we are conscious of it or not. Again, in time and beyond time, individuation must be reciprocal to be complete. To ignore in time, embodied individuation is out of the question. Seeing both together is a creative breakthrough view. Both need to be considered and understood if we are to have the entire picture for individuation.

To say that "in time," individuation work leads to the Self as some experience of wholeness, including the integration of our conscious and unconscious mind, is wonderful and accurate, but incomplete.

I mentioned to Murray in our discussions that this idea of wholeness felt vague and woolly to me. Because the intellect's ideas about what individuation is mistakes the box in time, for what's in the box, beyond time. The intellect either misses the revelation or makes a mess out of it. I think we need to back things up here so we reimagine matters with benefit of experience in the Natural State. I assure you, with some effort, you can learn the methods needed to understand and find it. These are no longer hidden in Tibetan monasteries, thank God.

The Natural State is very easy to find, but only after you find it. Until then, it's not so easy. Keep in mind the effortful sequence of learning a foreign language, how to ride a bike, skate on ice, dance, or play a musical instrument. Experiencing the Natural State starts with an introduction, an initiation, or a good intimation.

You may feel that somehow there's something or someone in you that Knows who you deeply are. But you don't know what that something is or how or where to find it. Then it's a little like a childhood friend whom you don't recognize until you do. The next time you see her, you'll know who she is. Once you connect to recognition of the Natural State, you turn in its direction. You then become increasingly familiar with the Natural State by finding it and being in it, again and again. Then you become confident that you know what it is and how to find it. As you get to know the Natural State more and more, you fall in love, and as lovers do, you reprioritize your energies so that you can stabilize and strengthen your relationship to it. Then you begin to bring your connection to the mind's innermost essence into your daily life. You bring the timeless into time with you. And then, if your thinking mind doesn't have the power to distract you, you can die in it. Dying in the Natural State is like having a good GPS in unfamiliar foreign territory.

The Dzogchen View that ultimate individuation can only be found in timeless, pure Gnosis is true, for me, beyond any doubt.

On a Possible Bridge between Individuation Theory and Dzogchen
Psychology: Challenges, Pitfalls, Opportunities for a Transcendent
"Third": A Dialogue between Murray Stein and Jim Manganiello

But it does not follow that psychological work on oneself aimed at a gradual, in time, progressive individuation is deluded and unnecessary. To say otherwise is an egoic misconception. In time, individuation is essential. Living embodied in the midst of madness and circumstances that leave us at risk of being imprisoned by unconscious forces — including merciless conditioning, in the 21st-century Western materialistic world — is a high art. Individuation in time is necessary if we are to craft our life into a work of art that be well-lived, loved, and understood.

The Tibetan Dzogchen tradition makes no provision for psychological work. It wasn't that the Tibetans were avoiding psychology; they just had no conception of psychology outside of a spiritual context. They understood the problem of conditioning and complexes, by other names, such as bag-chags and klesas. But the idea was that Dzogchen practice would eventually whiten, solve, and even prevent such problems. I think this was true long ago in Tibet. And it's possibly still true today for the grandfather Tibetan Dzogchen teachers. But not for the younger Dzogchen teachers in the West, who would benefit greatly from Jungian depth therapy or analysis. I am certain of this. Many so called-spiritual teacher-masters have become troubled and even aberrated in that role, including Dzogchen teachers.

Among the things that excite my imagination about meaningful conversation between Dzogchen psychology and Jungian Depth Psychology is that each can benefit from the view of itself from the other's lens. And together they may have important work to do if they can relinquish their respective biases. Depth psychologists must stop dismissing Eastern contemplative science by misreading Jung's cautions about Eastern spirituality and then by overvaluing their misconceptions. And Dzogchen psychologists must stop dismissing Jungian depth psychology as deluded Western nonsense without value. These respective criticisms arise to avoid seeing what depth psychology and Dzogchen psychology don't want to know about themselves. Typically, this is the signature of a position that has become riddled by formalisms.

Dzogchen psychology work can energize, deepen, and advance individuation work in time. To be able to access and experience our innermost core beyond time is to orient and inspire us to give ourselves deeply to the work of individuation in time. And depth psychology individuation work can do the same for Dzogchen psychology individuation work beyond time. As we become increasingly aware of and liberated from the unconscious forces that govern our lives, our personality structure becomes more capable of intuiting and honoring the self as our innermost identity.

Dzogchen is a contemplative science responsible for a remarkable discovery. Using direct experiential methods to systematically observe the mind, Dzogchen discovered the mind's root, essential nature. This discovery has only recently become known in the West, and it's barely recognized and understood. Tibetan Dzogchen has not transplanted well in the West because it has arrived in a form best suited to another time and place. Radical Dzogchen addresses these problems. As Dzogchen in its free position, it is independent of any cultural form or traditional formalisms.

As depth psychologists, we can learn about Dzogchen contemplative science and use its experimental methods to test its findings, and, if confirmed, then thoughtfully consider their implications for reimagining depth therapy and analysis in general and individuation in particular.

Let's consider Dzogchen contemplative science's discovery, as follows: The human mind has an all-pervasive root Nature that escapes our ordinary awareness. The detection and recognition of the mind's essential nature are not cognizable by the intellect. Thought and concepts, and Western scientific methods, will walk right by it and miss. The next step in psychology's "scientific evolution" must understand and use phenomenological methods to make reliable and valid deep inquiry into and about the mind. Third-person empirical study of the mind misses the mark. For Western psychology to use the empirical scientific method to investigate the mind is another variation on the materialistic nightmare that plagues life today.

On a Possible Bridge between Individuation Theory and Dzogchen
Psychology: Challenges, Pitfalls, Opportunities for a Transcendent
"Third": A Dialogue between Murray Stein and Jim Manganiello

Western science can no more understand the mind than a squirrel
can understand a mortgage agreement.

Dzogchen contemplative scientists used first-person
experiential methods to make their discovery about the mind's
essential nature. In the future, direct, firsthand experience of one's
own mind should rightly be understood as the *sine qua non* for
becoming a depth psychologist and for working with others as one.
Intellectual and conceptual knowledge and training are important but
insufficient.

We can consider Dzogchen psychology's discovery of the
mind's essential nature as similar to Copernicus's groundbreaking
discovery that the sun, not the Earth, is the center of our solar system.
Copernicus's discovery changed our vision of our solar system, and
in time, the science and practice of astronomy as well. Dzogchen
psychology research unveiled the Nature of Mind. We are only
just beginning to learn and understand the details of this important
discovery, one that could sit well with Jung's work as he imagined,
experienced, and lived it. Dzogchen contemplative science positions
the Self, not the ego, at the center of the mind as an accessible living
experience, not as a concept or theory.

Copernicus's research rocked the boat big time. He was
scoffed at and misunderstood initially by astronomers and other
scientists, as well as artists and church authorities. Yet his work
ultimately changed the role of astronomy in society. Similarly, if
we can understand and confirm decisively Dzogchen psychology's
discovery, then the unveiling of the Mind's innermost Nature will
have significant implications for us to reconsider depth psychology,
depth therapy, and analysis accordingly.

Dzogchen psychology also offers us an opportunity to
understand what a sound, healthy mind looks like and how to cultivate
and protect such a mind. Dzogchen gives us a unique experiential
lens to view the mind's difficulties and problems. A lens that also
sheds light on our social problems, including much of the hell that
characterizes human life.

Dzogchen psychology research shows "egocentrism" to be an affliction, one central to understanding the mind, and individuation in both its temporal and nontemporal aspects. Egocentrism means something different and more in Dzogchen psychology than the word usually implies in Western psychology. In Dzogchen, egocentrism is the hallmark of an unsound mind, separated from its innermost nature. Dzogchen contemplative scientists discovered its source and remedy.

The root of egocentrism is the mind's inherent tendency to mistakenly impute solid identity to itself from the flow of discursive thought in its stream of consciousness. Using Dzogchen contemplative science methods, we can replicate and confirm this critical finding through direct experience. For most people, this false-to-fact identity is wrongly presumed to be solid and real, and chronically vulnerable, based on a projected presumption of self and a projected view of external reality. This too can be easily confirmed.

At carefully chosen points, this method of experiential self-observation creatively can be carefully woven into sessions and integrated into depth therapy and analysis quite well. The benefits that come with this level of self-knowledge are clear. Impartial awareness gives rise to a consciousness better able to release from troublesome states of mind. To be able to recognize and stand free from anxious and depressive states of mind, for example, avoids identification with and possession by them. And awareness opens up a kind of free position that can create valuable opportunities for Active Imagination work.

Dzogchen psychology does not equate ego, as our conscious organizing and management function (and friend), with egocentrism, though the latter surely presents problems for the former. The term "ego" is often used to designate or characterize an exaggerated sense of self-importance. But in Dzogchen psychology, egocentrism is more, as noted: It's the signature of an unsound mind, a mind estranged from who and what it truly is. The imagined Eastern so-called "ego loss" and "egoless" ideas are probably a translation error of some kind. The target issue here is the attribution from the throughflow of fictive identity, as a solid permanent Self.

The egocentric mind takes itself very seriously. It imagines itself as an "I" or "me" as a starting and end point for all things. It's concerned, worried, and preoccupied with what it regards as its own needs and interests. It lacks the consciousness required for the reflection and echo needed to relativize its stance for course correction. Instead, it's prone to possession by whatever it's thinking and feeling. And it lacks the capacity for the attunement to others needed for empathy.

Egocentric self-identity experiences a strong and chronic need to protect and defend itself. It's preoccupied with advancing and safeguarding its own status and interests. It chases credentials, membership, wealth, reputation, "good reviews," and attractive appearance. Its primary concern is not the question: Who am I? It's: How do I look to others? And do I have the right stuff to win? And to avoid losing? The powerful seduction of discursive thought in our stream of consciousness is that it rings the bell loudly, and often over these preoccupations, daily. Thought can be addictive and dangerous.

When we follow discursive thought, we come to experience and believe in the content of those thoughts. Then, as a protagonist, we begin to fall into and live in the content of the narrative that those thoughts create. We follow our thoughts into a storyline as a fictional identity we mistake for who we truly are. This is not like a dream. It IS a dream. An expensive one. Imagination is reality.

All of this ongoingly feeds the recurring thought content that flows in our stream of consciousness. Most of us don't see this; we take our thoughts for granted. We even imagine that we have agency and that we are thinking our thoughts. This is true for our directed thinking, but not discursive thinking. Seen accurately in an experience of timeless awareness, thoughts are manifestations of energy. If left alone, if not liked or disliked or followed in any way, thought will liberate on its own. And the mistaken ascription of solid identity as protagonist in egocentric narrative and storyline releases as well. We can learn how to avoid this as we become more conscious. Then, thought flow in the stream of consciousness becomes like wind blowing across the desert. It comes and goes, leaving no traces, but we don't go with it. We stay undistracted and conscious, where the possibilities for life and for individuation are always the greatest.

The problem and remedy for egocentrism can be experienced directly using Dzogchen psychology methods. In many ways, discovering the problem is the remedy. Making conscious what's unconscious is the work. Dzogchen methods, including nonmeditation, also known as Trekcho, are skills that change the way the mind knows, experiences, and relates to itself. Dzogchen is often called a path of self-liberation. Its signature alchemical practice is to allow thought to simply liberate itself. In so doing, the egocentric process collapses, as does fictive identity. And what is unveiled is the mind's innermost nature.

The fictive "I" or "me" is a core problem because it becomes the heap on which family, social, cultural, and archetypal conditioning gets layered, as well as the array of complexes associated with them. As young children, we don't have the mind power to make sense of our circumstances and the problems therein. We don't realize, for example, that we are being raised by parents who are under the burden themselves of having become identified with a false identity. Not having the mindpower to reject or at least relativize parental projections, projections they insist are perceptions, we forfeit our direct experience and come to see ourselves as we are viewed by others. This coalesces into a self-image that, although fictional, nevertheless feels real, and determines much of what we think, feel, and do. And, as if this weren't enough trouble, through observational learning we take on additional burden by downloading features of our parent's personalities into our own.

We all become identified with our conditioned self-image until we develop the consciousness needed to see through and stand free from it. Our identification with this "I" or "me" is dominant and dangerous. It permeates all aspects of our psychological life. We live in it as something true and undeniable.

On a Possible Bridge between Individuation Theory and Dzogchen
Psychology: Challenges, Pitfalls, Opportunities for a Transcendent
"Third": A Dialogue between Murray Stein and Jim Manganiello

Let me illustrate how potent it is with a short story about Dr. Fred Farnsworth, a depth psychologist from the United States. Recall that Elvis Presley, in his day and long after, was widely considered by many millions to be the undisputed King of Rock and Roll. And indeed, Elvis was an amazing performer. Although he died many years ago, Elvis lives on in the hearts of his fans, some of who swear that he is still alive. These fans regularly report "Elvis sightings." Fred's fascination with Elvis became extreme. Here's his story:

> Fred wakes up one morning convinced that he is Elvis Presley. After jumping out of bed and singing one of Elvis's great songs, "You Ain't Nothin' But a Hound Dog," he turns to his wife and demands that she call him Elvis and treat him with the respect due the King of Rock and Roll. At breakfast Fred demands the same of his two children, and later at work that day, he demands that his group practice colleagues call him Elvis and treat him like the King as well.
>
> Initially, Fred's wife, children, and colleagues all got a kick out of Fred's bizarre performance, but by week's end, they've had quite enough.
>
> Together, they conclude that the best way to expose Fred's folly is to hire a lie detector expert. They reason that when a lie detector proves that Fred is not Elvis, then this foolishness will end.
>
> Somehow, Fred gets wind of their scheme.
>
> Upset and disappointed, he decides to spoil their plan by simply denying that he is Elvis.
>
> On the appointed day, everyone arrives at lie detector expert's office, on the 12th floor of the Tell the Truth Building. All are eager for the test to begin.
>
> The expert begins with obligatory questions. She asks Fred: "How old are you?"

"What town do you live in?" "What's your shoe size?" "What's your favorite holiday?" And so on.

Then the lie detector expert bears down and asks the key question: "Are you Elvis Presley?"

To everyone's surprise, Fred answers, "No."

But even more flabbergasting are the results. So deep is Fred's conviction that he is Elvis Presley that the lie detector reads that Fred is lying when he says that he isn't.

At some level, this is exactly our problem — no kidding.

In our self-image-based surface state of mind, we lack the awareness to know who we deeply are. And our soul lives and suffers in exile as a consequence.

To appreciate this dilemma, let's look at its relation to our important task of what I call "Remembering the Mustard." Did you ever go to the grocery store for mustard and then return home with two bags of groceries — but no mustard? At life's end, sitting on the edge of their bed, throngs of people reflect on their lives. They reflect on their wealth, family, credentials, and accomplishments. But, in the midst of these reflections, they suddenly are jolted and slap themselves hard on their forehead and yell, "Oh my God, I forgot the Mustard." The Mustard is becoming who we truly are. There is no other game in town. It is THE privilege of a lifetime.

Dzogchen psychology can signal and nudge Jungian depth psychology into a less formalized position to ensure that we approach Gnosis from the Heart, as Jung did, and not just from the intellect, as many of us do. What's important is what's _in_ the box, not so much the box itself. When Gnosis as revelation drops into form in this or that tradition, then the form itself becomes a kind of box, a container for the revelation. The danger is that the intellect becomes quickly fond of boxes, and, if too dominant, the intellect will push the heart aside and then mistake the box for the revelation

On a Possible Bridge between Individuation Theory and Dzogchen
Psychology: Challenges, Pitfalls, Opportunities for a Transcendent
"Third": A Dialogue between Murray Stein and Jim Manganiello

that's in it. The revelations are always "self-secret." No one can gain access to revelation from the intellect's vantage point. When the intellect opens the box to find the revelation, all it can see is the box. The revelation can only be seen by a consciousness that knows the experience of revelation. We can only understand divine wisdom while in the experience of divine wisdom; otherwise we're locked out. Let's experiment and use Dzogchen methods, methods that may grant us access to revelation as Nature of Mind. Sans Box. Boxes can mislead us terribly. They leave us at a loss for understanding what's really going on — like seeing Moses's Burning Bush and feeling compelled to find a fire extinguisher or being at the Last Supper and getting frustrated because the waiter is taking so long bringing the menus.

Ultimately, we are after the unseen essence of the Mystery, the formless dynamic power that is Gnosis, before it manifests in any form. The intellect mistakes the box of "form" for its contents; it sets up shop by "studying" Gnosis from the perspective of the container. Then it makes its inferences and draws conclusions, as if they were from the perspective of Gnosis. These get presented and published as theological or even esoteric scholarly findings. The more the form of a Gnostic container is assembled by conceptual minds, minds separated from direct experience of revelation, the greater the confusion and error. And the madness. Then, the storyline of the revelation will lean toward the literal and get lost in formalisms. So, people can kill one another insisting that their form is the only real box in town.

In contrast, the more a form-container arises spontaneously from the direct experience of revelation and transformed into images by the Creative Imagination, then it's like an abstract image loaded with power. Such a form-image, if unpacked properly with awareness and Active Imagination, can then grant access to the formless experience of revelation that originally gave rise to it. This is what I feel Jung managed to do with Christian Gnosis.

Dzogchen contemplative methods, with understanding and proper use, can lead us into the Natural State as formless Gnosis that is the nontemporal far side of individuation, known as nonidentity.

Murray Stein

It's a great pleasure to have this extraordinary opportunity to discuss with Jim Manganiello the various points of contact and some differences between Jungian depth psychology's theory of individuation and Dzogchen Psychology's discoveries concerning the human mind. I have to confess that I know next to nothing directly about Dzogchen Psychology, its methods, or its findings. Jim has brought my attention to some texts, but I have found them quite opaque. However, in the quite numerous discussions with Jim, and given his special ability to convey both the science and findings of Dzogchen and his experiences, I do get a glimpse, and I believe it is enough at least to make some preliminary assessment of possibilities of collaboration between the two schools.

To begin, I will state right off that I believe that we can find a basis for agreement between Dzogchen science and the theory of individuation, especially as Jung describes it in his last book, *Mysterium Coniunctionis*. This would be the theoretical part of a possible "transcendent third" position between the two schools. The common element is reflected in Dzogchen Psychology (DP's) concepts of Nature of Mind (NM) and Timeless Moment (TM) and Jung's concept of the Self as the transcendent center of the personality.

What Dzogchen Psychology can add to the alembic is a fulsome account of this experience, to describe its qualities and its effects on consciousness, and to offer methods for renewing the experience and building it into the localized consciousness with which we have to function in the everyday world. Heaven and Earth must find a way to coexist in consciousness in tandem, not in alteration (now a bit of this, mostly a lot of that).

On a Possible Bridge between Individuation Theory and Dzogchen
Psychology: Challenges, Pitfalls, Opportunities for a Transcendent
"Third": A Dialogue between Murray Stein and Jim Manganiello

I have written a good deal about individuation and, for
the sake of brevity, here will refer the reader to the References. In
general, I have described individuation as a process that unfolds
over the course of a lifetime in fairly discrete and distinct stages.
Jung speaks of the first half of life and the second half of life, the
first dedicated to ego and persona development and the second
to approximation of consciousness to the Self. As Jung states in
Memories, Dreams, Reflections, psychological development in
the first half of life is linear, while in the second half of life it is
circular, a circumambulation around the center. Jungians often use
the metaphor of a spiral to speak of this second type of process.
Each stage of the individuation process has certain specific tasks and
values, and the result of the process is cumulative. In the end, if one
is successful, the experience is psychological wholeness. This state
of wholeness is described in various ways, but in a nutshell, it refers
to self-knowledge of a wide and deep extent — knowledge through
experience, it should be emphasized. This type of self-knowledge
gained by personal experience could be called Gnosis, to use Jim's
language, in the sense that it is "knowledge of" and not "knowledge
about," and it is fundamentally grounded in personal experience of
the numinous center of the complex Self.

Jim is arguing that the apex of individuation, i.e., the
experience of the Self as center of the personality in psychological
terms, is experienced not as a product of previous work in becoming
conscious but as a sudden flash of realization, a visionary breakthrough
in which time and history disappear and the subject enters the
nontemporal far side of individuation, known as "nonidentity." It
is the Timeless Moment, and from this perspective, consciousness
views all of reality — Self, nature, the cosmos, history — as
relative and not substantial. This defining moment then forms the
centerpiece of consciousness when the subject returns to everyday
life and normal ego-functioning in time and space in order to manage
practical affairs in the social and interpersonal worlds. Basically, I
have no argument with this. It is absolutely the case that a glimpse
of the Self can come upon a person at any time in life, whether in

childhood, youth, adulthood or old age. But I would argue it is not as stable a realization and as effective in transforming the personality if it is not supported by other developments that have taken place earlier, and by tradition and supportive collectives surrounding the individual. It can also have an alienating effect upon the individual, but perhaps it can be alienation in the good sense of the word and not the pathological.

In Jungian work, moments of radical insight, such as Jim is speaking of as the Dzogchen discovery of NM and TM arrive in several packages: dreams, active imagination, synchronicities, and archetypal transference relationships. The following is an example of a dream in which the Self is experienced by a woman in her late 30s. The dream occurred after she had successfully passed through a severe midlife crisis and had found her voice perhaps for the first time in her life:

> I was in the clouds. The sky was pale, almost iridescent blue. I was ascending into the sky on a cloud until I saw an older Japanese man. My cloud stopped just below the one he was sitting on. He was dressed in silk. He gently extended a ring to me. It was clear that this ring was of high value. The ring had a gold band. In the ring's center was a white pearl. Surrounding the pearl was a circle of emeralds, but they were irregularly shaped. One extended out beyond the circle. We did not speak, we communicated telepathically. I asked if he was sure that he wanted me to take the ring. The man indicated that he did. Then I noticed that the ring was quite large on my finger. I looked on the inside of the band and saw the number 8, but it was stamped sideways into the metal, making it appear as an infinity sign. I said, "This is so big, I'm going to need to grow into it." The man smiled and shook his head, almost chuckling; my comment seemed to cause him great amusement. He communicated, "Don't worry."

On a Possible Bridge between Individuation Theory and Dzogchen
Psychology: Challenges, Pitfalls, Opportunities for a Transcendent
"Third": A Dialogue between Murray Stein and Jim Manganiello

The dream setting is clearly in a psychological space that is transcendent to the round of daily life and ego-functioning within persona identity. The pearl is a symbol of the archetypal feminine that resides at the core of the dreamer's being, the Self. It is set in a ring that represents the infinite, the eternal, and the ring symbolizes a permanent relationship with this level of the personality. The dream is an experience of the Timeless Moment and the Nature of Mind never to be forgotten. A difference with Dzogchen would be that the dreamer's identity is not eliminated but is rather enhanced and transformed. There is also the reference to time and further growth and development.

There are many further examples in the literature, and again I refer the reader to other writings of mine listed in the References. Such experiences of the Timeless Moment arrive in episodes of life that can take place either early or late. The Gnosis derived from them becomes woven into the individuation process of the individuals having these experiences, and their value for life depends upon how they are utilized. They are at least a kind of taste of what Dzogchen practice may deliver as experience of Timeless Moment.

In the concluding chapter of Jung's last book, *Mysterium Coniunctionis*, three stages of psychological and spiritual development are described using the work of the alchemist Gerhard Dorn. The sequence starts by moving from *unio naturalis*, a normal state of average ego-consciousness engaged in worldly interests and activities, to *unio mentalis*, a state of consciousness that includes much of what was previously shrouded in the shadow. Development takes place in the second half of life, and according to the usual individuation protocol, it is better at this time in life than earlier when there is a need for ego-building and identity-construction (persona). Adaptation to society and culture is generally seen as an important stage of psychological development, and psychotherapists try to facilitate it when it is lacking. When it comes to loosening the grip that social identity and ego have on consciousness, it is another matter. This is the stage of confronting the unconscious, analyzing and integrating the shadow, discovering the anima within, and eventually becoming oriented by the Self rather than the ego. This is a huge undertaking since it dismantles and relativizes what has previously been built up. But it does not destroy it. Relativization is a shift in the balance of forces, with the Self becoming more prominent and the ego less so. This means viewing personal and collective history from a broader perspective, seeing but not identifying with people, places and things, appreciating but not clinging to others, and taking into account one's finitude within the perspective of the timeless. This I take to be more or less equivalent to what Dzogchen means by Nature of Mind. Living by NM rather than ego would be, in Jungian terms, living by the Self rather than the ego. In neither psychology does this mean abolishing the ego or repressing thought and emotion. It's a question of distance from rather than attachment to.

The next stage of Dorn's series of conjunctions is the union of *unio mentalis* with body. Jung speaks of this as walking the talk, practicing the insights gained through the union of soul and spirit. Sometimes it yields a lifestyle that is considerably unconventional, though not aggressively so. The individual living in this state is guided in decision-making by an inner guidance system that is directed by the Self. It is this feature of the process that makes of a person a true individual. Every human being has this potential even if few realize the full potential resident in their nature.

The third and final stage of this process consists in a union with what the alchemists called *unus mundus*. The notion was that when God created the world, He left within His creation a part of Himself. This means that the natural world contains within it a Divine aspect. In philosophy, this has been called panentheism. It is different from pantheism in that God remains transcendent while at the same time immanent in creation. What Dorn was proposing was a union with the Divine as it could be found in and extracted from nature. This was the alchemical opus, to extract the Divine from the material and give it shape and form apart from its surround. The combination body/soul/self arrived at in the previous conjunction now joined with *unus mundus* to create a new being. This union was a mystical experience of joining the Divine and experiencing a state

On a Possible Bridge between Individuation Theory and Dzogchen
Psychology: Challenges, Pitfalls, Opportunities for a Transcendent
"Third": A Dialogue between Murray Stein and Jim Manganiello

of transcendence from the merely limited individual. When Jung writes about this, he says that it amounts to a state of total integration of conscious and unconscious. In other words, it is totality, and not only wholeness, that belongs to the previous stage.

Obviously, there are dangers here, namely grandiosity and inflation: I am like God, beyond good and evil! A Tower of Babel is about to be built when this becomes a conviction. This can only be avoided by rigorous self-awareness and continued sense of belonging to the ordinary, mundane, material world of human life on the planet Earth where the requirement for ethical awareness and reflection is never abridged. Communities are of immense help here because they keep the individual related to fellow human beings. Relationships also assist in keeping a framework of mortality and imperfection in mind. One thinks of the bickering elderly couple in assisting here as well. And of course, our body reminds us of our fragility and finitude. Taxes and the prospect of death help one stay grounded and out of danger of succumbing to inflationary pressures. And yet within all of that and in the midst of life, the individual can walk tall as Anthropos, the exemplar of *imago Dei* in flesh and blood. It requires an exquisite sense of balance.

Murray Stein and Jim Manganiello in Conversation

MS: Jim, you have practiced Dzogchen and you have had a lot of experience in Jungian analysis. My first question is: What does Dzogchen psychology have to offer Jungian practice and theory that will make it more fit for the 21st century? May we begin there?

JM: Yes, of course, a good way to begin. Dzogchen psychology arises from the discovery of the mind's innermost nature, the Nature of Mind. Jungian depth psychology now has an opportunity to learn how to test and confirm the discovery. If confirmed, then we can consider its implications as knowledge about the mind.

Dzogchen is not an eastern practice. It stands free. My experience is that it has profound implications for individuation

311

because it unveils who we truly are. It's beyond any literal or imagined geography. We can consider it as a contemplative science discovery. Contemplative science methods are experiential means to directly and systematically explore the mind. The methods increase awareness and consciousness. They grant access to the sine qua non for the consciousness required for stable recollection of God, i.e., as the sacred dimension of life: Entry into the Timeless Moment. Jung talks about this in *Memories, Dreams, Reflections* as a state of mind that's beyond temporality, a state in which there is no separation between past, present, and future. Once we can access the timeless moment at will, then we are always within earshot of the Delphic oracle's reminder.

MS: What about Dzogchen's origins? And how should Jungians view Dzogchen? Just what is it?

JM: Dzogchen has roots in the Tibetan indigenous spiritual tradition known as Yungdrung Bon and in Tibetan Buddhism. The Bon tradition gave Tibetan Buddhism its unique character. Though Bon and Buddhism have different origins, their Dzogchen teachings have been intermingled for so long that they are now inseparable. From a spiritual lens, Bon-Buddhist Dzogchen is considered the highest of spiritual teachings. It's the last stage of a nine-stage path of progressive development. But Dzogchen can stand free of both of these traditions. It is not a gradual path. It does not depend on anything prior to Dzogchen itself. A Radical Dzogchen is best suited for the West. Radical in the sense that it stands free from any Tibetan or any other cultural or institutional lineage. Radical Dzogchen eschews formalisms and is suspicious of organizations and institutions because they are soaked in proprieties.

As Jungian depth psychologists, it's more useful for us to view and consider Dzogchen as a contemplative science discovery about the mind rather than as a spiritual path. This discovery needs to be explored as direct experience in nontemporal states of mind. Dzogchen gives us precise methods to enter into these states.

On a Possible Bridge between Individuation Theory and Dzogchen
Psychology: Challenges, Pitfalls, Opportunities for a Transcendent
"Third": A Dialogue between Murray Stein and Jim Manganiello

If we can confirm the Nature of Mind, then we can consider
the discovery's implications for a revision of 21st-century depth
psychology, therapy, and analysis. Dzogchen psychology is a view
of the mind that sheds strong light on the problems we now face
as individuals and as a species. Psychology has ignored the fact
that everyone seems to have gone mad long ago. We just sit around
shaking our heads and writing papers in the face of horrors that are
barely imaginable, let alone tolerable. Dzogchen psychology can
clarify the dynamics behind the manifestation of madness reported
as history, including war, slavery, genocide, murder, child starvation,
global warming, vulture capitalism, and the rest of the materialistic
nightmare that we endure daily. In essence, the madness is a
psychological issue and must be understood and remedied as such.
These horrors are the signatures of an unsound mind. Through the
Dzogchen lens, we can grasp the psychological forces that create
and drive the madness. Once we can see the problem accurately, we
can then work to address it, instead of denying and avoiding it, or
assuming no solutions are possible.

MS: Thanks, Jim. I'm following you, but what you are saying is
an astonishing message at some levels. Help me let it sink in
so I can clearly understand. First of all, the Timeless Moment ...
Doesn't the word "moment" imply time? As we say, "a moment in
time." Temporality seems to rule ego-consciousness. As modern
(or postmodern) people, we are aware that we are living in the 21st
century. Indigenous people are aware of the passing of time in the
seasonal changes in nature. Your phrase, timeless moment, raises
a radical question about the place of temporality, as opposed to
atemporality, in our theory and practice. The individuation process,
as we conceive of it, is developmental and takes place in time and
advances in stages, or phases, or eras, such as childhood, adolescent,
adulthood.

The Jungian analyst thinks in these terms, especially in
dealing with early trauma. Even though we say that the unconscious
is timeless, dreams remind us of the past often, and very powerfully.

The analytic session is timed by the clock. Don't time and temporality have to occupy a central position in our theory and practice? Isn't development central to psychology? I wonder how awareness of the timeless moment would affect this preoccupation with time in depth psychology. I'm sure you have given a lot of thought to this, and I'm curious to hear your reflections.

JM: Your questions bring us into some important concerns. If we recognize the timeless moment and its importance, including its significance in the complete individuation picture, it doesn't mean we negate the temporal in Jungian work. The idea of timelessness seems like a fiction, or a mere thought experiment, until we experience it directly. On a relative level, time and timelessness are contrary notions. But on an absolute level, a level that's more than what it appears to be, we recognize time and timelessness as interdependent. Time is the manifestation of timelessness. And timelessness is the source of time.

Also, Murray, I feel that for us to explore and test Dzogchen's discovery of the mind's essential nature is to honor Jung by appreciating the importance of the sacred dimension in his work and life. If we are to follow Jung well, and with heart, we must follow him into his direct experience. Or we're just going to use his intellectual work as a kind of religious service we attend on weekends. Jung's inspiration and passion for sacred knowledge and wisdom drew many of us into him and his world.

Learning about Jung's Near Death Experience (NDE) confirmed his experience of nonduality. In *The Life and Ideas of James Hillman*, Hillman's first wife, Kate, wrote to him about Lilian Frey's observations of Jung after his NDE. A Near Death Experience, like a strong entheogen experience, tears down the obstacles to nondual consciousness. Kate puts it this way to Jim:

> He lives now in an "in-between" state
> somehow, most often he lets himself
> drop off into awake nondirective states,

314

On a Possible Bridge between Individuation Theory and Dzogchen
Psychology: Challenges, Pitfalls, Opportunities for a Transcendent
"Third": A Dialogue between Murray Stein and Jim Manganiello

> leaving the ego and mind out. He says he
> experiences truth as light, that is not with
> the consciousness that he has preached all
> these years, but another kind of awareness
> on a very deep level. ... Jung says he does
> not trust consciousness in the usual sense
> anymore ... it means giving up a great deal
> to enter into this state where truth so to say
> lingers on a different level, that Jung has
> always known about it, but not until now
> really taking it on as a change in himself.[1]

Murray, the words *"...not with a consciousness that he has preached all these years, but another kind of awareness on a very deep level"* appear to convey the difference between the conceptual mind and pure awareness. Both NDEs and entheogen-induced mystical experiences, in their timeless dimensions, absent the conceptual mind as pure awareness comes to the forefront. But we can't just keep almost dying or taking entheogens to keep that awareness refreshed. But with Dzogchen methods, we can do just that, with ongoing revelation in ongoing timeless moments.

As you note, Murray, seasons change, babies are born, age, grow old, and die. Every generation is on a train ride, and it mistakes its view out the window of life for reality. Jung's work and the treasures he left behind for us to use and enjoy arose on a particular train ride of time and circumstance. But it's important for us to recognize that what fed his best intellectual work was his direct experience of timeless Gnosis, as knowledge of the Sacred. And we must stay attuned to that part of his work. Perhaps our question is: Do we understand the importance of the nontemporal state for Jung and his work? And have we experienced it ourselves? The good news is that Dzogchen's methods, when learned and understood, can enable entry into the timeless moment as direct experience.

---

[1] D. Russell, 2013, pp. 468-469

Words like Gnosis, Sacred, and Divine are just words. And just words can have a purpose. But when looking to the experience of Gnosis, words are like photographs of food we think we can bake in the oven to create a gourmet meal. Many religions talk about timelessness and divinity and the sacred. For example, Christianity has as its center the symbol of the cross. The moment the vertical line intersects the horizontal represents the timeless sacred moment. As does the Catholic Mass and the Greek Orthodox liturgy. But timelessness only arises in direct experience, not its representations.

What Dzogchen, by any name, brings to the table is a precise method to experience the timelessness needed to unveil Gnosis as the mind's innermost Nature — as who we truly are. Dzogchen even eschews the idea of eternity, because it's a word, once removed from the experience. When Jesus was asked when the New Day would come. He said it was already here, NOW.

There is no reason why Jungian therapists and analysts can't learn to do their work with one leg in time and another in timelessness, as they see fit, if they know how.

MS: Jim, I'd like to ask you about Dzogchen psychology and how you see its relationship to our present form of working with people in our practices as Jungian analysts. It seems to me such a stretch to think of connecting my work with clients to Tibetan sages in their ancient and culturally remote contexts. Suppose a woman or man of our postmodern culture (doesn't have to be Western; could be Chinese or Japanese or Indian these days here in Zurich) comes to me with the usual complaints of anxiety, depression, burnout, "loss of soul" as Jung called it, or another of the common maladies of our times. How do you see Dzogchen contributing to the work of "care of the soul?" Would I want to introduce a form of meditation into my practice? If so, what is the Dzogchen form? As you well know, "mindfulness training" is all the rage in psychotherapeutic circles today, and there are many centers for practicing meditation. Should Jungians think of building meditation into the practice of analysis?

On a Possible Bridge between Individuation Theory and Dzogchen
Psychology: Challenges, Pitfalls, Opportunities for a Transcendent
"Third": A Dialogue between Murray Stein and Jim Manganiello

I'm asking now about "method" — for attaining the Timeless
Moment and the Natural State.

JM: Murray, no need to connect our work to Tibet or Tibetan sages,
though we owe them both deep appreciation and gratitude. We can
leave Tibetan cultural forms all at Mount Everest's base camp. That's
what Radical Dzogchen itself is doing on its journey to the West. We
don't drop Dzogchen into our work as tactics willy-nilly.

To use your example, a new patient presents with anxiety,
depression, burnout, "loss of soul." Her sufferings would still be the
prima materia for her individuation work. The only real difference,
at the outset, would be that her unconscious would realize that you
have direct knowledge of who you truly are. And so, her unconscious
would trust you. And from this trust, learn to trust itself to realize
who she truly is. But no need to introduce anything formulaic. As
her analyst, you're the artist who chooses what colors to use, when
and how, in her work. I have written about Dzogchen without using
the word. And in my practice, I seldom introduce anything called
Dzogchen until after much work has been done to prepare the ground
unless someone seeks me out because they know my depth therapy
work is informed by Dzogchen psychology. When I feel I am working
with someone who is capable and willing to meet Dzogchen, I'll
refer to it by name. And I do so when I teach and train in depth
therapy and Dzogchen practice. You are right about mindfulness
being inserted into therapy so much these days. If it's just dropped
in with no reference to the unconscious and individuation work, then
it turns out to be a mindless mindfulness. Another attempt to wax a
dirty floor.

As a creative analyst, you would intuitively find the times and
places in the relationship to spontaneously connect the dots. When
she had some foundation of self-knowledge and self-understanding,
for example, you might introduce her to methods to stay alert and
aware to her recurring patterns of thought and feeling. Once aware
of her complexes and persona-based identity, she can become alert to
her stream of consciousness and how to avoid its pitfalls and perils.

She can then understand and use the methods needed to gain access to her deep interior. She can learn as part of the work, that when she judges or follows her train of thought, she moves into a waking dream as a protagonist called "I" or "me." When she is ready, and if appropriate, you can lead her into deeper and deeper levels of awareness so she can experience directly that this "I" or "me" is a fictive identity. If the situation is ripe, you can lead her into methods to enter into the timeless moment and glimpse and then experience who she is, in her deepest nature.

MS: OK, Jim. This makes sense. If we discover that Dzogchen psychology indeed represents a monumental discovery about the mind's innermost essence, we can deeply consider its implications for Jungian theory and practice.

On the point of tradition and institutions, however, I'd like to press you a bit further regarding Dzogchen, and, of course, we should also consider also the issue of the institutionalization of Jungian psychology. But first Dzogchen. Is it really possible to shed all the Tibetan cultural baggage of Dzogchen psychology and still call it Dzogchen? Spiritual practices are carried through time and are supported and sustained by religious traditions. Strip away the tradition, can the "spiritual essence" and the psychological value survive, or does it become so abstracted away from its roots that one loses its deepest levels of experience? You are a gifted expositor of the great discovery of the Nature of Mind that was made and developed into a way of life in the mountains of Tibet. Is the experience of the Natural State, as you describe it taking place in the analytic setting, comparable? Or is it just a taste, a very faint taste at that, of what the Tibetan sages feasted on and lived? Doesn't one have to go to the Tibetan sages and learn their traditional practices in order to get the deep experience of the Natural State? I know you have studied with them. What was your experience?

I agree that in the temenos of the analytic relationship there are moments when one can step into a timeless moment. But as you have sometimes described the radical breakthrough into that

On a Possible Bridge between Individuation Theory and Dzogchen
Psychology: Challenges, Pitfalls, Opportunities for a Transcendent
"Third": A Dialogue between Murray Stein and Jim Manganiello

awareness, it comes as a thoroughly transformative experience never to be forgotten, a kind of psychic shock into an entirely new level of consciousness, the Natural State, in the mind's innermost core. I'd like you to give me a fuller picture of that, perhaps using your own experiences which I know are extensive. So, two questions: What about the Tibetan institutions and their emphasis on learning from a Master in order to really "get it"?

JM: As we consider Dzogchen and its possible role in helping us realize our purpose, we need to understand what Dzogchen is experientially, not just intellectually. Once the intellect is suffused with the mind's essential nature, it can better understand its role as a companion to direct experience, but not a substitute. The intellect can learn that there is intelligence and knowledge beyond thoughts, concepts, and memory. Only in direct experience can we find the ground of Being that is our source.

To set context for my answer to your first question about Tibetan institutions and their emphasis on learning from a Master, let's consider something very important to relieve you from the concerns that we are working with something that won't root or survive if ripped from its cultural moorings. Please understand that we are talking about Radical Dzogchen. My conviction is that as it comes West, Dzogchen itself is orchestrating its own journey into new territory. The Tibetan form can and should continue in Tibet, the gods willing. But not in the West. In the West, Dzogchen is now exploring opportunities. Jungian psychology is one of them. I only hope that Jungian psychology can see that and not miss it. A major problem in transplanting Dzogchen in the West in its Tibetan form is the role of the Teacher as a Divine Right Monarch. This model of spiritual teacher can still work in Tibet, but it's a dogma without basis or foundation in the West. Unlike in Tibet, we have no history, traditions, or institutions that can support and steward this model. Quite the contrary. Nor are we inoculated against or prepared for its excesses.

Not only will Dzogchen survive the rip from its cultural soil, but it can also prosper as a result. My hope is that Jungian depth psychology will experientially recognize what Dzogchen is and bridge it properly, to its own great advantage.

Dzogchen is allergic to institutions, including most monasteries. The formalisms, doctrine, and dogma of institutional life are anathema to Dzogchen. Dzogchen is not a philosophy, religion, or even an Eastern or Tibetan spiritual path, school, or tradition. Dzogchen is a word that refers to one thing: Our Real Nature. It's very ancient knowledge about who we truly are. Dzogchen was traditionally taught through oral transmission only, from one who has experienced Dzogchen to one aspiring to do so. Dzogchen was secret, never talked about. No one had access to the Dzogchen teachings, until or unless they demonstrated worthiness. Now they are available more readily because of the fear that this profound discovery could be lost. It must stay alive through experience. For Dzogchen, the intellect alone will always miss the mark. Inexperienced people who write about Dzogchen are just gargling with the alphabet. And they often footnote writings by other people who were also just gargling with the alphabet.

If we don't receive genuine and authentic instructions and methods from someone with experiential knowledge, we won't know what to do or how. But this "someone" who teaches us does not have to be a Master, Lama, or Guru, Tibetan or otherwise. We need the right methods and good enough instruction to get the results we are looking for. We need to be pointed in the right direction by someone who knows the right direction. Once pointed, what we begin to experience and recognize is in us. The Nature of Mind is in us; it's who we deeply are. That is who the real Teacher is. The Natural State can become an ongoing learning experience there are no words for. Let go of the Guru or Lama idea. We learned the alphabet from someone who knew it. Once we know it, and can read and write and so on, there's no need to wear a picture of our alphabet teacher around our neck. We don't require their instruction any longer. We should be

On a Possible Bridge between Individuation Theory and Dzogchen
Psychology: Challenges, Pitfalls, Opportunities for a Transcendent
"Third": A Dialogue between Murray Stein and Jim Manganiello

grateful, of course. And thankful for the remarkable intelligence in us that could learn the alphabet and use it.

At the end of the day, what's right now so exciting about the possibilities of Dzogchen for depth psychology (and depth psychology for Dzogchen) is that Dzogchen can stand free as a discovery about the mind's essential nature. And so, it has potential as a deeper understanding of mind, as it does for illuminating the farther reaches of individuation. No need to unnecessarily confuse the discovery with the discoverers. We don't regard Copernicus's discovery as Polish or even as Western. *Because it simply IS what is.*

MS: What we have here, Jim, is a binary: Jungian individuation of the West and Dzogchen psychology of the East. And we are looking for a trans-binary "third" that would in some way represent both of them and yet be something new and different from either one of them. You strike me as a trans-binary individual, Jim. You have partaken of both Jungian analysis and its practices and of Dzogchen psychology and its practices. Both come together in your experience, and you are an individual, a single unit of consciousness. So, can you speak about how you got to this place, how it began and developed in your life, and where you are now with the trans-binary position you have achieved? You are modest, and I don't want to set you up as a model or ideal, but you have an extent of experience with this that is quite special, maybe not unique, but housed in your background as a psychologist and a spiritual practitioner and with your abilities to articulate the result and its implications, you can suggest how this "third" might look.

JM: Yes, good point Murray. I think we have a third, but it's not yet entirely visible. It's in premanifestation mode. But I certainly feel it. Full disclosure: I brought Dzogchen into this book as a Trojan Horse. My intent is to deliver a monumental discovery to Jungian psychology.

Jungian psychology's view of individuation and Dzogchen psychology's view of individuation — i.e., becoming who we truly are — seem diametrically opposed — thankfully. I say thankfully because there's nothing like a seemingly impossible conflict of opposites to generate the heat and light needed for the birth of new ways of imagining and living psychology and spirituality. For Jungian Psychology, individuation is a gradual and progressive experience. That involves a good deal of inner work with dreams, fantasies, Active Imagination, etc. — all in the service of making what's unconscious conscious. Framed alchemically in three stages, we can say that the inner work proceeds, more or less, from the Nigredo, to and through the Albedo, on into the Rubedo — the final stage. When done well, this therapy/analytic work is a thing of beauty, whereby a great Oak Tree can see and experience itself in light of the acorn it once was.

Yet, for Dzogchen psychology, no gradual progression is possible because there is no path other than the intellect's "concept" of path. And even if there was a path, no entity with an identity can be found who could possibly walk it. For Dzogchen alchemy, who we truly are is and has always been — the Rubedo. For Dzogchen, the first step is the last step because it's the only step. But we must experientially awaken to and "realize" that the Rubedo is our true condition. For Dzogchen, individuation is an immediate experience of that realization. Because the timeless moment, to the discerning eye, is the only thing that's real. Psychologically, the past is always NOW. And when the future comes, it's always NOW. There is nothing prior to or beyond NOW.

Murray, my conviction is that the visions of depth psychology and Dzogchen psychology are both true and valid — but only from an experiential view that hasn't fully arisen as yet — the famous third. But I see it as partially arrived. While in a body, Jung had intimations that his conceptual mind could never hold a candle to what he experienced in his Heart — experiential knowledge. He left enough tracks for us to advance the possibility that his work can achieve, beyond his lifetime, what it couldn't during his lifetime.

On a Possible Bridge between Individuation Theory and Dzogchen
Psychology: Challenges, Pitfalls, Opportunities for a Transcendent
"Third": A Dialogue between Murray Stein and Jim Manganiello

MS: Jim, I know that you have a concern about the institutionalization of Jungian psychology. Can you share this concern? What is it that you think has gone amiss as Jungian psychology has been developed within the Jungian training institutes and societies?

JM: We shouldn't imagine the analytic hour today as fixed and final. If we come upon breakthrough knowledge about the mind, and so about individuation, we'll need to reimagine our work accordingly. Providing, of course, the new knowledge is reliable and valid. And that it advances our depth psychology aim and purpose — to bring light into the human heart and so enable people to awaken to who they truly are. A noble intent indeed, it's a blessing to be called to it. The Acid Test here is to experiment using Dzogchen methods on ourselves. As we were speaking a while ago, I imagined that Jung approached me and muttered: "*Läuten Sie zweimal im Jahr laut die Glocke des Chaos.*" Then in English, he explained: "Remember, for any organization to stay true and healthy, the bell of chaos must be rung loudly twice a year."

MS: Bravo! "Ring the bells that still can ring! Forget your perfect offering. There is a crack, a crack in everything. That's how the light gets in," to quote another visionary, our dear and lately departed Leonard Cohen. I feel certain that Jung would agree. Chaos is needed to keep things alive. We need enough organization to maintain and advance Jungian work, but not so much that it gets lost in institutional formalisms.

I congratulate you on your command of the local language, Jim. It's a rare visitor that grasps the meaning of German utterances in the Swiss dialect. And I'm so glad that we share such high esteem for Professor Jung, who gave us so much rich food for the soul.

JM: I am so glad that you and Professor Jung agree. I'd like to say a few more things about chaos before we conclude. Creative chaos is the antidote to institutional and organizational formalism. The Radical Dzogchen View asks us to be bold in our vision and capable of welcoming the chaos that becoming more conscious can create. Dzogchen represents an intelligence beyond the intellect, an intelligence asking us to stand naked and look over carefully who we are and what we are doing. In fact, this is our own intelligence; Dzogchen creates the occasion for our connecting to it. Murray, your description of Jung's reactions to using his name for training programs left me holding him in even greater regard for his very wise appreciation of chaos. Here I'll quote from your book *The Principle of Individuation*. When Jung was told about the training program idea by Joseph Wheelwright, "… Jung stared at him as if had been hit by a Mack truck." And when Wheelwright said, "I see you don't really want to hear about it." Jung replied: "To tell the truth, I can think of nothing less I would rather hear about Wheelwright."[2] All organizations and institutions contract into normative proprieties and skilled defenses against chaos. Hail the bell for chaos — may it ring loud and clear for Jungian analysis and depth psychology.

---

[2] M. Stein, 2006, p. 12

On a Possible Bridge between Individuation Theory and Dzogchen
Psychology: Challenges, Pitfalls, Opportunities for a Transcendent
"Third": A Dialogue between Murray Stein and Jim Manganiello

References and Suggestions for Further Reading

Dowman, K. (2020). *The Dzogchen View*. Morelos, Mexico: Dzogchen Now! Books

_____. (2020). *Dzogchen Nonmeditation*. Morelos, Mexico: Dzogchen Now! Books

_____. (2020). *Dzogchen Daily Practice*. Morelos, Mexico: Dzogchen Now! Books

Hoeller, S. (1982). *The Gnostic Jung and the Seven Sermons to the Dead*. Wheaton, IL: Quest Books

Jung, C. G. (1955-6/1970). *Mysterium Coniunctionis*. *CW* 14. Princeton, NJ: Princeton University Press

_____. (1950/1971). A study in the process of individuation. In *CW* 9i. Princeton, NJ: Princeton University Press

_____. (1961). *Memories, Dreams, Reflections*. New York: Vintage Books

Manganiello, J. (2013). *Unshakable Certainty*, 2nd rev. ed. [E-reader version] Retrieved from Amazon: http://bitly.ws/ocIF

_____. (2016). *Your Creative Imagination, Unlocked: Become Who You Truly Are*. Fresno, CA: Ashford Books

_____. (2021). Depth psychology and depth therapy — Reset and refreshed. In. B. Panter, Ed. *Psychological Studies of Art and Artists*. Vol. 3, pp. 105-122. Rancho Mirage, CA: AIMED Press

Norbu, N. (1989). *Dzogchen: The Self-Perfected State*, London: The Penguin Group

_____. (2006). *Dzogchen Teachings*. Ithaca, NY: Snow Lion Publications

Namdak, T. (2010). *Masters of the Zhang Zhung Nyengyud: Pith Instructions from the Experiential Transmission of Bonpo Dzogchen*. New Delhi: Heritage Publishers

Reynolds, J. (1989). *Self-Liberation Through Seeing with Naked Awareness*. Barrytown, NY: Station Hill Press

Ribi, A. (2013). *The Search for Roots: C.G. Jung and the Tradition of Gnosis*. Los Angeles and Salt Lake City: Gnosis Archive Books

Russell, D. (2013). *The Life and Ideas of James Hillman*. New York: Helios Press

Stein, L. (2021) *The Self in Jungian Psychology: Theory and Clinical Practice*. Asheville, NC: Chiron Publications

Stein, M. (2006). *The Principle of Individuation*. Asheville, NC: Chiron Publications

_____. (2020). *Individuation*. In *Collected Writings of Murray Stein*, Vol. 1. Asheville, NC: Chiron Publications

_____. (2021). *Transformations*. In *Collected Writings of Murray Stein*, Vol. 3. Asheville, NC: Chiron Publications

_____. (2022). *Four Pillars of Jungian Psychoanalysis*. Asheville, NC: Chiron Publications

Vyner, H. (2019). *The Healthy Mind*. New York and London: Routledge

EASTERN PRACTICES AND THE MATRIX

10

Yoga in Mayfair or Fifth Avenue, or in any other place which is on the Matrix, is a spiritual fake: What are the effects of Eastern spiritual practices on the individuation process and the revelation of the Self?

Royce Froehlich

Medialifeworld, the technological bubble in which we find ourselves, presents significant challenges to the individual psyche. C.G. Jung was an early critic of electronic media and he presciently warned of its disruptive tendencies. Another warning concerned Westerners going East. However, his theoretical, intuitive, and experiential understanding of Eastern practices suggests otherwise. Multimedia artist John Cage serves as an exemplar for bridging Jung's theory of a divided self and Eastern traditions to demonstrate a common ground of understanding of the healing power of the mind. The unifying element will be the application of aspects of Eastern and Western spiritual practices to treatment of some of the deleterious effects of living in Medialifeworld on the psyche.

By not making more of an effort to incorporate spirituality in treatment, we are doing a disservice to patients. [1]

---

[1] Rosmarin, 2021

Among the books in my library that are devoted to matters of the spirit, many inspiring ones came to me through tips from co-travelers, teachers of all types, theological studies, and, most relevant to us here, those who were brought to my attention by analysands. The book that put me "on the road" along with countless other "seekers," Hermann Hesse's *Siddhartha* remains a companion. So have Jack Kerouac's *Dharma Bums* and *Some of the Dharma*, and there's *The Psychedelic Experience* by the Harvard power trio — the self-proclaimed High Priest of a psychedelic society, Timothy Leary; Richard Alpert, AKA Ram Dass, author of the 1970s classic *Be Here Now*; and Ralph Metzner, who continued to research avenues toward the improvement of mental health and the relationship between humans and Earth — with their dedications to three forerunners who inspired the work: W.W. Evans-Wentz, who first brought The Tibetan books *Of the Dead* and *Great Liberation* to the West; the European Vajrayana Buddhist Lama, Anagarika Govinda; and C.G. Jung. I have a place on my bookshelves for all of these authors and would also include them in an infinite foreword.

Through Jung and other thinkers on the human condition, this chapter will address what may be one of the most important concerns of our day: *maintaining a time-sensitive understanding of the relationship between mental health and the religious attitude.* "Time-sensitive" in terms of being perceptive of the transformation in psychological conditions arising from being inescapably bound to what I'm calling *Medialifeworld*, the enframing technological bubble in which we find ourselves. The starting point is Jung: When we say that Jung wrote the book on Psychology and Religion,[2] we wouldn't be off base. Just keep in mind that we're reading it within the electromagnetic networks of Medialifeworld.

The title of this essay appropriates one of Jung's numerous exhortations to stay away from Eastern spiritual practices. "Yoga in Mayfair or Fifth Avenue, or in any other place which is on the

---

[2] CW 11

Yoga in Mayfair or Fifth Avenue, or in any other place which is on the Matrix,
is a spiritual fake: What are the effects of Eastern spiritual practices
on the individuation process and the revelation of the self?

telephone is a spiritual fake,"[3] is one of those instances, however, where he tells us to do as he says, not as he does. Jung often warns us Westerners — and few will be his readers who are not "Western" — to not ape such Eastern practices as Zen meditation or Hatha Yoga, yet he tells us outright that during his "confrontation with the unconscious," he used "certain yoga exercises in order to hold [his] emotions in check."[4] We wonder as to the nature of these exercises.

Prior to the publication of *The Red Book*, one might have more easily fallen for Jung's bluff about yoga: "I have never met a European who benefitted from this method."[5] However, the numerous texts in which he demonstrates his theoretical, intuitive, and experiential understanding of Eastern practices suggest otherwise. While more recent scholarship disputes some of Jung's observations and theoretical constructs regarding Eastern religious texts and practices,[6] we could say that those shady points are the "wrong means" in what are, overall, nevertheless the "right hands." Jung offers Westerners an opportunity to reflect on psyche through an Eastern-facing window and bring treasures to light for the individuation process.

Bridging Eastern and Western thought in his life and work, multimedia artist John Cage will serve as a touchstone. In the 1950s, Cage sat in classes on Zen and other Eastern traditions at Columbia University offered by D.T. Suzuki and found in them a model for a way of being that deeply affected his life and work. Cage would sit quietly for a good while in an anechoic chamber and discover that there is no such thing as silence, yet would say regarding zazen practice, "You will never find me sitting on a black cushion."[7] By

---

[3] Ibid., § 802

[4] Jung, 1963, p. 177

[5] Jung, 2020b, p. 17

[6] Tibetan Buddhism scholar Donald Lopez Jr. is an example of one who is critical of Jung's appropriation of the Bardo Thödol (The Tibetan Book of the Dead) and "other Asian texts . . . as raw material for his own theories . . . without acknowledging the violence (both epistemic and otherwise) that he did to the texts in the process" (Lopez Jr., 1998, p. 59)

[7] Pearlman, p. 64

the time of the lectures at Columbia, Jung had already written the foreword to Suzuki's *Introduction to Zen Buddhism*[8] and is credited with being another of the significant influences on the composer's way of approaching life. While he had only one disastrous session with a psychoanalyst, Jung's books helped Cage frame the question that was both spiritual and psychological: What is the mind that is so often divided against itself?[9]

Technology and Soul Work

While we may be living in a "global village," where electronic media create an atmosphere of interdependence, the inhabitants of this worldwide village appear to be suffering a loss of *kinship libido* — connection to others, desire for wholeness through relationship — which is a direct effect of the contemporary urban, mediated lifestyle. Anthony Stevens suggests that those of us who are "drawn into the caring professions are driven by a collective *enantiodromia* — a compensatory attempt to make good what has been lost."[10] Stevens's hypothesis offers a rationale for this paper, as some of the issues brought into consultation offices are concerns due to the effects of technology on the psyche. It therefore seems necessary to follow Wolfgang Giegerich when he says, "It is our psychological job finally to own and acknowledge physics and technology as inalienable parts of our soul work."[11] Part of that "soul work" will likely be related to working with internet addictions (gaming, news feeds, porn) or attention-related disorders. It has become common knowledge that methods employed in meditative exercises may be helpful in the treatment of psychological disorders due to electronic media.[12] The field of this essay, however, focuses on the effect of technology with soul work with individuals who are committed to

---

[8] Jung, CW 11, § 877-907
[9] Larson, 2012, p. 137
[10] Stevens, 1993, p. 90
[11] Giegerich, 1996
[12] Cf. Levy, 2016

Yoga in Mayfair or Fifth Avenue, or in any other place which is on the Matrix,
is a spiritual fake: What are the effects of Eastern spiritual practices
on the individuation process and the revelation of the self?

an Eastern form of spiritual practice and engage an analyst in their pursuit of, or discussions around, experiences of realizing a more equanimous or individuated way of being. This analyst, besides having read *Siddhartha*, pursued a master's degree in divinity and has graduate degrees in the field of media studies. Both areas of interest inform his practice. The menu in this chapter is therefore Jung and religion over a bed of technology.

Psychology and Religion and Technology

The *Scientific American* magazine cover story "Psychiatry needs to get right with God" sounds like a cry from the wilderness that is the field of mental health. Or is it a desperate call from the wasteland wrought by the effects of modernity? Jungian theory and practice support something that Jung and several Westerners saw: great potential for the expansion of consciousness through psychology or philosophy; and what the narratives of the East have known all along — cultivating a religious or spiritual attitude is a core element of mental health. Maintaining a spiritual component in daily life, something taken for granted in the farthest corners of Earth for millennia, now needs to be suggested as an additive to the formula for psychological well-being. Is that an evolutionary leap or a ball of confusion?

Theologian and media critic Mark C. Taylor suggests, "The way in which God is imagined determines the way in which the self and the world are conceived and vice versa."[13] Is your god a creator-being, organizing principle, chaos, or dead? What does it mean that Friedrich Nietzsche pronounced the death of God by human hands, "We have killed him — you and I,"[14] and drew the conclusion that the bright light of the arbiter of morality in the West, the Christian god, had died out? The structure that is typically provided by a central agent of a religious or social system appeared absent from the

---

[13] Taylor, 2007, p. 22
[14] Nietzsche, 1970, § 125, p. 181

world around him. For Nietzsche, belief in the Christian god became unbelievable. We can extrapolate from this image of the "dead" god any governing deity, unifying system, or organizing principle that no longer holds sway in a collective or personal psyche, Eastern or Western.

Here is where Jung and such fellow consciousness expansionists as Stanislaw Grof and John Gebser find their niche in contemporary times. "I am not addressing myself to the happy possessors of faith, but to those many people for whom the light has gone out, the mystery has faded, and God is dead."[15] The *Black* and *Red* books are Jung's testimony of his own experience of loss and alienation, and potential for recovery — a re-membering, what I call the *re-aster*.

As an illustration of what he observed, perhaps *learned,* is better, Jung would write, "in the world of spirits [the European] is a child of a troglodyte. He must therefore submit to living in a kind of prehistoric kindergarten until he has got the right idea of the powers and factors which rule that other world."[16] The other world that Jung is referring to, as we learn from *Liber Novus,* is "the depths." *The spirit of the depths* presents a compensatory balancing act to *the spirit of this time,* which is the force that inspires, animates, everything contemporary. Efficiency is a rationale for technological innovation, and Jung saw "the hero ideal of efficiency" as the pervasive force in the spirit of the collective consciousness of his day.[17] Along with the spirit of "instrumental reason," i.e., effective means to an end — think of the maxim "the end justifies the means" — come the notions of limitlessness, use, value, meaning, justification, and progress that also inform the spirit of this time.[18]

The zeitgeist, the spirit of the time, has only gotten faster since Jung's day. The computer is literally changing our minds as it

---

[15] CW 11, § 148
[16] CW 7, § 322
[17] Jung, 2009, p. 238 n. 85
[18] Cf Jung, 2009, p. 229

Yoga in Mayfair or Fifth Avenue, or in any other place which is on the Matrix,
is a spiritual fake: What are the effects of Eastern spiritual practices
on the individuation process and the revelation of the self?

hegemonizes the collective nervous network. Filmmaker and media theorist Joan Grossman suggests that what we are seeing may be the birth pangs of an evolutionary shift to a new way of being human, which she sees as being the psychological side effects of living in *Medialifeworld*.

> *This pervasive invasion may merely be part of the new ontological order of being. But it also portends dissociative and pathological traits that might be characterized as a generalized media disorder (a neurosis yet to be categorized by the psychiatric profession), in which we fail to perceive the body's limits (if such a thing is still relevant), let alone the limits of memory and intelligibility.*[19]

GMD: Generalized Media Disorder

Before he began to explore the effects of electronic media, Marshall McLuhan, in a 1944 Christmas letter to two Catholic priest friends, lauds Jung's work. "Increasingly, I feel that Catholics must master C.G. Jung. The little self-conscious (unearned) area in which we live today has nothing to do with the problems of our faith. Modern anthropology and psychology are more important for the Church than St. Thomas to-day."[20] In another 20 years, he would note, "As the Western world has invested every aspect of its waking life with visual order, with procedures and spaces that are uniform, continuous, and connected, it has progressively alienated itself from needful involvement in its subconscious life."[21]

Jung made an observation in 1932 that McLuhan would have agreed with and is no less applicable today: "We are living undeniably in a period of the greatest restlessness, nervous tension, confusion,

---

[19] Grossman, 2009, p. 22

[20] McLuhan, 1987, 166. To Walter Ong, SJ and Clement McNaspy, SJ, 23 December 1944.

[21] McLuhan & Parker, 1968, 1

and disorientation of outlook."[22] Later, in the 1950s, instead of war or other disquieting social traumas, Jung attributed the etiology of these symptoms of disorientation to electronic media and the rise of noise. Noise interferes with the reception of a message, and what if it's a message from psyche? Anticipating the media critiques of Guy Debord's *Society of the Spectacle* and Neil Postman's *Amusing Ourselves to Death*, Jung writes:

> *Panem et circenses* [bread and circuses] — this is the degenerative symptom of urban civilization, to which we must now add the nerve-shattering din of our technological gadgetry. ... [There is] a widespread though not generally conscious *fear* which *loves noise* because it stops the fear from being heard. ... Fear seeks noisy company to scare away the demons.[23]

What are the demons? Following Jung's understanding, they are typically conflicts of conscience, one of "the chief causes of neurosis," along with "difficult moral problems that require an answer."[24] Jung sees such a conflict as a conflict of duty that forces us to examine our conscience and likely discover unsavory elements of our personality. While distraction can be a helpful tool for coping with traumatic memories, what is meant here is the distraction of "bling," or things that light up and go "bling," that draw one away from present and immediate duties inherent in any social order. Peter Kingsley laments the ineffective ways in contemporary times of attempting to counter one's psychic demons. "Distracting ourselves may feel innocent and carefree on the surface, but in fact it's a very intense activity that requires a huge amount of energy. The more

---

[22] CW 11, § 514

[23] Jung, Letter to Karl Oftinger, September 1957. *Letters Vol. 2*, p. 389

[24] Jung, Foreword to Neumann, *Depth Psychology and a New Ethic*. In CW 18, § 1408

Yoga in Mayfair or Fifth Avenue, or in any other place which is on the Matrix,
is a spiritual fake: What are the effects of Eastern spiritual practices
on the individuation process and the revelation of the self?

frightened of the reality inside us, the more hyperactive we're sure to become."[25]

Medialifeworld makes noise, and noise causes psychological disruption, which calls for more noise. We are living in "The Age of Disruption,"[26] where an "off" button, whether for lights or sound, is increasingly more difficult to find and earplugs aren't effective. A prescient Jung will say how "the fault [the inability to concentrate] lay with the cinema, the radio, television, the continual swish of motor cars and the drone of planes overhead. For these are all distractions."[27] He had already weighed in on humankind's menacing genius in a 1949 letter to the editors of the Swiss Federal Institute of Technology, responding to their question concerning "the effect of technology on the human psyche." Writing four years after the atom bomb made history and brought the curtain down on the Pacific theater of World War II, Jung wonders "whether man is sufficiently equipped with reason to be able to resist the temptation to use [technology] for destructive purposes, or whether his constitution will allow him to be swept into catastrophe. . . . a question which experience alone can answer."[28]

In that same year, 1949, Martin Heidegger began lecturing on what may turn out to be the mother of all problem children, technology. He posed questions that still guide us while we are beset with generations for whom media-induced Post-Traumatic Stress Disorder and Attention-Deficit/Hyperactivity Disorder are commonplace. The media technologies in which we are immersed affect the personal and collective nerve networks whose ages-old internal wiring cannot be easily updated or reprogrammed to meet digital standards. Computers do not require sleep or other human

---

[25] Whittaker, 2011

[26] Stiegler, 2019

[27] Jung, 1977, p. 249

[28] Jung, Letter to the Editors, *Zürcher Student, ETH* 14 September 1949, in CW 18, § 1403-1407

necessities to function, yet that's what many of us are competing with.

Grossman coined a possible entry for a future *Diagnostic and Statistical Manual of Mental Disorders*: GMD. "This pervasive invasion [of communication technologies] ... portends dissociative and pathological traits that might be characterized as a *Generalized Media Disorder* (a neurosis yet to be categorized by the psychiatric profession), in which we fail to perceive the body's limits (if such a thing is still relevant), let alone the limits of memory and intelligibility."[29]

Disaster: Between the Changing of the Gods

When teaching opportunities come my way and the material calls for it, I invoke an old phrase traditioned by Gurdjieff, "Let God kill him who himself does not know and yet presumes to show others the way to the doors to His Kingdom."[30] A photo of Jung with keys in his hand, about to open the door to his home, above which is the Latin inscription *Vocatus Atque Non Vocatus Deus Aderit* (*Called or not called the god will be there*). The foundational principle, the guiding image that gives Jung the *chutzpah*, the audacity to position himself as a prophet leading people out of psychic disaster is his insight into the psycho-historical evidence of the dissolution of no-longer vital gods while offering evidence for a remnant, a leftover of "the supreme meaning that never dies." Because of the amorphous nature of the god-image, with the potential for new, transcendent development, Jung will say that the trajectory of a god is that the god first "turns into meaning and then into absurdity, and out of the fire of their collision the supreme meaning rises up, rejuvenated anew."[31] This rejuvenation comes at a cost. A god is like a valuable territory, one doesn't want to give it up, especially when the god is holding

---

[29] Grossman, 2009, p. 22
[30] Gurdjieff, 1963, p. 185
[31] Jung, 2009, p. 230

Yoga in Mayfair or Fifth Avenue, or in any other place which is on the Matrix,
is a spiritual fake: What are the effects of Eastern spiritual practices
on the individuation process and the revelation of the self?

some enticing image of paradise or better things to come in Heaven after living a righteous life here on Earth.

Marshall McLuhan takes Nietzsche's phrase to mean the death of the Newtonian god, who made a clockwork universe and disappeared. "The phrase 'God is dead' applies aptly, correctly, validly to the Newtonian universe, which is dead."[32] Algis Mickunas also addresses another one of the issues that plague contemporary times: the condition of a mind that tends to forget limits and lacks the awareness that nothing lasts forever. Mickunas suggests that "the term 'god' does not imply an entity, but a culturally devised symbol of permanence. Other cultures will use other available means to symbolize permanence."[33] As the song goes, "And he shall reign forever and ever, hallelujah!" Whether or not this was Nietzsche's intention behind his death of God statement, the attribute of "permanent status" in the minds of a god's adherents expands what the death of a god can mean. And it's not only philosophers who find the prevalent cultural attitude of limitlessness problematic. "All of us find it clear," says Jungian Luigi Zoja, "that revising the notion of unlimited growth and replacing it with a concept of limits is of at least as much concern to psychologists as to any other group of specialists."[34]

Godlessness can imply an uncomfortable sense of unending impermanence or a permanent hell. Having no sense of direction is a *dis-aster*, the sailing ship navigator's nightmare: to be *without a guiding star* and, consequently, at risk of being off course, lost. This archetype that describes the postmodern condition in which the center cannot hold — being thrown into a world of chaos — has premodern roots in many cultural examples of sailors being lost at sea, wanderers in a desert, Jonah redux, etc., each wondering whereto and why.

Besides the devout atheists who have something to hold onto, the price for a godless worldview, following Nietzsche, is a

---

[32] McLuhan, 1967, p. 146
[33] Mickunas, nd, p. 14
[34] Zoja, 1995, p. 170

EASTERN PRACTICES AND INDIVIDUATION

vacuum of meaning in personal existence that gives rise to endemic alienation and separation anxiety. A concomitant rise in social disease is shown in the growing demand for psychotherapeutic relief. We may wonder how much longer it will be before any notion of a social and personal center point fully gives way, while Yeats's rough beast continues to slouch toward bedlam.

The Divided Mind: where East and West Meet

> When an idea is the expression of psychic experience which bears fruit in regions far separated and as free from historical relation as East and West, then we must look into the matter closely. For such ideas represent forces that are beyond logical justification and moral sanction; they are always stronger than man and his brain.[35]

Jung, speaking of the archetypal nature of ancient rituals and scripture, brings them into a psychologically oriented language suitable for contemporary readers to learn from, and wrestle with, regarding the religious attitude in relationship to the individuation process and self-realization. By many accounts and the simple fact of the presence of Jungian societies in Japan, Korea, China, and Taiwan, Jung's interpretations of Eastern practices, texts, and "art" indicate that he caught more than just a mere glimpse of those traditions and processes of perception. He may be doing for the East what the Rolling Stones did for American Blues music: brought the Blues back home to the U.S. and re-presented it to a much wider audience.

Questioner, a prepubescent youngster: How do you know when you have an orgasm?
Respondent: You'll know.

---

[35] Jung, 1939, p. 48. In the revised version that appears in CW 16, § 147, instead of the East-West apposition, Jung makes it "psychology and physics."

"We are faced with something that cannot be expressed originally with words."[36] What, then, are we talking about when we're talking about Eastern spiritual concepts and practices? We find an endless list of words that elude adequate, never mind precise, communicative reflection.

> You see, I maintain that — I don't know, whatever you call this; I don't like to use the words enlightenment, freedom, moksha, or liberation; all these words are loaded words, they have a connotation of their own, this cannot be brought about through any effort of yours. It just happens. And why it happens to one individual and not another, I don't know.[37]

Zen master Shunryu Suzuki offers an answer to the question — and then turns it on its head: "Zen is *not* something to talk about. It is also something *to* talk about."[38] Talking about Zen and other Eastern traditions invariably brings one to such terms as emptiness and fullness, nothingness and being, spontaneity, simultaneity (synchronicity), immediacy and indeterminacy. Inspired by Eastern thought, John Cage, would in turn arouse the neo-dadaist art movement Fluxus and various versions of personal and communal spontaneity, e.g., "acid tests" and their contemporary version, *raves*. Yet, as anarchic and extemporaneous as they seem, many works by Cage clearly reflect the influence of the Zen tradition. In his music, the so-called "silent piece," *4'33"*, is the crowning exemplar, with *Ryoanji* being a more dynamic reflection. Cage's "Lecture on Nothing" is longer than his lecture "Lecture on Something." What is it about a live performance of *4'33"*, by the Berlin or London Philharmonic, for instance, that the audience is applauding? Here, *nothing* appears to be appealing, which is not always the case.

---

[36] Nishitani, 1982, p. 125
[37] U.G., 1992, p. 3
[38] Suzuki, 2021, p. 2, emphasis added.

Religion, for Jung, "means the special frame of mind that has been changed by experience of the numinous."[39] He admitted that the main interest of his work was *not* in the treatment of neuroses, but "with the approach to the numinous,"[40] and as Umberto Eco notes, "it doesn't take long for the experience of the numinous to unhinge the mind."[41] Regarding the *mysterium tremendum et fascinans*, Paul McCartney describes an encounter with divine numinosity during a psychedelic experience: "We were immediately nailed to the sofa. And I saw God, this amazing towering thing, and I was humbled."[42] Not an unusual report from the hallucinogenically brokered universe.

Questioning another's meeting with the numinous, asking about the personal rendering of an uncanny experience, could elicit a response similar to the answer given to our young questioner above: *experience* — you'll know it when it happens. An endless number of books offer us new ways to talk about Nothing, and there's a plethora of dissertations on aspects of Silence, each its own translation of what lies beyond language and hidden within it. "It's just one of those mystifying ... sayings — until it happens to you."[43] Yet something appears to be traditionable — transmissible. We talk about it like fingers pointing to the moon.

> The radical difference from a clearly definable term is that these basic expressions, such as 'nothing' and 'emptiness', are not given any ontological or theological status, e.g., 'creation out of nothing' or cosmic waves pulsating out of 'emptiness.' It is rather the ability to become a 'place' (basho) where the world 'thinks and reflects itself.' The Buddha, the Zen master, and noh images can 'represent' this empty state.[44]

---

[39] Jung, quoted in Schaer, 1950, p. 19
[40] Letter to P. W. Martin, 20 August 1945 in Jung, Letters, Vol. 1, pp. 376-7
[41] Eco, 1989, p. 6
[42] Quinn, 2018
[43] Larson, 2012, p. xiv
[44] Algis Mickunas, personal correspondence with the author.

Yoga in Mayfair or Fifth Avenue, or in any other place which is on the Matrix,
is a spiritual fake: What are the effects of Eastern spiritual practices
on the individuation process and the revelation of the self?

Does discussion around this empty state in analysis have any therapeutic value?

The Place of Meditation in Therapy. Or Is It: The Place of Therapy in Meditation?

> Psychotherapy essentially seeks to assist in the transformation of conscious-ness, from a lesser state to a higher state. The lesser state is usually one of psychic malaise, existential pain, dysphoria in all its myriad forms, from all manner of persistent depressions and paralyzing anxieties to painful self-esteem and self-image issues. The coveted higher states of consciousness, on the contrary, imply relief, or even liberation from these dysphoric challenges.[45]

The foundational link between psychotherapy and a spiritual life is shown by Devrishi Ojaswan. "Both start from the mind. When the mind is cluttered, stressed-out, there is need for a psychotherapist."[46] Personal anecdotal evidence, as well as independent empirical studies, conclude that psychotherapy interconnected with meditative practices, East or West, can be highly beneficial.[47] However, it may well turn out that the meditation practice, which may initially have been engaged as an aid to psychotherapy, in some cases reduces the need for psychotherapy. In the process of finding liberation from dysphoric challenges, "meditation thus goes beyond being an adjunct for psychotherapy to becoming an individual discipline aiming for personal transcendence."[48]

Jungian Walter Odajnyk emphasizes the social value of integrating Zen and Analytical Psychology.

---

[45] Sunnen, 2019
[46] Personal conversation, December 18, 2021
[47] Rubin, 1996
[48] Sunnen, 2019

Like the Nazi epidemic, the present-day re-
actionary movements are unconscious collective attempts at individuation and wholeness.
They seek to heal the split between modern
secular rational consciousness and the powerful archetypal forces rooted in our instinc-
tive nature. Here, Jungian psychology, with its
emphasis on integrating the conscious and the
unconscious, and Zen enlightenment, with its
experience of the paradoxical uniqueness and
universality of every individual, have an important contribution to make to the sanity of
individuals and the unity of humankind.[49]

Stay Here Now

Odajnyk sees the analysis-and-meditation process as
bidirectional. "I sometimes think of this method as hatching an egg.
Psychotherapy chips away at the protective ego structure from the
outside while meditation supplies the necessary psychic energy for
the archetype of the Self to form and eventually break through from
the inside."[50] His colleague Christopher Whitmont feels that "not all
problems need or can be solved. We can also sit down. When you cannot
solve your problem, the question is, really, *can you sit down?* And if
you can sit down, are you sitting on thumbtacks or a grassy meadow?"[51]

Most often, the response to Whitmont is *tacks*. Sitting down
is not easy. There are many books devoted to cultivating the ability
to "just sit." Jeffrey Rubin, a psychoanalyst with a long-standing
engagement with Buddhist practices, addresses the difficulties that
one encounters when sitting down in terms of *ego defenses*. He
contrasts the old-school, judgmental views of various hindrances to
sitting meditation practice with a more contemporary psychoanalytic
understanding of what may be underlying contributory factors for
those who report finding it difficult just to sit quietly. In the East, an

---

[49] Odjanyk, 1993, p. 103
[50] Ibid, p. 169
[51] Whitmont, Audio recording, "Lecture 14." Kristine Mann Library, New York

Yoga in Mayfair or Fifth Avenue, or in any other place which is on the Matrix,
is a spiritual fake: What are the effects of Eastern spiritual practices
on the individuation process and the revelation of the self?

old Zen master might call one who is unable to fulfill a commitment to a regular sitting practice "lazy" or "slothful," words designed to make a person work harder through shame, which generally turns out to be counterproductive. Pushing back against that strategy, Jung finds that the "habit of rushing in to correct and criticize is already strong enough in our tradition, and it is as a rule further reinforced by fear ... a fear of all these things that cause so many of us to flee from being alone with ourselves as from the plague."[52]

What drives us from ourselves? Jonathan Lethem puns, "We have nothing to fear except nothing itself, or that which masks itself as nothing, the ubiquitous invisible swirling everywhere."[53] And we are living in a time when individuals are running from both a plague that is swirling everywhere and themselves, with nowhere to go. Fleeing from being alone is not an unusual source of resistance to meditation, where resistance is understood to be an ego-defense strategy for avoiding psychic discomforts.[54]

I've found it important to ask analysands who are Hatha Yoga instructors how their personal yoga practice is going. The same for those who claim to want to meditate but for one reason or another don't. The question "How's your personal practice going?" is often met with expressions of being "too busy" to attend to a personal regimen. Whether or not I respond with a paraphrase of philosopher Jean Gebser's observation that people who say they have no time are really saying they have no life[55] depends upon the moment.

Disindividuation

I descended away from you to serve the earth as a day-laborer;
but instead of a day laborer I became a slave:
matter fettered me with magical arts.[56]
We're all texting while driving.[57]

---

[52] Jung, 1935, in CW 7 § 323
[53] Lethem, 2012, p. 78
[54] Rubin, 1996
[55] Steiner & Gebser, 1962, p. 22
[56] "Soul's Lament," Synesius of Cyrene, quoted in Ribi, 2019, p. 33
[57] Poem of patient Tom Lee, 2018

Our discussion has come to a point that has as much to do with the effect of the death of a god as with the alienating effects of technology on the psyche. Both cause a loss of connection with a personal center. Technology needs to be understood not as physical objects or instruments but rather how to be human in relation to the forms that technologies adopt. They are not "neutral," they create a framework for knowledge. McLuhan points out the flaw in thinking that technology has no voice in the outcome: "'The products of science are not in themselves good or bad; it is the way they are used that determine their value,' *that is the voice of the current somnambulism.* ... If the slugs reach the right people firearms are good."[58] Heidegger would agree. "Everywhere we remain unfree and chained to technology, whether we passionately affirm or deny it. But we are delivered over to it in the worst possible way when we regard it as something neutral; for this conception of it to which today we particularly like to do homage, makes us utterly blind to the essence of technology."[59] The essence of technology, according to Heidegger, is that it is enframing, it subordinates the movement toward the wholeness of one's being to suit technology's requirements. In a Medialifeworld, a world of immediacy, no separation is possible. "You can't drop out. It's part of technology's 'set-up.'"[60]

What seems to be developing is a media-driven "self-erasure," a subtle and largely unconscious dehumanization, a destruction of the self that seems to be taking place through a hijacking of the creative process that contributes to what Bernard Stiegler (after Gilbert Simondon) calls *disindividuation.*[61] This is a condition attributed to an unmanageable set of demands compounded by behavior patterns (complexes) that develop in particular ways that can be traced directly to the presence and influence of information and communication technologies. Individuation aims toward a state

---

[58] McLuhan, 1964, p. 11, emphasis added.
[59] Heidegger, 1977, p. 4
[60] Babich "'The Danger' in Heidegger's Bremen Lectures"
http://digital.library.fordham.edu/cdm/ref/collection/VIDEO/id/468 (Last accessed 3/1/2022)
[61] Stiegler, 2009, p. 4

Yoga in Mayfair or Fifth Avenue, or in any other place which is on the Matrix,
is a spiritual fake: What are the effects of Eastern spiritual practices
on the individuation process and the revelation of the self?

of being at one with oneself, while disindividuation means the loss of one's individuality.

Remembering that Jung identified a chief cause of a neurosis as a conflict of conscience or duty,[62] the state of *cognitive dissonance* — two or more incompatible truths/realities causing a psychic split — manifests when one is caught between the sense of obligation to the outer world's call and a call of duty to oneself. The collective anxiety around the growing sense of isolation to which a Medialifeworld significantly contributes is simultaneously creating the end of absence altogether. "The instantaneous world of electronic informational media involves all of us, all at once. No detachment or frame is possible."[63] As a result of the ubiquity of the Net, we're always on call. Another part of the "setup" is living in a world that is perpetually on *standby*. The motto of the Boy Scouts of Switzerland, *Allzeit bereit* (always ready), has become the motto of Medialifeworld, where everyone and everything is set up for mechanized consumption and for whom the world appears as a standing reserve, ready to use when wished for, like an Eveready® battery, but one that, theoretically, never dies out. Paradoxically, the individual is conditioned to be on standby for the world, always on call for duty — Ding!

This predicament of being always on call can be understood archetypally as an imbalance of eros, the feminine characteristic of receptivity and holding. Jung's associate, Erich Neumann, describes the elementary aspect of the Great Mother as "the Great Container, [which] tends to hold fast to everything that springs from it and surrounds it like an eternal substance."[64] The imbalance, the overstimulation by electronic media, can be seen as a function of the negative pole of the archetypal feminine. The "Gaia" politic and notion of interconnectedness that values the positive mother archetype distracted us from her restrictive nature. Medialifeworld,

---

[62] Jung, Foreword to Neumann, 1969, p. 11

[63] McLuhan & Fiore, 1967, p. 53

[64] Neumann, 1955, p. 25

AKA The Matrix or global village, offers complete connectivity and containment in a boundaryless and limitless world. Held on a short tether, beholden to till Her field, a net suspends the Great Container's subjects in ever-ready standby.

The web of electronic media generates psychological consequences that must be considered when we attempt to address the current human condition, and while Jung was critical of Heidegger,[65] he would have agreed with the philosopher's view that "it is not [only] that the world is becoming entirely technical which is really uncanny. Far more uncanny is our being unprepared for this transformation, our inability to confront meditatively what is really dawning in this age."[66] It is our task now to see whether the imperative implied here, i.e., to find a meditatively informed confrontation with the spirit of this time, can manifest.

Reaster: Healing the split

> The man of today needs a deeper will to live, to overcome our complexities. He must resolve all opposites in himself; be all these in one.[67]

"We are split, and we can heal the split" was the mantra recited by Jungian Armin Wanner during his Basics of Analytical Psychology course at the Jung Foundation of New York. An axiom of the depth psychologies is that psyche has an inherent tendency to heal itself — under the right conditions. The inward-looking introverted attitude brings with it a psychological space that is conducive for contents to rise from the unconscious. In that vein, "The role of the music," says John Cage's biographer Kay Larson, "is to reveal the life that invisibly flows in and through us at all moments."[68] Cage discusses the atomized multiplicity of dissociated self-parts and the

---

[65] Jung to Arnold Künzli. In Letters, Vol. 1, p. 330
[66] Heidegger, 1966, p. 52
[67] Wilson, nd, p. 4
[68] Larson, 2012, p. 141

Yoga in Mayfair or Fifth Avenue, or in any other place which is on the Matrix,
is a spiritual fake: What are the effects of Eastern spiritual practices
on the individuation process and the revelation of the self?

role that music can play in reconnecting a splintered psyche. While music holds no monopoly on the healing process, it serves as a model for a type of treatment plan for wholeness.

> There are two principal parts of each personality: the conscious mind and the unconscious, and these are split and dispersed, in most of us, in countless ways and directions. The function of music, like that of any other healthy occupation, is to help bring those separate parts back together again. Music does this by providing a moment when, awareness of time and space being lost, the multiplicity of elements which make up an individual become integrated and he is one.[69]

Cage finds music to hold the potential to help free one from oppositional thinking: "A quiet mind is a mind that is free of its likes and dislikes," and can also "sober and quiet the mind, thus making it susceptible to divine influences."[70] When he says, "No illustrations need to be given to make clear the necessity in the field of form for individuality rather than adherence to tradition,"[71] Cage the student became a friend of Zen scholar D.T. Suzuki, also seems to be describing the personal freedom offered by a psychotherapy that incorporates the Jungian notion of individuation.

Phil, an analysand with express interests in Eastern traditions, brought my attention to a book I'd been meaning to read: Sri Nisargadatta's *I Am That*, which became the centerpiece for exchange over a few consecutive sessions and, five years later, continues to serve as a touchstone. Further along in our work, passages in Longchenpa's *Treasury of Natural Perfection* became a focal point after Phil's commitment to an American *Vajrayana* (Diamond Path)

---

[69] Ibid., p. 137
[70] Ibid., p. 134
[71] Ibid., p. 144

Buddhist teacher waned and shifted to a teacher who, as part of the diaspora, eventually came to the U.S. from Tibet.

At the same time, our meeting on "spiritual" grounds could not prevent some of Phil's personal truths and reservations around Buddhist "precepts" (guidelines) from being revealed during a psychotic episode requiring psychiatric care. Another unfortunate example of what I call the *Zen casualty*, demonstrating Jung's reasoning behind his warning about Westerners going East is: "If we do not try hard and dare to commit many errors in assimilating it to our Western mentality, we simply get poisoned."[72] Phil's ego could not withstand the pressure of his conscience, and when Phil could not admit to having committed errors in his ways, things fell apart. The Western psyche is typically not prepared for the extreme introversion demanded of Eastern practices. Sometimes the unconscious contents that arise during sitting periods of contained nonmovement cause trouble. During the long periods of "noble silence" maintained during weeklong retreats and at-home meditation sessions prior to his break, Phil's mind was overrun with issues of personal conflict. If there was a last straw, it was the death of his cat that opened floodgates of self-loathing and irruptions of paranoid thoughts.

Phil's Buddhist practice was an example of the homeopathic notion of the *pharmakon*: a medicine that is both a poison and a cure. Sometimes his attitude toward practice was a great source of guilt and shame for "not upholding the Dharma." Other times he took comfort in "seeing the emptiness" of his thoughts and emotions. In the years after the psychotic break, some of the contributing factors of Phil's split, having little or nothing to do with his Buddhist studies, became and remain the central points of focus in our work. I also receive regular updates on the ups and downs of his personal Vajrayana practice and his professional energy healing practice that he maintains with a modest number of clients.

---

[72] Jung, 1996, p. 14

Mystery and Mental Health

A Zen master said, "Yes, there is sudden enlightenment, but *you*? Sit on the cushion." Individual degrees of enlightenment, individuation, cultivation of wisdom and compassion, whatever we may call goals of a spiritually attuned lifestyle are byproducts of living in an atmosphere of openness to the mystery of the numinous. People develop from an effect of a unique process of orientation toward wholeness, rather than their will or conscious intention being the cause of individuation. To sit on a cushion, or meditate in any form, is to offer oneself to the mystery. Sometimes the mystery responds. I call that *collateral positive*.

Henry is an example of such a collateral positive. He had been an Israeli soldier in the 1967 war: "It burned in my flesh and soul since so many eighteen- and nineteen-year-old children, on both sides, lost their lives in the war. I heard that philosophy is a search for wisdom, and that yoga leads to the same. I turned to both and practiced them diligently."[73] After years of studying Plato and Kierkegaard and developing his personal yoga practice in New York City, Henry would eventually become a successful yoga teacher in the perennially hip St. Mark's Place and wrote about his personal experience, attempting to describe something of a transcendental nature "that transforms everyday life. The yogi retains the memory of the experience, and a tranquil fountain of joy opens in his heart, which will nourish him even if disaster strikes."[74] While I'm not sure that it is always the case that a memory can *always* nourish a yogi even if disaster strikes, the memory of a glimpse is sometimes enough to get one through rough waters. The years of practice leading to his self-described inner atmosphere of a transcendent nature was likely an important aspect of the re-membering process brought about by the transformative experience that offered Henry nourishment for a reaster, a coalescing of his shattered ego. It isn't

---

[73] Kochan, p. 2
[74] Ibid., p. 5

that Henry is perennially happy and problem-free; he's become a master at relativizing difficulties. It is also true that his nuclear family of four came to Israel with nothing and lived in a small shack for several years, which certainly provides Henry with a frame of reference for relativizing "the small stuff," as he referred to it. The lessons learned in his formative years, however, weren't enough to answer the questions brought about by his experience of war, and his modest quarters during the COVID-19 restrictions hearken the early days of the shack. His spirit, enlivened by yoga, is being tested.

How did I get here?

> Shunryu Suzuki Roshi was asked, "How do you know you're enlightened?" He responded: "When you no longer complain."[75]

I can't speak firsthand about enlightenment or what it means to finally be individuated, but I do know about a core ego strength that owes much to the blessing of the parents I was born to and continue to be fortified ever since. First-generation American, I was raised with a combination of lessons on how to survive and thrive, taught by Shoah refugees who faced nightmarish adversities and made it through them — battered and permanently scarred but more or less intact. From their words, and the various manifestations of their survivors' guilt, I learned to relativize my own moments of misery, knowing that things really could be worse. When such commonly used words as "unbearable," "unacceptable," "need," and "no" are met with a laugh, glare, sneer, a rifle butt, or its discharging barrel, one sees how meaningless these "privileged" utterances are. Extreme as such a harsh standard may be, it's just one end of an archetypal spectrum that allows for a middle ground somewhere between absolute deprivation and limitless resources and influence — one standard of reference among many.

---

[75] Chadwick, 2021, p. 41

Yoga in Mayfair or Fifth Avenue, or in any other place which is on the Matrix,
is a spiritual fake: What are the effects of Eastern spiritual practices
on the individuation process and the revelation of the self?

Along with the tribal elders of my family were those co-travelers I mentioned at the outset: friends, co-workers, and chance encounters — real or imagined. I've had one experience of not knowing whether an encounter with another person was actual or imaginal, which has lent itself to my acceptance of far-out psychic stories. This event, along with the type of synchronicity I'd first heard of in the golden oldie, *My Grandfather's Clock*, that "stopped short when the old man died," convinces me that theirs is more to Heaven and Earth than what's in an exclusively rational philosophy or psychology. Goosebumps raised up when I learned that the living room clock stopped in my friend Jerry's living room just around the time his dad died. As Ziv the kabbalist said to the entranced group of seekers gathered around a table after one of his mystical tales over tea at Kathmandu's Yin-Yang Café, "You believe it, or you don't."

My mystical tale is like the one Rudi (Swami Rudrananda) tells of being 6 years old and playing in a park when "two Tibetan lamas appeared out of the air and stood before me."[76] I wasn't much more than 10, living in Washington Heights, Manhattan, also known as *The Fourth Reich* and *Frankfurt on the Hudson* because of all of the native German language speakers who found refuge there in flight from the Nazis. The neighborhood was home to "Black Hats," not a Tibetan sect but Orthodox Jews. The memory I have is of walking down my block and encountering such an Orthodox type who said to me, "The Kabbalah is a one-way street. Once you go in, you never come out." That's all. I don't know if it really happened, or how I would have, at that age and growing up in an ultra-Reform household without a Bible, known what the Kabbalah even was. How this event attached to my memory is a mystery to this day. Nevertheless, reframing "Kabbalah" to mean "an esoteric symbol system," it is evident that the phrase has proved to be true to my experience. It informs me and my practice. I still wonder about these things.

---

[76] Mann, ed., 1984, p. 1

Then, along with the various *chochmas*, wisdom offerings from friends and kin — like Chris, "Where does stress live? Between your ears" — I also take to heart Nietzsche's challenge through the question asked by his adaptation of the theory of *the eternal recurrence of the same*. Would I say "yes" to reliving my life, every moment of it, without change? Am I able to meaningfully reflect the Japanese saying, *Nichinichi kore kōnichi* (every day is a good day) or Jung's "You can experience God every day"?[77] These questions help me to bring my inner gyroscope into balance, and surely the spiritual teachings by the holy men of India, including Siddhartha Gautama Buddha, have been of great help and support to me — informing my worldview, personal comportment — to some degree at least, and psychotherapy practice.

In February 2020, just before the coronavirus first hit New York, where I live and practice psychotherapy, another form of help for ego strength came at what in hindsight was a critical juncture for developing deeper roots for ill winds to come. A book that didn't belong to me but had been on a shelf for years suddenly called out — as books do from time to time, if they don't fall directly on one's head. *The Holy Fire: Teachings of Kalonymus Kalman Schapira, Rebbe of the Warsaw Ghetto*, suddenly compelled my attention and became of prime importance. I would soon come to appreciate why. Here was one from whom something about the force of character can be learned. Trapped in a vortex of three years of unrelenting horror and tragedy at the hands of unspeakable evil, yet reluctant to focus his teachings on the actual details of the abject suffering that the Jews were enduring under the Nazis, the rebbe delivered homilies that drew from archetypal narratives, Talmudic and biblical sources, and, finally, would remind his ever-dwindling number of Hasidim of the incomprehensibility of God's ways. After going through a two-month period of psychogenic mutism in the summer of 1940, he found a way to "return to self-possession after initial collapse" — an

---

[77] Jung, 1977, p. 250

Yoga in Mayfair or Fifth Avenue, or in any other place which is on the Matrix,
is a spiritual fake: What are the effects of Eastern spiritual practices
on the individuation process and the revelation of the self?

example of a *reaster* — and continued to inspire those who survived until the final deportation from the Ghetto in 1943.

> In the face of death and bereavement, I have found the strength to rejoice and have inspired others to joy as well. When others observed my self-possession and joy in the face of such great troubles, they too found strength in the face of their own troubles, through my example. This inner strengthening will itself have the effect of turning evil into good. 'Bless thy people Israel.'[78]

In the coming times, we therapists are going to be called to dig down deep and deeper and deeper to accompany those who are looking to us for support — and sometimes only a glimmer of hope, a glimpse of a way to ameliorate suffering. What do we offer when the light goes out and numinous mystery is replaced by dread and trembling fear? The Rebbe of Warsaw, who likely did not know the *Four Noble Truths* of Buddhism that aim toward the cessation of suffering, reflects the figure of one who has returned from hell and provides support for others, a true *therapeutes*[79] in the darkest of times. A bodhisattva. May his memory be blessed.

Onward

In 1941 and the midst of World War II, Jung was asked whether happiness was found through spiritual means. His response made me laugh out loud: "An attainable sausage is as a rule more illuminating than a devotional exercise." Then, after affirming

---

[78] Polen, 1994, p. 26

[79] Therapeutae, Greek Therapeutai ("Healers," or "Attendants"), singular Therapeutes, Jewish sect of ascetics closely resembling the Essenes, believed to have settled on the shores of Lake Mareotis in the vicinity of Alexandria, Egypt, during the 1st century AD. https://www.britannica.com/topic/Therapeutae (Last accessed 3/3/2022).

the enlightening value of a sausage, he refrains Meister Eckhart's maxim that to know releasement, one must already be released, "to find happiness in the spirit one must be possessed of a 'spirit' to find happiness in."[80] Enlightenment-individuation-awareness-equanimity-*Gelassenheit*: Apparently, it happens when it does, if it does. "The highest god," says Jung, "is the god born in man, Buddha himself."[81] With no transcendent god to redeem us, Herbert Guenther concludes, "humankind redeems itself by itself, and that is what the individuation process is about."[82] "It is only by our *thinking the death of God*," suggests Greg Mogenson, "here at the abyss-edge of the split in the world, that the birth of man, and along with this the challenge of *becoming self* (in contradistinction to *having a relationship to the Self* on the model of a relation to God) truly comes into its own."[83]

Muriel, an intuitive massage therapist, asked, "If it's all about resonance between our patients and us, and if we are not whole ourselves, how much can we connect others to their wholeness?" I said, "You're right, it's a liability of our trades," and shared the psychotherapeutic axiom of not being able to take another farther than one has gone oneself; then added, "We do the best we can, and we keep going." Like it says on Ken Kesey's magic bus, "Furthur."

---

[80] Jung, CW 18, § 1346
[81] Jung, 2020c, p. 47
[82] Herbert Guenther, 1994, p. 16
[83] Greg Mogenson, 2010, p. 261

Yoga in Mayfair or Fifth Avenue, or in any other place which is on the Matrix,
is a spiritual fake: What are the effects of Eastern spiritual practices
on the individuation process and the revelation of the self?

References

Babette, B. (2013). "'The Danger' in Heidegger's Bremen Lectures: Con-stellating Technology." http://digital.library.fordham.edu/cdm/ref/collection/VIDEO/id/468 (Last accessed February 13, 2015)

Chadwick, D., ed. (2021). *Zen Is Right Now*. Boulder, CO: Shambhala Publications

Eco, U. (1989). *Foucault's Pendulum*. New York: Harcourt Brace Jovanovich

Giegerich, W. (1996). The opposition of 'Individual' and 'Collective' — Psychology's basic fault: Reflections on today's magnum opus of the soul. *Harvest: Journal for* Jungian Studies, 42(2), pp. 7-27

Grossman, J. (2009). *Blackout: On Memory and Catastrophe*. New York: Atropos Press

Guenther, H. (1994). *Wholeness Lost, Wholeness Regained*. New York: SUNY Press

Gurdjieff, G.I. (1963). *Meetings With Remarkable Men*. A.R. Orage, Trans. London: Routledge & Kegan Paul, Ltd

Heidegger, M. (1966). *Discourse on Thinking*. J. Anderson & E. H. Freund, Trans. New York: Harper & Row

_____. (1966a). "Only a god can save us." *Der Spiegel*, September 23. W. Richardson, Trans. http://www.ditext.com/heidegger/interview.html (Last access 3/1/2022)

_____. (1977). *The Question Concerning Technology*. W. Lovitt, Trans. New York: Garland Publishing, Inc

Jung, C.G. (1939a). *Modern Man in Search of a Soul*. W.S. Dell & C.F. Baynes, Trans. New York: Harcourt, Brace and Company

_____. (1963). *Memories, Dreams, Reflections*. A. Jaffe, Ed. C. Winston, Trans. New York: Random House

_____. (1973). *Letters* 2 Vols. G. Adler & A. Jaffé, Eds. R.F.C Hull, Trans. Princeton, NJ: Princeton University Press

_____. (1977). *C.G. Jung Speaking*. W. McGuire & R.F.C. Hull, Eds. Princeton, NJ: Princeton University Press

_____. (1996). *The Psychology of Kundalini Yoga*. S. Shamdasani, Ed. Princeton, NJ: Princeton University Press

_____. (2009). *The Red Book*. S. Shamdasani, Ed. M. Kyburz, J. Peck, S. Shamdasani, Trans. New York: W.W. Norton & Co.

_____. (2020a). *The Black Books* (7 vols). S. Shamdasani, Ed. M. Liebscher, J. Peck, S. Shamdasani, Trans. New York: W.W. Norton & Co

_____. (2020b). *Psychology of Yoga and Meditation*. M. Liebscher, Trans. Princeton, NJ: Princeton University Press

_____. (2020c). *On Theology and Psychology*. M. Jehle-Wildberger, Ed. Princeton, NJ: Princeton University Press

Kochan, H. (nd). *Hatha Yoga*. Privately printed

Larson, K. (2012). *Where the Heart Beats*. New York: Penguin Press

Lethem, J. (2012). *Fear of Music*. New York: Continuum International Publishing Group

Levy, D.M. (2016). *Mindful Tech.* New Haven, CT: Yale University Press

Lopez Jr., D.S. (1998) *Prisoners of Shangri-La*. Chicago: Chicago University Press

Mann, J., ed. (1984). *Behind the Cosmic Curtain*. Arlington, MA: Neolog Publishing

McLuhan, M. (1964). *Understanding Media*. New York: McGraw-Hill Book Company

_____. (1967). *The Medium Is the Massage*. New York: Random House

_____. (1967). The Fordham University Lectures, Tape 1.c https://www.youtube.com/watch?v=WfnHB5f6FZM (Last accessed July 18, 2021)

_____. (1987) *Letters of Marshall McLuhan*. M. Molinaro, C. McLuhan, & W. Toye, Eds. Toronto: Oxford University Press

_____. (1968). *Through the Vanishing Point*. New York: Harper & Row

Mickunas, A. (nd). *Nietzsche: Life And World*, unpublished manuscript.

Mogenson, Greg. (2010). Post mortem dei. *Spring 84, 207-270*

Neumann, E. (1955). *The Great Mother*. R. Manheim, Trans. New York: Pantheon Books

_____. (1969). *Depth Psychology and a New Ethic*. E. Rolf, Trans. New York: G.P. Putnam's Sons

Nietzsche, F.W. (1974). *The Gay Science*. W. Kaufmann, Trans. New York: Random House

Nishitani, K. (1982). *Religion and Nothingness*. J.V. Bragt, Trans. Berkeley: University of California Press

Odajnyk, V.W. (1993). *Gathering the Light.* Boston: Shambhala Publications, Inc.

Pearlman, E. (2012). *Nothing and Everything – The Influence of Buddhism on the American Avant Garde*. Berkeley, CA: Evolver Editions

Polen, N. (1994). *The Holy Fire*. Northvale, NJ: Jason Aronson, Inc.

Quinn, B. (2018). https://www.theguardian.com/music/2018/sep/02/paul-mccartney-saw-god-after-taking-drugs-during-beatles-heyday. (Last accessed August 8, 2021)

Ribi, A. (2019). *Turn of an Age*. M. Kyburz, Trans. Los Angeles: Gnosis Archive Books

Rosmarin, D.H. (2021). "Psychiatry needs to get right with God," *The Scientific American*. https://www.scientificamerican.com/article/psychiatry-needs-to-get-right-with-god/ (Last accessed 3/3/2022)

Rubin, J. (1996). *Psychotherapy and Buddhism*. New York: Plenum Press

Schaer, H. (1950). *Religion and the Cure of Souls in Jung's Psychology*. R.F.C. Hull, Trans. New York: Pantheon Books

Steiner, H. and Gebser, J. (1962). *Anxiety*. P. Heller, Trans. New York: Dell Publishing Co.

Stevens, A. (1993). *The Two Million-Year-Old Self*. College Station, TX: Texas A&M University Press

Stiegler, B. (2009). *Acting Out*. D. Barison, D. Ross, & P. Crogan, Trans. Stanford, CA: Stanford University Press

Stiegler, B. (2019). *The Age of Disruption*. D. Ross, Trans. Medford, MA: Polity Press

Sunnen, G. (2019). Experiencing "pure consciousness": A catalyst in psychotherapy? http://www.triroc.com/sunnen/topics/experiencepureconsciousness.htm (Last accessed October 3, 2021)

Suzuki, D.T. (1927). *Essays in Zen Buddhism (First Series)*. London: Luzac and Co.

Taylor, M.C. (2007). *After God*. Chicago: University of Chicago Press

U.G. (1992). *The Mystique of Enlightenment*. R. Arms, Ed. Bangalore: Akshaya Mudrana

Whitmont, C. (nd). Audio recording, "Lecture 14". Kristine Mann Library audio archive

Whittaker, R. (May 21, 2011). Interview with Peter Kingsley: Remembering What We Have *Forgotten*. https://www.conversations.org/story.php?sid=285 (Last accessed October 8, 2021)

Wilson, C. (nd). *Some Notes on Beats and Angries*. Cornwall: Abraxas

Zoja, L. (1995). *Growth and Guilt*. H. Martin, Trans. New York: Routledge.